THE TOTALLY FOOTBALL BOOK

Edited by Nick Miller

2022

CORONET

First published in Great Britain in 2022 by Coronet
An imprint of Hodder & Stoughton
An Hachette UK company

1

Copyright © The Athletic Media Company 2022

A CIP catalogue record for this title is available from the British Library

Hardback ISBN 9781529346787
eBook ISBN 9781529346817

Typeset in Berthold Akzidenz Grotesk by Palimpsest Book Production Ltd,
Falkirk, Stirlingshire

Printed and bound in Great Britain by Clays Ltd, Elcograf S.p.A.

Hodder & Stoughton policy is to use papers that are natural, renewable
and recyclable products and made from wood grown in sustainable forests.
The logging and manufacturing processes are expected to conform to
the environmental regulations of the country of origin.

Hodder & Stoughton Ltd
Carmelite House
50 Victoria Embankment
London EC4Y 0DZ

www.hodder.co.uk

Contents

THE TOTALLY FOOTBALL BOOK

Edited by Nick Miller

2022

CORONET

For unrivalled football insight...
...subscribe to The Athletic
theathletic.com/totally
The Athletic

Introduction
by James Richardson

Welcome reader, to a brand new *Totally Football Book*.

Another year has passed — how was it for you?

Good, I'm guessing, if you're a fan of Champions League drama, crypto-backed fan initiatives, or dizzying RPMs on Watford's managerial merry-go-round.

Not so great perhaps, if you're a supporter of Derby, if you're Ralf Rangnick's PR guy, or run events management for major finals in Paris.

Here at Totally Towers, *we* enjoyed the season so much we went back and watched it again, and took extensive notes! *What did we discover?*

It was the season when football *almost* got back to normal, with the return of crowds*, and the end of social distancing — unless you were a Manchester United defender.

A season that brought resurrections for Ronaldo and the extraordinary Christian Eriksen, but also the year we lost Steve Bruce, Mike Dean and poor Rebekah Vardy's phone there in the North Sea, sinking like some cellular Norwich, or the value of John Terry's NFTs.

Has it all marked a new chapter for the game? Only time will tell, but in the meantime, here's a set of 'em from us, to cement your memories of this golden age.

In this edition of the *Totally Football Book*, we've set out to capture the flavour as well as the facts of this season, and the result is a time capsule of treasures from 2021-2022, box fresh from the cream of Team Totally.

We've got James Horncastle on Giorgio Chiellini, who brought the curtain down on his Juventus and Italy career this year. What's next for the grizzled old warhorse and most respected man in Italian football? We'll find out, as soon as he's finished his expenses for this Chiellini piece.

Julien Laurens is here too and, unusually for him, talking about PSG: why is it, despite having Neymar, Lionel Messi, Kylian Mbappé and all the foie gras they can guzzle, nobody there seems happy?

Similarly, Rafa Honigstein weighs in with how Bayern Munich's many fans are almost as upset by the mention of Qatar as Italy supporters.

Alvaro Romeo explains a Spanish football scandal – the leaked recordings that reveal who really runs things in the land of El Chiringuito, exposing the grubby underbelly of Spanish football, and how Florentino Pérez and Gerard Pique remain the men pulling the strings.

There's Carl Anka tackling the legacy of COVID-19 on football and its lungs, Daniel Storey on the heart-breaking predicament of Ukraine's footballers and Charlie Eccleshare, looking the world square in the eye and asking why Son Heung-min isn't a global superstar.

Curious about Patrick Vieira rebuilding Palace in his image? Dom Fifield has a piece just for you. Confused by the philosophical question: what is Frank Lampard? Adam Hurrey's been considering that very topic. And if you've ever wondered who the Premier League's most statistically average footballer is, well, Duncan Alexander has a paragraph or two you're going to love.

Elsewhere, Nick Miller strokes his luscious beard and wonders whose fault Paul Pogba's six years at Manchester United were, and Tom Williams mulls over the strange dichotomy of Gareth Bale: loved in Cardiff, loathed in Madrid.

Maher Mezahi profiles Aliou Cissé, the man who appropriately enough would not stop in his bid to see Senegal crowned Africa Cup of Nations champions in 2022.

Our top tactics man Adrian Clarke tells us about a batch of coaches so young they barely remember the Millennium bug, while Elias Burke tells the tale of Wayne Rooney at Derby and his extraordinary first full season as a manager.

It's a lot, and on top of all that there's also a day-by-day diary of the 2021-22 season, plus quiz questions galore in case you want to stage your very own Inter Totally Cup (just don't invite Jack Lang). Best of all, if you flick to the back of the book you'll find not only a rather fine On This Day section, with a potted history of football in 365 slices, but also the sweet release of the ending.

What are you waiting for? Dive in, and happy reading!

*you came down here looking for a joke about the Emirates, didn't you?

Editor's notes

by Nick Miller

Life got a bit easier for most people in 2022.

After the worst of the COVID-19 pandemic eventually started ebbing away, though the virus will never go away completely, things began returning to . . . something approaching normal life. We could go out and do things. Go to bars and restaurants and friends' houses without counting how many people you were with and whether you were breaking any rules.

Weddings could take place, people could mourn collectively, human contact became a little bit easier. The pressure on businesses that rely on the population being able to move around relented. Masks became a less and less frequent sight, for better or worse.

But most pertinently for this book, football came back. Proper football, with fans present — the collective experience that the game is supposed to be. We were able to be in grounds, to suffer agonising tension and beautiful joy and spirit-crushing disappointment. Football no longer felt like a sterile TV show, the equivalent of when you see behind-the-scenes footage from big CGI sci-fi films but just with the green screen and not the special effects that made it so spectacular in the first place. We were getting the full picture again.

All of which was good, but something wasn't quite right with football.

There was an aggression that wasn't there before. Fans seemed more violent. The rash of pitch invasions at the end of the season where players genuinely feared for their safety was troubling. Anyone who attended a decent-sized game will tell you how prevalent cocaine became in the stands. Frequently, the experience of a game — travelling to one and being around one — would be unpleasant.

Maybe it was like this before and we all just forgot about it, like we blocked out the bad bits of an experience we idealised when we couldn't have it. Maybe football has always had the capacity to be unpleasant and we were just more aware of that than before after a year away.

But it didn't feel like that. It felt like something had changed. There will be plenty of theories about how this translates to broader life, about how the world has simply forgotten how to behave. And there might be something in that. But it might just be something specific to football too.

It was almost as if, while football in empty stadia was horrible and a brutally watered-down version of this great game, we at least knew where we were. There was certainty — if temporary certainty. We couldn't be there, so we just had to make the most of watching from afar.

Now we've all gone back, it's like we don't know how to deal with it all. Like all these complicated emotions, built up from so long spent inside and away from the games, burst out in many different directions and we weren't able to control where they were going.

Which is probably to be expected. You can't just take something away for a year, then bring it back and expect everything to be the same. It's like astronauts who return to earth and are unable to readjust to normal life: we have all been through a fairly transformative experience, and it's going to take us all a little while to recalibrate.

Throw in things like the war in Ukraine and the knock-on effects it had on football, the return of the Taliban to Afghanistan

— and the dire consequence for sportswomen in particular — and the takeover of Newcastle by a Saudi regime with an abysmal human rights record and it would be easy to paint a picture of 2022 as a year when we all lost our faith.

But it's not quite as straightforward as that. Equally, there were plenty of joyous and remarkable things that happened. Aliou Cissé gaining some form of redemption by winning the Africa Cup of Nations for Senegal. The US Women's National Team, their equal pay campaign and the example it sets. Nottingham Forest returning to the Premier League after 23 years of frustration and disappointment. Wales qualifying for their first World Cup since 1958. The incredible Clasico in the Women's Champions League.

This book is an attempt to paint a picture of where football is in 2022. It's not just a blow-by-blow account of a season (although if you do want that: there's The Diary, starting on page 15), in the same way that the previous edition was, but more a collection of writing about the people and events that defined the game — for good and bad, in significant and in minor ways, to be celebrated or otherwise — in 2022. Plus, some quizzes. Because everyone loves quizzes.

Enjoy, and thanks for reading.

When will football be normal again?

by Carl Anka

Football since 2019 has been . . . weird. Do these seasons that have been impacted by the COVID-19 pandemic just not count? Or should we accept that it's always been weird?

'Last season doesn't count because they changed the rules.'

This book looks at where football stands in 2022, but the above sentiment has been bubbling under for several years now. Football used to be one thing, but in the last few years something has fundamentally shifted and it's become harder to properly evaluate.

Does Liverpool's Premier League win in 2019-20 count if it was finished behind closed doors? Can we really say Real Madrid were the best team in Europe in 2021-22, considering their bizarre run to Champions League glory? The comic book readers among you will know what I mean if I said the past three seasons have felt like 'non-canon' football experiments. The non-comic book readers will hopefully understand what I mean if I said the COVID-19 pandemic both disrupted and exacerbated a number of traditional football conventions, leaving the last few years of football a little weird. Strangeness invites suspicion, and opposition football fans love doing anything that could take the shine off their rivals' achievements.

Put this all together and we've entered an era of Too Weird, Doesn't Count football.

The oddity starts with the 2019-20 season – the first Premier League season with VAR, which ended up being hated by nearly everyone and revealed we've all watched football with a very particular, very personal rulebook in our heads that rarely matched up with the person sat next to us watching the same game. The 2019-20 season also saw what constituted handball change and we spent an awful amount of time watching offside lines being drawn on a pitch looking for errant elbows, heels and other pointy parts of the body.

It had a 110-day pause due to the pandemic, and then the Premier League came back with five substitutions and games behind closed doors. Oh, and the Champions League and Europa League had (really fun, should be repeated) single-legged knockout games in Lisbon and Cologne respectively for their closing stages. For several weeks at the tail end of the English season, football below the Championship didn't really exist. Over in the Netherlands, Ajax probably would have won the Eredivisie, but in late April 2020 everyone decided to pack it all in on account of *gestures to lockdowns* . . . you know.

Too Weird. They changed the rules. Doesn't count.

The 2020-21 season saw the return of three substitutes in the Premier League while a number of other European leagues continued with five. The majority of Premier League games were played behind closed doors in a confusing series of events that first saw certain clubs play in front of limited crowds due to their geographical location; there was a real moment where clubs in the south of England had a soft home advantage playing in front of fans compared to those in the north.

Eventually, everyone realised the tier system introduced by the government didn't quite work and everyone had to play behind closed doors, and it all too often felt like a slog. Playing behind closed doors probably led to a bunch of differences on how football teams played that we are still struggling to quantify to this day. The Premier League saw more teams win away from home, but no one is 100 per cent sure *why* that happened.

Nearly every Premier League game of 2020-21 was televised and we all slowly learnt that watching more than three games of football in a weekend can feel like gorging on too much cake.

The Champions League and Europa League had two-legged knockout games, but some of them had to be played in neutral locations due to travel restrictions and other rules that still make little sense now. It was a minor miracle we crammed all of 2020-21's fixtures into a timeframe several weeks shorter than a regular European league season, but we had to make space for Euro 2020. Which was held in 2021.

Oh, and the Euros may have been a lot of fun, but it had way too many host cities that probably gave a sporting advantage to nations that didn't have to travel much. Still, it was nice to watch England reach the final, even if they did lose on penalties.

Too Weird. Weirder than 19-20, which we thought would be the weirdest season in modern football. Doesn't count.

Now we come to the 2021-22 season, which had thicker lines for offsides on VAR decisions, and then the handball rule got tweaked again. Fans returned, in full voice and even fuller fervour. But there were also a bunch of games postponed due to COVID-19 outbreaks. Everyone was knackered after the Euros. There was a new European competition that was sort of fun in theory but didn't make for loads of fun in practice until the last eight stage. (Which feels different, but kind of tracks with how the modern-day Champions League works?)

Kind of weird. Some rule changes. Vibes were off. This might be the normal season? Might not count.

Apologies for writing every tweak that happened to football over the past few years, but sometimes one has to read it all in one go and have a 'What on earth are we doing?' moment. When did football get this weird and why are we doing this? The obvious answer is 'because it makes money', but we will be here again after the 2022-23 Premier League season crams 16 matchdays before the World Cup break on 13 November 2022, before resuming on Boxing Day. There's going to be a return to five subs in the Premier League because clubs realised that actually, the Project Restart section of 19-20 had some good ideas.

Too Weird. Going to be the weirdest season we've seen. A Winter World Cup? A summer AFCON tournament? A January transfer window opening up a fortnight after the World Cup Final? Too weird. Doesn't count.

And so on.

This is not an experience unique to football. Flick through enough Reddit threads and basketball blogs and you can find some very intelligent people applying an asterisk to each and every NBA title from the last 30 years. Every season can feel off and non-canon if one thinks about it too much. The last three seasons of COVID-19-affected football have brought about some very strange seasons, but the sport has constantly been in a state of recalibration and soft reboots.

Across the last 30 years, European leagues have seen multiple rebrands and revamps of the European Cup format. We've had the Bosman Ruling, the arrival of sovereign wealth funds as club owners, the introduction of VAR and more. A Premier League player suiting up in 2022 is very different to one in 2012, and both are operating under different rules, and living different lives to any player who kicked a ball about in 1992.

A fun illustration of the strange new reality of football came in early January 2022, where former Manchester City and QPR defender Nedum Onouha said that when he first emerged into senior team dressing rooms in 2004, a Premier League player earning £100,000 a week would enter rarefied air and be discussed in hushed tones. In 2022, Aleksandar Mitrović was thought to be earning such a figure at the top end of the Championship.

Football is forever changing in such a way that it can be hard to pinpoint when the last 'normal' season was, let alone predict when the sport might return to normalcy again. The Super League may have come and gone in the space of 48 hours in 2021, but present-day football is heading towards . . . *something*. The 2022 World Cup in Qatar was shifted to the winter as its summer temperatures were not conducive to healthy football games, but temperatures taken across major American cities in the summer of 2022 suggest the next World Cup might see the USA, Mexico and Canada be a little too hot for games in 2026, which will see 48 nations compete.

The 'Swiss Format' of the Champions League, due to be introduced in 2024, is going to take a while to figure out, as will the level of prestige that fans afford the Europa Conference League and the various Nations League tournaments that keep popping up.

UEFA and the South American Football Confederation (CONMEBOL) seem to be aligning themselves closer together for ~reasons~ while FIFA President Giovanni Infantino appeared to be particularly focused on the state of African football, possibly to create his own Super League, but more probably to secure a solid voting bloc for future elections. Everyone is aware that there are too many games and it causes too much stress on players' minds and bodies, but no one can agree on which games should be removed from the calendar to ease the burden. The football we're currently watching is subtly changing and reforming itself for reasons that are hard to fathom beyond 'it makes more money this way'.

This isn't really a good enough answer, but it's hard to figure out what happens next. Football is meant to be one of the important things on a list of unimportant things in life. At its essence, it is a children's game that is popular because it is so simple and cheap to play; because anyone can play a game of football, everyone can take something of interest from the game. It is one of the most absurd hobbies we have, and we have reached a point where multi-billion dollar companies are willing to spend hundreds of millions of dollars on players in order to thrill us. In 2022 Kylian Mbappé is less a football player and more a powerful geopolitical tool for both the French and Qatari governments. That is absurd. Too Weird. Probably shouldn't count.

There might never be another 'normal' season of football again, but that might be ok because football was never really normal to begin with.

THE TOTALLY FOOTBALL BOOK

The Diary

From the traditional curtain-raiser of the Community
Shield, through to a team ending a 23-year wait for
promotion in the playoffs with plenty in-between: this
is the story of the 2021-22 season, day-by-day . . .

The diary of the 2021–22 season

by Nick Miller

August 7

The traditional curtain-raiser to the English domestic season saw
FA Cup holders Leicester City beat Premier League champions
Manchester City 1-0, thanks to a late Kelechi Iheanacho penalty.
Jack Grealish, who had completed his British record, £100 million
move from Aston Villa to Manchester City a couple of days earlier,
made his debut off the bench.

August 8

The Harry Kane transfer saga continued after the England captain
belatedly reported to Tottenham training following a confusing
episode where it initially appeared as if he had gone on strike to
force a move to Manchester City. However, the Kane camp
insisted that he was reporting for duty at the appointed time after
an extended post-Euro 2020 break.

August 9

Liverpool were dealt a blow with the news that Andy Robertson
would potentially miss the first month of the season with an ankle
injury suffered in a pre-season friendly against Athletic Bilbao.

'It could have been worse,' said Jürgen Klopp. Meanwhile in other injury news, Sergio Agüero learned he would miss the first 10 weeks of his Barcelona career with a calf injury.

August 10

It actually happened. Lionel Messi officially left Barcelona, where he had spent his entire senior career, to sign a two-year contract with PSG. The 34-year-old left Barca after it became clear their financial restrictions would not allow them to re-sign him, so he instead linked up with Neymar and Kylian Mbappé in Paris. 'The club and its vision are in perfect harmony with my ambitions,' Messi said.

August 11

The much-maligned Kepa Arrizabalaga was the hero for Chelsea as they beat Villarreal on penalties to win the European Super Cup. Thomas Tuchel had made the bold move to bring on the Spaniard in place of Édouard Mendy specifically for the shootout, after the game finished 1-1, and he saved two penalties as Chelsea prevailed 6-5.

August 12

Romelu Lukaku completed his return to Chelsea, signing from Inter for around £100 million, 10 years after he joined them for the first time and seven after he left for Everton. Lukaku had won Serie A with Inter, scoring 64 goals over two seasons in Italy. 'I'm happy and blessed to be back at this wonderful club,' he said after the transfer was confirmed.

August 13

The Premier League season began with a bang as Brentford cele-brated their return to the top flight for their first time since 1947 by beating Arsenal 2-0. Goals from Sergi Canos and Christian Nørgaard were enough to defeat the Gunners, whose new signing at centre-back, Ben White, had a chastening evening, although Mikel Arteta's side were missing a number of first-choice players.

August 14

The first Saturday of the season began with Manchester United hammering their rivals Leeds United 5-1, shortly after confirming the signing of Raphaël Varane from Real Madrid. Liverpool beat Norwich 3-0, Rafa Benítez's first game as Everton manager ended in a 3-1 win over Southampton while Watford sealed a winning return to the Premier League as they beat Aston Villa 3-2.

August 15

Legendary German striker Gerd Müller died at the age of 75. Müller scored a record 365 goals for Bayern Munich and 68 for West Germany, including the winner in the 1974 World Cup final. In the Premier League, Nuno Espírito Santo got off to a perfect start as Tottenham manager, as a Son Heung-min goal was enough for them to beat Manchester City 1-0.

August 16

Carli Lloyd announced her retirement from all football, after a career that took in a whopping 316 caps and 134 goals for the USA, with whom she won two World Cups and two Olympic gold medals. Barcelona president Joan Laporta revealed the extent of the club's debt, which stood at £1.1 billion, pointing to a 'dreadful inheritance' left by his predecessor Josép Maria Bartomeu.

August 17

Tammy Abraham completed a £34 million move from Chelsea to join José Mourinho at AS Roma. Abraham's services were no longer required after the arrival of Romelu Lukaku from Inter, who in turn signed Edin Džeko from Roma. The Italian club had also hoped to sign Granit Xhaka from Arsenal, but the Swiss midfielder instead signed a new three-year contract at the Emirates.

August 18

Arsenal Women made an ideal start to life under new manager Jonas Eidevall by strolling through their first round of Champions League qualifying, beating Kazakh side Okzhetpes 4-0. Celtic's men won their own qualifier, this time in the Europa League, as Kyogo Furuhashi and James Forrest scored the goals in a 2-0 win over AZ Alkmaar.

August 19

Manchester United legend Denis Law announced that he had been diagnosed with mixed dementia. Law, 81, said he wanted to be 'open' about his condition, adding: 'I do understand what is happening and that is why I want to address my situation now whilst I am able, because I know there will be days when I don't understand and I hate the thought of that right now.'

August 20

Arsenal completed a double signing, after they paid £34 million for Real Madrid midfielder Martin Ødegaard, and quickly followed that up with a £30 million deal for goalkeeper Aaron Ramsdale, who joined from Sheffield United. Ødegaard had spent the second half of the previous season on loan at the Emirates, while Ramsdale was signed to compete with Bernd Leno for the No.1 jersey.

August 21

Jack Grealish scored his first goal for Manchester City in their 5-0 thrashing of Norwich, Diogo Jota and Sadio Mané scored in Liverpool's 2-0 win over Burnley, while Patrick Vieira secured his first point as Crystal Palace boss as they drew 0-0 with Brentford and Raphinha bagged Leeds United's second equaliser as they twice came from behind to draw 2-2 with Everton.

August 22

Romelu Lukaku scored the first goal of his second spell at Chelsea as they easily flexed Arsenal aside 2-0 at the Emirates. Reece James scored the other goal in a game that seemed to lay bare the gulf in class between the two London rivals. Earlier in the day, Harry Kane returned for Tottenham as they beat Wolves 1-0, while Manchester United drew 1-1 with Southampton.

August 23

Michail Antonio scored two rapid-fire goals in West Ham's comprehensive 4-1 win over Leicester City, who had to play the whole second half with ten men after Ayoze Pérez was sent off. Antonio celebrated his first goal by running over to the sidelines and lifting a cardboard cutout of himself high over his head, recreating a scene from *Dirty Dancing* with . . . himself.

August 24

Real Madrid, who had been relatively reticent in the transfer market for a few years, made a £137 million bid to bring their long-term target Kylian Mbappé to Spain from PSG. The 22-year-old's contract was due to run out at the end of the season, and he was expected to leave the French champions at some point: Real were attempting to bring that move forward.

August 25

After a little deliberation, PSG rejected the offer for Mbappé as being 'very far' from his value, but sporting director Leonardo admitted that the player did want to leave the club. 'Kylian Mbappé feels like leaving, this seems clear to me,' he said. 'If a player wants to leave it must be under our terms. This applies not just to Kylian but to all players.'

August 26

Harry Kane confirmed he would be staying at Tottenham, after his attempts to force through a move to Manchester City proved unsuccessful. Kane had hoped to join the Premier League champions, but a series of offers were deemed insufficient by Spurs. 'I will be staying at Tottenham this summer and will be 100% focused on helping the team achieve success,' Kane said.

August 27

A blockbuster transfer from virtually nowhere: Manchester United agreed a deal to bring Cristiano Ronaldo back to the club from Juventus. Ronaldo had looked certain to move to Manchester City, who turned to him after failing to sign Harry Kane, but an intervention from Sir Alex Ferguson persuaded the hierarchy to move for the man who left them for Real Madrid in 2009.

August 28

Arsenal's start to the season moved into 'farce' territory after they were ripped apart by Manchester City, who shared around the goals in a 5-0 win after Granit Xhaka was sent off. Chelsea also had a man sent off, but they held out for a 1-1 draw against Liverpool at Anfield despite Reece James's dismissal for handball just before half-time.

August 29

Mason Greenwood scored the only goal in Manchester United's 1-0 win over Wolves, Son Heung-min sealed Tottenham's third 1-0 win in three games as they beat Watford, while Patrick Bamford scored a late equaliser for Leeds as they drew 1-1 with Burnley. In France, Lionel Messi made his debut for PSG, coming off the bench to play the final 24 minutes of their 2-0 win over Reims.

August 30

Another indignity befell Arsenal as Ainsley Maitland-Niles voiced his desire to leave the club on Instagram, posting: 'All I want to do is go where I'm wanted and where I'm going to play @Arsenal.' That seemed to be Everton, who were interested in taking him on loan for the season, but after a meeting with Mikel Arteta, Maitland-Niles ultimately stayed.

August 31

A relatively low-key transfer deadline day ended with Chelsea signing Saúl Ñiguez on loan from Atlético Madrid, Arsenal paying Bologna £15.5 million for Takehiro Tomiyasu, Salomón Rondón joining Rafa Benítez for a third time as he signed for Everton while Dan James moved to Leeds. Real Madrid didn't get Kylian Mbappé, but did sign promising 18-year-old midfielder Eduardo Camavinga.

September 1

Cristiano Ronaldo became the highest scorer in men's international football history with two late goals for Portugal against Ireland in a World Cup qualifier. Ireland looked set for a famous win with 89 minutes gone, but the Manchester United man popped up with two headers to seal the win, and take him to 111 international goals in 180 games, two ahead of previous record-holder Ali Daei.

September 2

England eventually recorded a comfortable 4-0 win in their World Cup qualifier against Hungary in Budapest, with goals from Raheem Sterling, Harry Kane, Harry Maguire and Declan Rice. But attention after the game was on the home fans, who racially abused Sterling and Jude Bellingham with monkey chants, prompting Gareth Southgate to demand more protection for his players.

September 3

Arsenal Women landed a significant coup when they completed the signing of Tobin Heath, after the US international left Manchester United, joining Mana Iwabuchi and Nikita Parris as new Gunners arrivals. Heath's old club United kicked off the Women's Super League season with a 2-0 victory over Reading, thanks to goals from Kirsty Hanson and Ona Batlle in Marc Skinner's first game in charge.

September 4

UEFA president Aleksander Čeferin expressed 'serious reservations and grave concerns' about the ongoing plans for a biennial World Cup. FIFA and Gianni Infantino had been pressing on with the proposals to host the tournament every two years instead of every four — in the face of significant opposition — but Čeferin said UEFA 'stands with the fans on this important issue'.

September 5

Italy were held to a 0-0 draw by Switzerland in their World Cup qualifier after Jorginho missed a second-half penalty, but the stalemate was Roberto Mancini's side's 36th consecutive unbeaten international game, which matched the world record set by Brazil in the 1990s. Elsewhere England beat Andorra 4-0, while Wales defeated Belarus 3-2 thanks to a Gareth Bale hat-trick.

September 6

Police were investigating after Brazilian health officials caused a World Cup qualifier between Brazil and Argentina to be abandoned. Four England-based Argentina players had breached COVID-19 regulations relating to entry into the country, apparently providing 'false information' in their health declaration forms, and officials from the Anvisa agency entered the field of play during the game.

September 7
Barcelona president Joan Laporta insisted that the flame of the European Super League, seemingly snuffed out the previous April, was still very much burning. Laporta told a Spanish TV station that 'the project is alive', despite every club involved apart from Barca, Real Madrid and Juventus pulling out of the proposed league in the face of overwhelming opposition from fans.

September 8
Gareth Southgate defended his decision not to make any substitutions in England's World Cup qualifier against Poland, after a late Damian Szymański goal earned the Poles a 1-1 draw in Warsaw. Elsewhere Manchester City crashed out at the qualification stage of the Women's Champions League, defeated 2-1 on aggregate by Real Madrid over two legs.

September 9
Vivianne Miedema helped herself to a hat-trick as Arsenal beat Slavia Prague 4-0 on the night, 7-0 on aggregate to qualify for the group stages of the Women's Champions League. Meanwhile Lionel Messi bagged a hat-trick for Argentina against Bolivia, which made him the top scorer in South American international history with 79 goals, taking him above Pelé who had 77.

September 10
UEFA threatened to boycott any future World Cup over FIFA's plans to hold the tournament every two years, instead of four. 'We can decide not to play in it,' said UEFA president Aleksander Čeferin. 'As far as I know, the South Americans are on the same page. So good luck with a World Cup like that.' Čeferin added that while they would make more money, the proposal would 'kill football'.

September 11

Cristiano Ronaldo marked his second debut for Manchester United by scoring twice in their 4-1 rout of Newcastle at Old Trafford. However a banner with the slogan '#BelieveKathrynMayorga' was flown over the ground during the game by protest group Level Up, in reference to rape allegations against Ronaldo from 2009, about which criminal and civil complaints were dismissed.

September 12

Liverpool's 3-0 win over Leeds United was overshadowed by a horrible injury to youngster Harvey Elliott, who dislocated his left ankle in a challenge with Pascal Struijk. 'The whole team was shocked and we lost rhythm,' said Jürgen Klopp afterwards. In the WSL, Spurs shocked Manchester City 2-1, while Sam Kerr scored twice in Chelsea's 4-0 win over Everton.

September 13

Andros Townsend scored a sensational strike from 25 yards and Demarai Gray got his third in three games as Rafa Benítez's fine start at Everton continued with a 3-1 win over Burnley at Goodison Park. Things weren't looking so great for Burnley, as they started the season without a single victory from their four games in the Premier League so far.

September 14

Manchester United's Champions League campaign got off to a calamitous start as a Jesse Lingard error presented Young Boys with a 2-1 win. Life was a little easier for Chelsea, who beat Zenit St Petersburg 1-0 thanks to Romelu Lukaku. Elsewhere Bayern Munich won 3-0 at Barcelona and there were four first-half penalties in Sevilla's 1-1 draw with Red Bull Salzburg.

September 15

Liverpool completed a comeback win in a fizzing first Champions League group game against Milan, Jordan Henderson scoring the winner in a 3-2 victory. There was another thriller in Manchester as City beat RB Leipzig 6-3, with a Christopher Nkunku hat-trick not enough for the German side. Leo Messi made his first start for PSG, but they could only draw 1-1 with Club Brugge.

September 16

Nottingham Forest sacked Chris Hughton as manager after an abysmal start to the season, one that had seen them take just a point from their first seven games. In the Europa League, Leicester drew 2-2 with Napoli, while Tottenham came from behind to secure the same scoreline against Rennes, while Declan Rice and Michail Antonio both scored as West Ham beat Dinamo Zagreb 2-0.

September 17

Derby County were given a 12-point penalty which sent directly to the bottom of the Championship after their financial problems forced them to enter into administration. They were already facing a separate points deduction for breaking Financial Fair Play rules. In the Premier League, Allan Saint-Maximin equalised for Newcastle to earn them a 1-1 draw with Leeds after Raphinha had given the visitors the lead.

September 18

Southampton sprung a surprise by holding Manchester City to a 0-0 draw, Liverpool made short work of Crystal Palace with Sadio Mané opening the scoring in their 3-0 win at Anfield, Martin Ødegaard got the only goal as Arsenal beat Burnley 1-0 while Norwich's winless start to the season continued, their 3-1 home defeat to Watford their fifth loss in a row.

September 19

Jimmy Greaves, who scored 44 goals in 57 international games for England and was Tottenham's all-time record scorer with 266, passed away at the age of 81. Two of his former teams faced each other, with Chelsea winning 3-0 at the Tottenham Hotspur Stadium, while Manchester United won 2-1 at West Ham, for whom Mark Noble came off the bench just to take a late penalty, which he missed.

September 20

James Rodríguez, a marquee arrival at Everton only a year earlier, travelled to Qatar to seal a transfer to Al Rayyan. The Colombian signed for the Toffees from Real Madrid and, after a fine start, his time at Goodison Park was hampered by injuries and, after Carlo Ancelotti had returned to Madrid his future was always uncertain. He had yet to feature under Rafa Benítez.

September 21

England Women followed up an 8-0 thrashing of North Macedonia with another mismatch, beating Luxembourg 10-0 with Ellen White, Alex Greenwood and Millie Bright all scoring twice. In the men's Carabao Cup, QPR beat Everton on penalties, Takumi Minamino scored twice as Liverpool beat Norwich 3-0 and Manchester City hammered Wycombe 6-1 after initially falling behind.

September 22

Tottenham and Chelsea both progressed in the Carabao Cup on penalties, beating Wolves and Aston Villa respectively, while West Ham gained some revenge for their recent league defeat to Manchester United by knocking them out of the competition thanks to a Manuel Lanzini strike. Eddie Nketiah capped Arsenal's 3-0 win over Wimbledon with a cheeky backheeled goal.

September 23

The grim situation at Derby appeared to worsen after Wayne Rooney criticised former owner Mel Morris following the confirmation of their 12-point penalty for entering administration. Rooney called Morris 'disrespectful' over his apparent lack of communication, revealing that he had to call him on the club doctor's phone in order to speak directly.

September 24

In Scotland, Leigh Griffiths was charged by the police after the Dundee striker kicked a smoke bomb that had been thrown onto the pitch back into the stands. Griffiths claimed he was just trying to 'remove it from the pitch', but the police described it as 'culpable and reckless conduct.' In the Championship, West Brom beat QPR 2-1 and Coventry defeated Peterborough 3-0.

September 25

Gabriel Jesus scored the only goal as Manchester City grabbed a 1-0 win over Chelsea at Stamford Bridge, which Pep Guardiola described as their 'best performance of the season'. Brentford held Liverpool to a thrilling 3-3 draw, Newcastle's poor start to the season continued as they drew with Watford, while Bruno Fernandes missed a late penalty as Aston Villa beat Manchester United 1-0.

September 26

Arsenal produced an emphatic performance to beat Tottenham 3-1 in the North London derby, with all three goals arriving by the 34 minute mark. Raúl Jiménez scored his first league goal since returning from a head injury as Wolves beat Southampton. In the WSL, defending champions Chelsea hammered Manchester United 6-1, while Arsenal stunned Manchester City 5-0.

September 27

Neal Maupay popped up with a 95th-minute equaliser to claim a point for Brighton in their clash with rivals Crystal Palace. A Wilfried Zaha penalty had given Palace the lead, but Maupay scored deep into injury time to deny them the victory. Elsewhere the national fuel crisis started to hit football, with several non-League fixtures in England having to be postponed.

September 28

Roger Hunt, one of England's World Cup winners in 1966, died at the age of 83. Hunt played a key role in Liverpool's rise from the Second Division under Bill Shankly, and was their all-time top scorer until Ian Rush broke his record in 1992. In the Champions League, Leo Messi scored as PSG beat Manchester City 2-0, Liverpool hammered Porto 5-1 and FC Sheriff, minnows from Moldova, beat Real Madrid.

September 29

Manchester United had to rely on Cristiano Ronaldo to dig them out of a hole against Villarreal, as he scored in the 95th minute to grab a 2-1 victory, after which Ole Gunnar Solskjær admitted they were 'lucky'. In Italy, Federico Chiesa got the only goal as Juventus beat Chelsea 1-0 in their group game, while the pressure on Ronald Koeman increased after Barcelona lost to Benfica.

September 30

Tottenham enjoyed some respite from their poor league form with a Harry Kane hat-trick against Mura in the Europa League, a game Spurs won 5-1. West Ham beat Rapid Vienna 2-0 although the game was marred slightly by missiles thrown by the Austrian team's support, while Leicester's European campaign took a turn for the worse after they were beaten 1-0 by Legia Warsaw.

October 1

Sparta Prague responded to accusations of racism on the part of their fans, who had booed midfielder Glen Kamara during their Europa League game, by claiming any boos came from children who should not be attacked. Kamara had been racially abused by Slavia Prague's Ondřej Kúdela the previous season. In Australia, Daniel Sturridge signed for A-League side Perth Glory.

October 2

Another adverse result for Manchester United came as Andros Townsend equalised to secure a 1-1 draw for Everton at Old Trafford. Brighton had the better of a 0-0 draw against Arsenal, Timo Werner scored late to help Chelsea to a 3-1 win over Southampton, Norwich got their first point of the season thanks to a goalless draw with Burnley and Leeds enjoyed their first win, beating Watford 1-0.

October 3

Mo Salah scored a stunning goal that wasn't enough for Liverpool to beat Manchester City in a thriller at Anfield, with Phil Foden and Kevin De Bruyne scoring the defending champions' goals in a 2-2 draw. Crystal Palace came from 2-0 down to draw with Leicester, Yoane Wissa sealed a 2-1 win for Brentford against West Ham with the last kick of the game while Spurs beat Aston Villa 2-1.

October 4

Watford appointed Claudio Ranieri as their new manager, after defeat to Leeds proved the end for Xisco Muñoz. Ranieri's most recent job in England was at Fulham, where he steered them in the direction of relegation, but he'd done solid work in Italy with Roma and Sampdoria in the interim. Manchester City alleged that a Liverpool fan had spat at their bench during the teams' 2-2 draw.

October 5

Arsenal were outclassed by an unstoppable-looking Barcelona in the Women's Champions League. Alexia Putellas and Lieke Martens were among the scorers for the Catalan side in their 4-1 win, with Frida Maanum claiming a consolation. James Ward-Prowse was called up to an injury-hit England men's squad for their World Cup qualifiers against Hungary and Andorra.

October 6

Ferran Torres scored twice for Spain as they beat European champions Italy in the Nations League semi-final. Lorenzo Pellegrini scored for Italy, but couldn't prevent their first defeat since September 2018. In the Women's Champions League, Pernille Harder scored a late equaliser for Chelsea in a 3-3 thriller against Wolfsburg, who were 3-1 up at one stage thanks to some calamitous defending.

October 7

The long Newcastle takeover saga came to an end after the Saudi Arabia Public Investment Fund completed their £300 million purchase of the club from Mike Ashley. Amnesty International called the takeover 'a clear attempt to sportswash the Saudi's appalling human rights record.' In the Nations League, France roared back from 2-0 down to Belgium to win 3-2 and earn a place in the final.

October 8

In the 2022 World Cup qualifiers, Dan James earned a point for Wales as they drew 2-2 with the Czech Republic in Prague. Elsewhere Germany beat Romania 2-1, the Netherlands defeated Latvia and Turkey drew 1-1 with Norway. England's game in Andorra was briefly in doubt after a fire at the Estadi Nacional, but it was ultimately confirmed that the World Cup qualifier would go ahead.

October 9

Jack Grealish rounded off the scoring as England strolled to a 5-0 victory against Andorra and all but sealed their qualification for the World Cup. It wasn't so hot for Northern Ireland, who lost to Switzerland, while Scotland took a huge step towards securing second place in their group with a 94th minute Scott McTominay winner over Israel. The Manchester derby in the WSL ended 2-2.

October 10

France added the Nations League to their World Cup win after they defeated Spain in the final in Milan, a goal by Kylian Mbappé 10 minutes from time enough to seal the 2-1 victory for Didier Deschamps's side. Arsenal stayed on top of the WSL after they beat Everton 3-0, while Chelsea defeated Leicester City 2-0 but had to wait until the last 10 minutes to break the deadlock.

October 11

Germany became the first team to qualify for the World Cup after Timo Werner and Kai Havertz were among the scorers in their 4-0 victory over North Macedonia, sealing their spot in Qatar. Wales remained on track to join them after an early Kieffer Moore strike was enough to earn a 1-0 win over Estonia, while Turkey scored two late goals to beat Latvia.

October 12

England limped to a 1-1 draw against Hungary at Wembley, John Stones scoring their goal, but attention was mainly focused on the stands where a section of the visiting support fought with police near the start of the game. Denmark qualified for the World Cup after beating Austria while Scotland stayed on course for a play-off spot by beating the Faroe Islands 1-0.

October 13

Chelsea earned a sensational first win of their Women's Champions League campaign, as goals from Erin Cuthbert and Pernille Harder were enough to beat Juventus 2-1 in Turin. The win took Chelsea second in the 'Group of Death', behind Wolfsburg. The Bournemouth midfielder David Brooks was diagnosed with cancer, but his prognosis was good and he began treatment immediately.

October 14

Arsenal bounced back from a thrashing by Barcelona in their previous Women's Champions League game by emphatically beating Hoffenheim 4-0, with Tobin Heath scoring in her second start for the club. Despite much speculation that he would be sacked, it was confirmed that Steve Bruce would remain in charge for the new Newcastle owners' first game, against Tottenham.

October 15

Jürgen Klopp joined those questioning Newcastle United's takeover by the Saudi Arabia Public Investment fund. After Premier League clubs called an emergency meeting to discuss the takeover, Klopp asked why there had been no explanation from Premier League chief executive Richard Masters. 'We all know there are obviously some concerns over human rights issues,' he said.

October 16

Ole Gunnar Solskjær was under more pressure after his Manchester United team were ruthlessly beaten 4-2 by Leicester. Roberto Firmino scored a hat-trick and Mo Salah hit another stunner as Liverpool hammered Watford 5-0, Wolves scored three times after the 80th minute to come back from 2-0 down at Aston Villa, while Southampton got their first win of the season, beating Leeds 1-0.

October 17

The first game of the new era at Newcastle ended in defeat — despite the Magpies going ahead against Tottenham, first Tanguy Ndombele then Harry Kane and Son Heung-min scored to claim a 3-2 win. Afterwards Steve Bruce said his future was 'out of my hands'. David Moyes enjoyed a return to Goodison Park after an Angelo Ogbonna header gave West Ham a 1-0 win over Everton.

October 18

UEFA gave a two-match crowd ban (the second suspended) to England at Wembley, plus a €100,000 fine, as punishment for the violence at the Euro 2020 final. The ban would be for England's next competitive UEFA fixture, their first home game of the 2022-23 Nations League. In the Premier League, Alexandre Lacazette scored a late equaliser as Arsenal and Crystal Palace drew 2-2.

October 19

Mo Salah scored a penalty in Liverpool's lively 3-2 victory over Atlético Madrid in the Champions League, with Antoine Griezmann scoring twice but getting sent off for the hosts. Manchester City made short work of Club Brugge, Riyad Mahrez scoring twice in their 5-1 win, while a Leo Messi Panenka penalty gave PSG a 3-2 win over RB Leipzig in Paris.

October 20

The inevitable was confirmed when Newcastle announced the dismissal of Steve Bruce as manager. In the Champions League, Cristiano Ronaldo completed Manchester United's comeback from 2-0 down against Atalanta to win 3-2, while things were a little more straightforward for Chelsea and Bayern, who both won 4-0 against Malmö and Benfica respectively.

October 21

Tottenham were embarrassed in the Europa Conference League as Nuno Espírito Santo's decision to play a second-string side against Vitesse backfired, the Dutch side winning 1-0. It wasn't quite as bad as José Mourinho's Roma, who were humiliated 6-1 by Bodø/Glimt. West Ham had a better time, as they beat Genk 3-0, while Rangers beat Brondby 2-0.

October 22

Emile Smith Rowe capped a fine individual performance with a goal as Arsenal easily beat Aston Villa 3-1 in the Premier League, with Thomas Partey and Pierre-Emerick Aubameyang scoring the other goals for Mikel Arteta's side. Five men appeared in court in Belgium after a Manchester City fan was attacked before their Champions League game against Club Brugge.

October 23

Joshua King scored a hat-trick for Watford as they shocked Everton with a 5-2 win at Goodison Park. Mason Mount also hit three as Chelsea battered Norwich 7-0, a Callum Wilson overhead kick earned Newcastle a 1-1 draw against Crystal Palace and Rodrigo rescued a point for Leeds against Wolves. Beth Mead scored a hat-trick for England Women as they beat Northern Ireland 4-0.

October 24

Ole Gunnar Solskjær called Manchester United's 5-0 home defeat to Liverpool his 'darkest day' as the club's manager. Mo Salah got a hat-trick while Diogo Jota and Naby Keïa got the others. Michail Antonio scored the only goal as West Ham beat Tottenham 1-0. James Maddison scored the winner for Leicester as they beat Brentford 2-1. In Spain, Real Madrid beat Barcelona 2-1.

October 25

Barcelona condemned 'violent and disdainful acts' against their coach Ronald Koeman, after his car was blocked from leaving the Camp Nou following their defeat to Real Madrid. Fans verbally abused Koeman and kicked the car as he attempted to drive away. 'The club will take security and disciplinary measures so that such unfortunate events do not happen again,' a statement read.

October 26

Walter Smith, the legendary manager of Rangers who guided the Scottish giants to 21 major trophies in two spells at the club, passed away at the age of 73. Smith won seven league titles in his first stint as Rangers boss and three in his second, as well as reaching the 2008 UEFA Cup final. Smith also managed Scotland, Everton and was Sir Alex Ferguson's assistant at Manchester United.

October 27

A 1-0 defeat to Rayo Vallecano was the final straw for Barcelona as they dismissed Ronald Koeman as their manager. The loss left Barca ninth in La Liga and after some poor results in the Champions League, the club's board felt they could leave it no longer. In Australia, Adelaide United player Josh Cavallo received widespread support after he came out as gay.

October 28

England and Northern Ireland were drawn together in the Women's European Championships, to be held in England in 2022, with Austria and Norway making up the other teams in Group A. Defending champions the Netherlands were drawn with world No 2 side Sweden, as well as Russia and Switzerland, while Germany and Spain in Group B looked like a spicy pairing.

October 29

One of the more bizarre stories of the year became more real as Hollywood actors Ryan Reynolds and Rob McElhenney gave their first press conference after taking over National League side Wrexham. 'We'd be lying if the dream wasn't the Premier League,' said Reynolds. 'We want to get back in the Football League and continue our way upwards.'

October 30

Goals from Conor Gallagher and Wilfried Zaha gave Crystal Palace a 2-0 win over Manchester City, then Brighton came back from two down to claim a 2-2 draw against Liverpool. Manchester United beat Tottenham 3-0, Aaron Ramsdale produced heroics as Arsenal beat Leicester 2-0, while Burnley got their first win of the season, 3-1 over Brentford.

October 31

Chelsea and Arsenal reached the delayed 2020-21 Women's FA Cup final as they beat Manchester City and Brighton in their respective semi-finals. In the men's Premier League, West Ham took advantage of Ezri Konsa's red card to sweep Aston Villa aside 4-1 at Villa Park, while Raphinha and Rodrigo scored the goals for Leeds as they beat struggling Norwich 2-1.

November 1

Nuno Espírito Santo's reign as Tottenham manager ended after just 17 games in charge, as he was sacked following their defeat at home to Manchester United and general unhappiness from the stands at their dismal style of play. Wolves beat Everton 2-1 to pile pressure on Toffees manager Rafa Benítez. In Spain, Sergio Agüero was ruled out for three months with cardiac problems.

November 2

Tottenham moved quickly to appoint Antonio Conte as their manager, with the former Inter and Chelsea boss signing a two-and-a-half year contract to replace Nuno. In the Champions League, Cristiano Ronaldo saved Manchester United with an injury-time equaliser to salvage a 2-2 draw with Atalanta, while Chelsea edged past Malmö 1-0 thanks to a Hakim Ziyech goal.

November 3

Liverpool booked their spot in the Champions League knockout rounds after Diogo Jota and Sadio Mané scored a pair of early goals in their 2-0 win over Atlético Madrid. Manchester City were on the brink of joining them following their 4-1 victory against Club Brugge. In the Championship, Fulham hammered Blackburn Rovers 7-0 at Ewood Park.

November 4

Tottenham won their first game under Antonio Conte, hanging on after scoring three early goals to beat Vitesse Arnhem 3-2 in the Europa Conference League. In the Europa League, West Ham drew 2-2 with Genk in David Moyes's 1,000th game as a manager, while Leicester drew 1-1 with Spartak Moscow. Jadon Sancho was dropped from the England squad for their upcoming World Cup qualifiers.

November 5

An early Adam Armstrong goal was enough for Southampton to inflict a fifth successive league defeat on Aston Villa, who edged closer to the relegation zone. In managerial news, Eddie Howe looked set to take the vacant position at Newcastle after Unai Emery turned it down, while Xavi agreed a deal in principle to return to Barcelona from Al-Sadd in Qatar.

November 6

Manchester City cruised to a straightforward 2-0 win over Manchester United, an Eric Bailly own goal and one from Bernardo Silva securing the points. Matěj Vydra scored a late equaliser for Burnley as they grabbed a surprise draw at Chelsea, Norwich finally got their first league win of the season, 2-1 over Brentford, while Newcastle drew 1-1 at Brighton with Eddie Howe watching on.

November 7

West Ham moved above Liverpool in the table after an extraordinary 3-2 win over Jürgen Klopp's side, uncharacteristic mistakes by Alisson contributing to the result. It was 0-0 between Everton and Spurs, Leicester and Leeds drew 1-1 while Arsenal beat Watford 1-0. Dean Smith was sacked by Aston Villa, while in the Championship Chris Wilder replaced Neil Warnock at Middlesbrough.

November 8

Eddie Howe was officially confirmed as Newcastle manager, replacing Steve Bruce but with the side second bottom of the Premier League without a win to their name. Another long-expected appointment was confirmed, with Xavi officially taking over as Barcelona head coach. Emile Smith Rowe was called up to the England squad after Marcus Rashford and James Ward-Prowse dropped out.

November 9

Emma Hayes had warned Chelsea not to take Servette lightly in the Women's Champions League, but they didn't need those warnings as they beat the Swiss side 7-0. The prospect of a narrative-fuelled relegation battle loomed as Aston Villa looked to be interested in Steven Gerrard as their new manager, while Norwich considered Frank Lampard to replace Daniel Farke.

November 10

An extraordinary story in France saw PSG women's midfielder Kheira Hamraoui hospitalised after she was dragged out of her car and attacked by two masked men, while police questioned her team-mate Aminata Diallo over the incident. Diallo was later released without charge. In the Women's Champions League, Arsenal thrashed HB Køge 5-1. Liverpool sporting director Michael Edwards announced he was stepping down at the end of the season.

November 11

Aston Villa confirmed the appointment of Steven Gerrard as their new manager, the former England international signing a three-and-a-half year contract after leaving Rangers. In the World Cup qualifiers, Ireland held Portugal to a 0-0 draw as Pepe was sent off, Spain edged past Greece 1-0, Germany beat Lichtenstein 9-0, while Croatia hammered Malta 7-1.

November 12

Harry Kane scored a hat-trick in England's 5-0 World Cup quali-fying win over Albania, Scotland confirmed a play-off spot after beating Moldova 2-0 but Italy's qualification was in doubt after they drew with Switzerland. Brazil became the first South American side to qualify after they beat Colombia 1-0. Ron Flowers, a member of England's 1966 World Cup squad, died aged 87.

November 13

Belgium and France booked their places at the World Cup with 3-1 and 8-0 wins over Estonia and Kazakhstan respectively. The Netherlands had to wait after losing a two-goal lead to draw 2-2 with Montenegro, but Wales's hopes were still alive after Aaron Ramsey starred in a 5-1 win over Belarus. In the WSL, Vivianne Miedema equalised in injury time to earn Arsenal a 1-1 draw with Spurs.

November 14

Portugal would have to go through the play-offs to make the World Cup after a late Aleksandar Mitrović goal gave Serbia a 2-1 win and an automatic spot in Qatar. Álvaro Morata scored a late winner over Sweden to seal Spain's passage while Croatia also qualified. Chelsea humiliated WSL rivals Manchester City with a 4-0 win, putting City boss Gareth Taylor's position under pressure.

November 15

European champions Italy joined Portugal in the World Cup play-offs after they could only muster a 0-0 draw with Northern Ireland. England confirmed their qualification after beating San Marino 10-0, Switzerland did the same after thrashing Bulgaria 4-0, while Scotland beat Denmark 2-0. Dean Smith was confirmed as Norwich City's new manager, just a week after leaving Aston Villa.

November 16

Wales ensured they would be at home for their World Cup qualifying play-off after a 1-1 draw with Belgium, while the Netherlands secured automatic qualification by beating Norway 2-0. Derby were deducted a further nine points — taking their total deficit to 21 points — for breaking EFL rules over the sale of Pride Park to a company controlled by former owner Mel Morris.

November 17

Argentina's 0-0 draw with Brazil ensured their spot at the World Cup, but Uruguay lost 3-0 to Bolivia and thus were in real danger of not making it to Qatar. Arsenal all-but sealed their place in the knockout rounds of the Women's Champions League by beating HB Køge 3-0. Reading were deducted six points for exceeding financial losses allowed in EFL profit and sustainability rules.

November 18

Chelsea were made to work surprisingly hard for their 1-0 win in the Women's Champions League over Servette, but Sam Kerr eventually got the only goal. Rangers appointed former player Giovanni van Bronckhorst as their new manager, replacing Steven Gerrard. In the FA Cup, Exeter would have to replay their game against Bradford — which they had won 3-0 — due to using too many substitutes.

November 19

An extremely 2021 story saw Manchester City suspend a partnership with cryptocurrency firm 3Key — initially announced as their 'official regional partner in decentralised finance trading analysis' — after doubts emerged whether the company actually existed. Manchester United faced up to three months without Paul Pogba, after the Frenchman sustained a thigh injury on international duty.

November 20

The end looked nigh for Ole Gunnar Solskjær after Manchester United were humiliated 4-1 by Watford. Arsenal's good run ended after they were dismantled by Liverpool, Sadio Mané scoring first in a 4-0 win. Late goals gave Steven Gerrard a winning start as Aston Villa manager as they beat Brighton 2-0, while Dean Smith also won his opener for Norwich, 2-1 over Southampton.

November 21

The inevitable was confirmed as Manchester United sacked Ole Gunnar Solskjær after almost three years in charge, with Michael Carrick taking temporary charge. Manchester City beat Everton 3-0 while Antonio Conte got his first Premier League win as Spurs boss, beating Leeds 2-1. Vivianne Miedema scored yet again as Arsenal beat Manchester United 2-0 in the WSL.

November 22

Gareth Southgate signed a contract extension that would keep him in charge of England until Euro 2024. There was recrimination and blame after the weekend saw Lyon's game against Marseille abandoned, due to L'OM's Dimitri Payet being struck by a bottle thrown from the crowd. It was the latest such incident in a Ligue 1 season marred by repeated incidents of crowd trouble.

November 23

Chelsea emphatically made it to the last 16 of the Champions League after they hammered Juventus 4-0. Michael Carrick won his first game in charge of Manchester United, as they beat Villarreal 2-0. Bayern Munich's 100% record continued as they beat Dynamo Kyiv 2-1, while Barcelona's qualification hopes were left in doubt as they could only draw 0-0 with Benfica.

November 24

Manchester City ensured they would top their Champions League group after coming from behind to beat PSG 2-1. Liverpool cruised past Porto, beating them 2-0. Real Madrid and Inter both sealed their qualification, but Borussia Dortmund were out after losing 3-1 to Sporting. Ben Chilwell was expected to miss the rest of the season after suffering a cruciate ligament injury.

November 25

Antonio Conte said he truly understood how difficult his job at Spurs was following their shock 2-1 defeat in the Europa Conference League to Slovenian side NS Mura. Sheffield United appointed Paul Heckingbottom as their new manager after sacking Slaviša Jokanović. Wigan striker Charlie Wyke was in a stable condition in hospital after collapsing during training.

November 26

Manchester United were in advanced talks to appoint Ralf Rangnick, the man who was the architect of the Red Bull football empire, as the man to replace Ole Gunnar Solskjær as their manager until the end of the season. Czech billionaire Daniel Křetínský agreed to purchase a 27% stake in West Ham, which included an option to take over the club in full.

November 27

Goals from Bukayo Saka and Gabriel Martinelli were enough for Arsenal to beat Newcastle 2-0. Diogo Jota scored twice as Liverpool beat Southampton 4-0, while Steven Gerrard's good start as Aston Villa boss continued as they beat Crystal Palace 2-1. Ellen White celebrated her 100th cap by scoring the only goal for England as they beat Austria 1-0 in a Women's World Cup qualifier.

November 28

Manchester United claimed a battling point at Stamford Bridge, with Jorginho saving a 1-1 draw for Chelsea after Jadon Sancho had opened the scoring. Everton's misery continued as an Ivan Toney penalty gave Brentford a 1-0 win, making it seven winless games for Rafa Benítez's side. Manchester City beat West Ham 2-1 while Leicester defeated Watford 4-2.

November 29

Ralf Rangnick was confirmed as Manchester United's interim manager until the end of the season, with the German set for a consultancy role at the club after that. Rangnick arrived from Lokomotiv Moscow, where he had been director of football. The Ballon d'Or winners were announced, with Leo Messi winning his seventh men's title and Barcelona's Alexia Putellas winning the women's trophy.

November 30

Raphinha scored a 94th minute penalty to help Leeds to a 1-0 win over Crystal Palace and ease them a little further clear of the bottom three. Newcastle thought they were on course for their first win of the season until Teemu Pukki's equaliser earned Norwich a 1-1 draw. Ellen White became England's record goalscorer as she helped herself to a hat-trick in a 20-0 thrashing of Latvia.

December 1

Mo Salah scored twice as Liverpool swept Everton away in the Merseyside derby, Jordan Henderson and Diogo Jota getting the others in a 4-1 win. Bernardo Silva starred and scored in Manchester City's 2-1 win over Aston Villa, Chelsea beat Watford 2-1 thanks to a Hakim Ziyech winner and Neal Maupay scored a sensational bicycle kick to earn West Ham a draw with Brighton.

December 2

Michael Carrick left Manchester United after guiding them to a 3-2 comeback win over Arsenal, Cristiano Ronaldo scoring their winner. Carrick had been expected to stay under Ralf Rangnick, but announced his departure after the game. Tottenham were made to work hard for their 2-0 win over Brentford, with Son Heung-min scoring the clinching goal in the second half.

December 3

Christian Eriksen returned to Odense, the Danish club with whom he started his career, to train as he started to inch his way back into football. Eriksen, who suffered a cardiac arrest while playing for Denmark at Euro 2020, had been unable to play for Serie A champions Inter due to regulations in Italy preventing footballers fitted with defibrillators from playing in the country.

December 4

A remarkable fluke by Arthur Masuaku completed an extraordinary win for West Ham, as they came back to beat Chelsea 3-2. Manchester City went top after beating Watford 3-1. Divock Origi popped up in the 94th minute to score a dramatic late winner as Liverpool beat Wolves 1-0. Callum Wilson scored the only goal as Newcastle finally won a game, 1-0 over Burnley.

December 5

Sam Kerr scored twice, one of them a delicious chip, as Chelsea beat Arsenal 3-0 in the Women's FA Cup final. This was the 2020-21 cup, with the previous season's final postponed due to COVID-19. Ralf Rangnick won his first game in charge of Manchester United, 1-0 over Crystal Palace, Patrick Bamford grabbed a late point for Leeds against Brentford while Spurs beat Norwich 3-0.

December 6

Demarai Gray scored an absolutely sensational long-range winner for Everton, as they beat Arsenal 2-1 at Goodison Park to relieve a little of the pressure on manager Rafa Benítez. It was an eventful day for Everton, after their director of football Marcel Brands had departed following disagreements with Benítez and the board about the direction of the club.

December 7

Liverpool made it six wins from six in their Champions League group after Mo Salah and Divock Origi scored in their 2-1 away win to Milan. Manchester City's group stage ended flatly as they were beaten 2-1 by RB Leipzig in Germany. Atlético squeaked through to the knockouts after beating Porto 3-1 and Real Madrid topped their group after beating Inter 2-0.

December 8

Chelsea had to settle for second in their Champions League group after a frantic 3-3 draw with Zenit St Petersburg. Manchester United drew 1-1 with Young Boys having already qualified, but Barcelona went out after losing to Bayern Munich. In the Women's Champions League, Sam Kerr knocked a pitch invader to the ground in Chelsea's 0-0 draw with Juventus.

December 9

Barcelona outclassed Arsenal 4-0 in the Women's Champions League, Jenni Hermoso scoring twice in a one-sided affair at the Emirates. An already qualified West Ham were beaten 1-0 by Dinamo Zagreb in the Europa League, while Tottenham's Europa Conference League fixture with Rennes and their Premier League game against Brighton were postponed due to a COVID-19 outbreak.

December 10

Brentford were losing to Watford in the 84th minute but two late goals, including a 96th-minute penalty by Bryan Mbeumo, turned things around as they secured a comeback victory. Paul Pogba's Manchester United future became less clear after Ralf Rangnick insisted he wouldn't try to persuade the French midfielder, whose contract was up at the end of the season, to stay.

December 11

Pierre-Emerick Aubameyang was dropped for 'disciplinary reasons' by Mikel Arteta for Arsenal's 3-0 win over Southampton. Mo Salah's penalty was enough for Liverpool to beat Aston Villa on Steven Gerrard's return to Anfield, Jorginho scored from the spot in injury time as Chelsea beat Leeds 3-2, Manchester City beat Wolves 1-0 and Manchester United beat Norwich 1-0.

December 12

Leicester made short work of Newcastle as James Maddison led the way in a 4-0 victory at the King Power Stadium. Conor Gallagher scored twice for Crystal Palace as they comfortably beat Everton 3-1, while Nick Pope made a series of fine saves to salvage a 0-0 draw for Burnley against West Ham. Manchester United beat Brighton 2-0 in the WSL.

December 13

There were farcical scenes at the Champions League draw, after an error forced UEFA to scrap the first attempt and redo the draw. The second try saw Liverpool paired with Inter, Manchester United would face Atlético Madrid, Chelsea against Lille, Manchester City versus Sporting but the biggest tie of the last 16 would be PSG and Kylian Mbappé against Real Madrid.

December 14

Kevin De Bruyne scored twice and pulled the strings as Manchester City thrashed Leeds 7-0 in the Premier League. Jacob Ramsey and Ollie Watkins scored for Aston Villa in their 2-0 win over Norwich, but plenty of other games were either called off or under threat, as dozens of fresh COVID-19 cases emerged in the Premier League, threatening to throw the season into chaos.

December 15

Sergio Agüero announced his retirement from football, after it was decided that the heart issues that caused him to leave a game in November were too serious for him to continue playing. Agüero had only played 165 minutes and scored one goal after signing for Barcelona in the summer. In the Premier League, Arsenal beat West Ham 2-0 and Wolves beat Brighton 1-0.

December 16

It was a bad night for both Chelsea sides as their men's team could only draw 1-1 with Everton in the Premier League, while the women were knocked out of the Champions League after being thrashed 4-0 by Wolfsburg. Liverpool beat Newcastle 3-1, but the Premier League rejected calls for a break in the season, despite being forced to postpone six games due to COVID-19 outbreaks.

December 17

Christian Eriksen and Inter agreed to a mutual termination of the Dane's contract, after he was prevented from playing in Italy due to regulations against the cardioverter-defibrillator he had fitted following his cardiac arrest at Euro 2020. The Premier League held talks with club owners and managers over the increasing numbers of COVID-19 cases that had decimated the league programme.

December 18

Gabriel Martinelli scored twice in the only Premier League game that survived the outbreaks of COVID-19, as Arsenal thrashed Leeds 4-1 at Elland Road. Aston Villa's game against Burnley was called off just three hours before kick-off. In the Championship, Bournemouth's poor run continued as they lost 1-0 to a Middlesbrough side resurgent under new manager Chris Wilder.

December 19

Andrew Robertson scored and was sent off in a dramatic 2-2 draw between Liverpool and Tottenham, with Son Heung-min grabbing a late equaliser for Spurs. Chelsea's attempts to get their game against Wolves postponed were unsuccessful, and the match ended in a 0-0 draw. Manchester City made short work of Newcastle, winning 4-0 at St James's Park.

December 20

Arsenal were given a tough draw in the Women's Champions League after they were paired with Wolfsburg, but the standout tie of the last-16 fixtures was Barcelona against Real Madrid. Tottenham's exit from the Europa Conference League was confirmed after UEFA awarded Rennes a 3-0 win following the postponement of their final group game earlier in December.

December 21

Arsenal made it into the semi-finals of the Carabao Cup after an Eddie Nketiah hat-trick helped them to a 5-1 hammering of Sunderland. Pep Guardiola dropped Jack Grealish and Phil Foden after they were pictured on a night out earlier in December. 'I pay a lot of attention to behaviour on and off the pitch,' said Guardiola. 'And when off the pitch is not proper they are not going to play.'

December 22

Liverpool, Chelsea and Spurs joined Arsenal in the Carabao Cup semi-finals: Liverpool beat Leicester on penalties after a thrilling 3-3 draw in normal time, Jorginho's late penalty sealed Chelsea's 2-0 win over local rivals Brentford, while Steven Bergwijn and Lucas Moura scored in Tottenham's 2-1 win over West Ham. Barcelona agreed a €55 million fee for City's Ferran Torres.

December 23

Pep Guardiola suggested that Premier League players could go on strike as concerns over COVID-19-related player welfare increased, with more games postponed but no official break in the fixture list forthcoming. 'Just through words it's not going to be solved,' said Guardiola. 'For FIFA, the Premier League, the broadcasters, the business is more important than their welfare.'

December 24

Everton's trip to Burnley became the latest Boxing Day fixture to be called off, after the Toffees eventually convinced the Premier League that the number of COVID-19 cases in their squad meant they didn't have enough players for the trip. That game joined Leeds United's trip to Liverpool and Wolves versus Watford as matches struck off from the traditional December 26 programme.

December 25

Steven Gerrard would miss Aston Villa's two games over the Christmas period after he tested positive for COVID-19. At least those games, against Chelsea and Leeds, were scheduled to take place; as well as the postponement of three Premier League games, a further 22 fixtures in the EFL had been called off after outbreaks at just about every club in the top four divisions.

December 26

There were plenty of goals in the Premier League games that did survive on Boxing Day: Manchester City and Leicester shared nine of them as the reigning champions won 6-3, Bukayo Saka scored twice as Arsenal hammered Norwich 5-0, Tottenham beat Crystal Palace 3-0 while Jorginho scored two penalties for Chelsea as they beat Aston Villa 3-1.

December 27

Newcastle looked like they were on track for a win over Manchester United following Allan Saint-Maximin's early goal at St James's Park, but Edinson Cavani saved Ralf Rangnick's side with a late equaliser. Meanwhile, the Premier League announced a record new 103 COVID-19 cases as the virus continued to decimate the fixture list, a situation Antonio Conte called 'a big mess'.

December 28

Jürgen Klopp described Liverpool's performance in their 1-0 defeat to Leicester as 'very bad', as they lost ground in the title race thanks to Ademola Lookman's goal. Ten-man Southampton held Tottenham to a 1-1 draw, while West Ham completed a comprehensive 4-1 victory over Watford at Vicarage Road. Ferran Torres completed his €55 million move from Manchester City to Barcelona.

December 29

Manchester City went eight points clear at the top of the Premier League, after Phil Foden scored the only goal in their 1-0 win over Brentford. They took advantage of Liverpool's loss the previous day, and also Chelsea's draw against Brighton, for whom Danny Welbeck scored a 91st-minute equaliser. Mikel Arteta became the latest manager to test positive for COVID-19.

December 30

Cristiano Ronaldo and Scott McTominay were among the scorers as Manchester United emphatically beat Burnley 3-1 at Old Trafford, the goals all coming in the first half. In the Championship, Bournemouth moved four points clear at the top following a 3-0 victory over Cardiff, while Derby defied their points deduction to claim their third straight win, 2-1 over Stoke.

December 31

Romelu Lukaku's future at Chelsea appeared uncertain just six months after he returned to the club. The Belgian striker had claimed that he was 'not happy' with his lot at Stamford Bridge, prompting head coach Thomas Tuchel to declare his irritation. 'We don't like it,' Tuchel said. 'It brings noise that we don't need and it's not helpful.'

January 1

Rodri scored a 93rd-minute winner for Manchester City in a game that Arsenal dominated, but somehow conspired to lose 2-1. Davinson Sánchez left things even later for Tottenham against Watford, heading home in the 96th minute to seal a 1-0 win. Manuel Lanzini scored twice in West Ham's 3-2 win over Crystal Palace. Everton signed Ukrainian left-back Vitaliy Mykolenko.

January 2

Chelsea came back from two goals down against Liverpool to earn a 2-2 draw, with Mateo Kovačić and Christian Pulisic levelling things up after Sadio Mané and Mo Salah scored early on. Elsewhere Brighton heaped more pressure on Rafa Benítez by beating Everton 3-2, Mads Roerslev scored a late winner for Brentford over Aston Villa and Leeds beat Burnley 3-1.

January 3

A late strike from João Moutinho gave Wolves a remarkable win over Manchester United, to which interim United manager Ralf Rangnick reacted by saying they failed 'individually and collectively'. Romelu Lukaku was welcomed back into the Chelsea fold after a brief expulsion following an interview he gave to Italian media in which he suggested he was unhappy with life in London.

January 4

Christian Eriksen, who left Inter in December, said that his aim was to start playing again and represent Denmark at the World Cup in Qatar. Former Brighton midfielder Davy Pröpper announced his retirement from football, claiming that he 'gradually lost the love for the game'. A consortium led by Serbian media mogul Dragan Šolak completed their takeover of Southampton.

January 5

A combination of a Kai Havertz strike and calamitous own goal by Ben Davies gave Chelsea a 2-0 victory over Tottenham in the first leg of their Carabao Cup semi-final at Stamford Bridge. The other semi-final, due to take place the following evening between Liverpool and Arsenal, was postponed due to a COVID-19 outbreak, which included Reds' manager Jürgen Klopp.

January 6

Manchester United announced that Ed Woodward would step down as their chief executive, to be replaced by managing director Richard Arnold. There were scenes of high farce in Italy, as Inter showed up for their game at Bologna, but their hosts did not: due to a series of COVID-19 cases, the local health authority insisted the squad had to quarantine, and Inter were awarded the game 3-0.

January 7

Newcastle completed the signing of Kieran Trippier from Atlético Madrid for £12 million, their first purchase since the takeover by the Saudi Arabian Public Investment Fund. Aston Villa agreed the loan signing of Philippe Coutinho from Barcelona. A much-changed Manchester City side beat Swindon Town 4-1 in the third round of the FA Cup, youngster Cole Palmer playing a starring role.

January 8

Newcastle United, theoretically the richest club in the world, were knocked out of the FA Cup by League One side Cambridge United, with Newcastle fan Joe Ironside scoring the only goal. In the championship Huddersfield beat Burnley 2-1, non-League Boreham Wood made it to the fourth round after beating Wimbledon and Everton needed extra-time to get past Hull City.

January 9

Arsenal were knocked out of the FA Cup by Championship side Nottingham Forest for the second time in four years. Liverpool went behind to Shrewsbury but ultimately won 4-1, while West Ham beat Leeds 2-0. In the WSL, Birmingham shocked Arsenal by beating them 2-0 while Manchester City beat Brighton 6-0. The Africa Cup of Nations began as hosts Cameroon beat Burkina Faso.

January 10

A Scott McTominay header gave Manchester United a 1-0 win, although they made heavy work of beating Aston Villa in the FA Cup. Barcelona were finally able to register Ferran Torres, their signing from Manchester City, after Samuel Umtiti agreed to defer some of his salary and thus freed some room in their budget. Sadio Mané scored a penalty as Senegal beat Zimbabwe 1-0.

January 11

Southampton cruised to a 4-1 win over Brentford in the Premier League, on-loan Chelsea forward Armando Broja among the scorers. Fulham notched up their second 7-0 win of the season in the Championship, Reading the victims this time. Kelechi Iheancho scored the only goal as Nigeria beat Egypt 1-0 in the Africa Cup of Nations, while Algeria drew 0-0 with Sierra Leone.

January 12

Antonio Rüdiger scored the only goal of the Carabao Cup final second leg as Chelsea went through to the final, beating Spurs 3-0 on aggregate. A shambolic AFCON game saw Mali beat Tunisia 1-0, but not before referee Janny Sikazwe blew for full-time first on 86, then 89 minutes. Gambia beat Mauritania in the day's other game in their first ever appearance at the tournament.

January 13

The delayed first leg of the other Carabao Cup semi-final ended 0-0 between Liverpool and 10-man Arsenal, who had Granit Xhaka sent off. Newcastle made their latest signing, after triggering the £25 million release clause in Burnley's New Zealand striker Chris Wood. Aston Villa completed the signing of Lucas Digne from Everton, after the full-back had fallen out with manager Rafa Benítez.

January 14

An 87th-minute Joachim Andersen own goal gave Brighton a 1-1 draw in their game against Crystal Palace. Morocco became the first team to qualify for the Africa Cup of Nations knockouts after they beat Comoros 2-0, but Ghana were in danger of missing out after they could only draw 1-1 with Gabon, while Senegal drew 0-0 with Guinea and Malawi beat Zimbabwe 2-1.

January 15

Kevin De Bruyne scored the only goal as Manchester City beat Chelsea — an easier victory than the 1-0 scoreline might suggest. Philippe Coutinho starred on his Aston Villa debut, scoring the 87th minute equaliser as they came back to draw 2-2 with Manchester United. Nigeria qualified for the AFCON last 16 by beating Sudan, while Mo Salah scored in Egypt's 1-0 win over Guinea-Bissau.

January 16

Everton confirmed the inevitable as they sacked Rafa Benítez, following a 2-1 defeat to Norwich that meant they had taken just six points from their previous 13 games, and left them six points above the relegation zone. Jack Harrison scored a hat-trick as Leeds beat West Ham 3-2. Equatorial Guinea produced a huge shock by beating defending AFCON champions Algeria 1-0.

January 17

Everton suffered their first blow in finding a replacement for Benítez after the Belgian FA rejected the possibility that Roberto Martínez could combine his role as their head coach with a return to Goodison Park. Pierre-Emerick Aubameyang left the Gabon's Africa Cup of Nations squad after he was found to have 'cardiac lesions', although that apparently wasn't as serious as it sounded.

January 18

Chelsea continued to stumble as an Adam Webster header gave Brighton a 1-1 draw with the European champions. Paco Gento, the Real Madrid great who won six European Cups, died aged 88. Ghana's AFCON humiliation was complete after they were beaten by Comoros, consigning them to bottom place in their group. Senegal went through after drawing 0-0 with Malawi.

January 19

Steven Bergwijn's goals in the 95th and 97th minutes stole an extraordinary 3-2 win for Tottenham against Leicester. Manchester United beat Brentford 3-1, but Cristiano Ronaldo wasn't happy after being substituted in the second half. Egypt ensured they would be in the AFCON knockouts after beating Sudan 1-0, while Nigeria topped their group by beating Guinea-Bissau 2-0.

January 20

Diogo Jota's brace saw Liverpool through to the Carabao Cup final, after they beat Arsenal 2-0 in the second leg of their semi-final at the Emirates. Defending champions Algeria were dumped out of the Africa Cup of Nations by a 3-1 defeat to Ivory Coast, with Equatorial Guinea progressing thanks to a 1-0 win over Sierra Leone. Tunisia went through despite losing to the Gambia.

January 21

Things were looking grim for Claudio Ranieri and Watford as they were beaten 3-0 by relegation rivals Norwich City, for whom Josh Sargant scored twice. Eddie Howe defended the decision to take Newcastle on a mid-season break to Saudi Arabia. Sam Kerr became Australia's all-time leading goalscorer as she scored five in their 18-0 rout of Indonesia at the Women's Asian Cup.

January 22

Southampton impressively held Manchester City to a 1-1 draw, with Aymeric Laporte's goal ensuring it wasn't even worse for the defending champions. Marcus Rashford popped up with an injury-time winner as Manchester United beat West Ham 1-0. Emi Buendía scored the only goal of Aston Villa's 1-0 win over Everton. Newcastle grabbed a crucial 1-0 win over Leeds.

January 23

Antonio Conte's unbeaten start at Spurs ended when Chelsea beat them 2-0. Liverpool held off Crystal Palace to claim a 3-1 win, while Burnley took a 0-0 draw against Arsenal. In the Africa Cup of Nations last 16, Tunisia beat Nigeria 1-0 while Burkina Faso defeated Gabon on penalties. In the WSL, Manchester City and Arsenal drew 1-1 while Manchester United beat Spurs 3-0.

January 24

Claudio Ranieri's spell as Watford manager lasted just 14 games, after he was sacked following their defeat to Norwich. Cameroon's last 16 win over Comoros at the Africa Cup of Nations was over-shadowed after eight people were killed in a crush outside the stadium. Another 38 were injured after a build up of people caused a gate to be opened, and dozens were crushed.

January 25

Roy Hodgson ended his brief retirement to take over from Claudio Ranieri at Watford, the 22nd job of his 46-year managerial career: he took over the Hornets in 19th place, but only two points from Premier League safety. Senegal beat Cape Verde to reach the quarter-finals of the Africa Cup of Nations, while Morocco joined them thanks to their 2-1 victory over Malawi.

January 26

Mo Salah scored the decisive penalty as Egypt beat Ivory Coast on penalties at the Africa Cup of Nations, following a 0-0 draw after extra time. New COVID-19 rules were introduced: Premier League teams would have to have four cases in their squad to get a game postponed, after concerns that some teams were simply using a few cases to put off fixtures when they had other injuries.

January 27

Barcelona completed the surprise loan signing of Adama Traoré from Wolves, Juventus sealed the £63 million signing of Dušan Vlahović from Fiorentina while Newcastle agreed terms for the transfer of Brazilian midfielder Bruno Guimarães from Lyon. Goals from Beth Mead and Vivianne Miedema completed Arsenal's comeback in the WSL as they beat Brighton 2-1.

January 28

Derby manager Wayne Rooney claimed he had turned down the opportunity to interview for the vacant Everton manager's job, as the club dithered over whether to appoint Frank Lampard or Vítor Pereira. Liverpool looked to have gazumped Tottenham for the signing of Porto's Colombian winger Luis Díaz: Spurs thought they had their man, but Liverpool swooped and agreed a fee.

January 29

Toko Ekambi scored two quick second-half goals to give hosts Cameroon a 2-0 win in the Africa Cup of Nations quarter-final over the Gambia. They would be joined in the semi-finals by Burkina Faso, who beat Tunisia 1-0. Georgia Stanway helped herself to a hat-trick as Manchester City beat Nottingham Forest 8-0 in the Women's FA Cup, while Chelsea beat Aston Villa 3-1.

January 30

Frank Lampard agreed a deal to become Everton's new manager, and it looked like he would be followed by Manchester United midfielder Donny van de Beek, who picked a loan move to them over Crystal Palace. Mo Salah scored as Egypt beat Morocco 2-1 in extra time to reach the AFCON semi-finals, then Senegal made it through after beating Equatorial Guinea 3-1.

January 31

Brentford signed Christian Eriksen, who hadn't played football since suffering a cardiac arrest at Euro 2020, until the end of the season. Pierre-Emerick Aubameyang moved to Barcelona on a free transfer, Spurs signed Rodrigo Bentancur and Dejan Kulusevski from Juventus, Dele Alli joined Everton while Matt Targett and Dan Burn joined Newcastle from Aston Villa and Brighton respectively.

February 1

Raith Rovers invited significant criticism by signing striker David Goodwillie. In 2017 a civil court found Goodwillie and another man raped a woman, although he denied the claims and criminal charges were never brought. Tyler Rattray, the captain of Raith's women's team, resigned and the author Val McDermid cancelled her sponsorship of the club's shirts.

February 2

Senegal made it to the Africa Cup of Nations final after Sadio Mané and Idrissa Gueye scored in their 3-1 semi-final win over Burkina Faso. Valérien Ismaël was dismissed as West Brom manager following three defeats in four, as the club feared they would drop out of the play-offs. Everton Women sacked their manager Jean-Luc Vasseur after just 10 games in charge.

February 3

A narrative-laden Africa Cup of Nations final was set up after Mo Salah's Egypt beat Cameroon on penalties in the semi-final. Salah would face his Liverpool team-mate and Senegal forward Sadio Mané in the final. Steve Bruce was appointed as West Brom manager. Raith Rovers admitted 'we got it wrong' and said David Goodwillie would not play for them, amid significant protests.

February 4

Middlesbrough piled the latest ignominy on Manchester United's season by knocking them out of the FA Cup. The match ended 1-1 after normal time, but Anthony Elanga blazed his penalty over the bar in the shootout, meaning the Championship side went through. To make things even worse for the home fans, a 'technical fault' meant no food or drink was available to purchase at Old Trafford.

February 5

National League side Kidderminster were seconds away from knocking West Ham out of the FA Cup, only for Declan Rice to score an injury-time equaliser before Jarrod Bowen scored the winner in the final minute of extra time. There was victory for Frank Lampard in his first game as Everton boss as they beat Brentford 4-1. In the WSL, Arsenal struck late to draw 1-1 with Manchester United.

February 6

Sadio Mané was the hero for Senegal as they won the Africa Cup of Nations on penalties, beating Egypt after the game ended 0-0. Mané had missed an early penalty in general play. Nottingham Forest claimed their second Premier League scalp in the FA Cup, beating Leicester City 4-1. Chelsea went within two points of Arsenal at the top of the WSL after they beat Manchester City 1-0.

February 7

England, Scotland, Wales, Northern Ireland and Ireland launched a joint bid to stage Euro 2028, after deciding that it was preferable to hosting the 2030 World Cup. 'We think it's a brilliant opportunity for the five federations and governments to come together,' said the English FA's Mark Bullingham. This was despite the trouble that marred the Euro 2020 final, held at Wembley.

February 8

Jay Rodriguez scored a second-half equaliser for Burnley to earn a 1-1 draw against Manchester United. Kieran Trippier's exceptional free-kick sealed a 3-1 win for Newcastle over Everton. Kurt Zouma played in West Ham's Premier League game over Watford, despite footage of him kicking a cat at home emerging. West Ham won the game 1-0.

February 9

Romelu Lukaku scored the only goal for Chelsea as they beat Saudi side Al-Hilal in the semi-final of the Club World Cup in Abu Dhabi, putting them through to face Palmeiras in the final. Tottenham twice threw away a lead as Che Adams scored Southampton's winner in their 3-2 victory, Manchester City beat Brentford 2-0 while Aston Villa and Leeds drew in a 3-3 thriller.

February 10

Diogo Jota bagged a couple as Liverpool beat Leicester 2-0, keeping alive some distant hopes of hunting down league leaders Manchester City: the defending champions remained nine points clear. Gabriel scored the only goal for Arsenal as they won 1-0 at Wolves, but they had to play the last 20 minutes with 10 men as Gabriel Martinelli got sent off for two yellow cards in a minute.

February 11

The WSL top two played out a 0-0 draw, as Arsenal maintained their two-point lead over Chelsea at the sharp end of the table. 'I think it's the best game that has been played in the league so far,' said Arsenal manager Jonas Eidevall. Alex Neil became the latest manager to attempt to drag Sunderland out of League One, after he was appointed to replace Lee Johnson.

February 12

Chelsea won the Club World Cup, after a Romelu Lukaku strike and a Kai Havertz penalty in extra time secured their 2-1 win over Palmeiras. Che Adams got the goal to secure a 1-1 draw for Southampton against Manchester United, Raheem Sterling helped himself to a hat-trick in Manchester City's 4-0 win at Norwich, and there was relief for Everton after they beat Leeds 3-0.

February 13

Fabinho stabbed home the sole strike in Liverpool's 1-0 win at Burnley. Early goals from Raùl Jiménez and Leander Dendoncker ensured Wolves beat Tottenham 2-0. Craig Dawson headed home a 91st-minute equaliser for West Ham at Leicester to seal a 2-2 draw. Kieran Trippier scored another free kick but was injured in Newcastle's 1-0 win over Aston Villa.

February 14

Newcastle confirmed that Kieran Trippier had broken his foot in their victory over Aston Villa. The right-back had excelled since moving from Atlético Madrid in January, but the injury put the rest of his season in doubt. UEFA announced that they would cover the costs of 30,000 tickets for the finals of their various men's and women's competitions at the end of the season.

February 15

Kylian Mbappé showed Real Madrid why they were so keen to sign him after he scored a late goal against them for PSG to win the first leg of their Champions League last 16 game at the Parc des Princes. Bernardo Silva starred for Manchester City as they strolled to a 5-0 win against Sporting. In the Premier League, Cristiano Ronaldo scored in Manchester United's 2-0 victory against Brighton.

February 16

Liverpool left it late but came away from their Champions League last 16 first leg trip to Milan with a 2-0 win over Inter, the goals coming from Roberto Firmino and Mo Salah. In the night's other game, Red Bull Salzburg looked like they had grabbed a shock win over Bayern Munich, but Kingsley Coman popped up in the final minute to salvage a 1-1 draw.

February 17

Rangers produced an extraordinary performance to beat Borussia Dortmund 4-2 in the first leg of their Europa League knockout tie in Germany. Leicester also took a commanding lead in the second leg of their Europa Conference League tie against Danish side Randers, sealing a 4-1 home victory, but Bodø/Glimt were in control of their tie against Celtic, winning 3-1 in Glasgow.

February 18

Tottenham told Antonio Conte to stop giving interviews to Italian media outlets after he told Sky Italia that his squad had been 'weakened' in the January transfer window, although some suspect translation may have been responsible for the consternation his comments caused. Manchester City looked close to completing the signing of Brazilian winger Savio from Atlético Mineiro.

February 19

An extraordinary game between Manchester City and Spurs saw Harry Kane score a 95th-minute winner, after a 92nd minute Riyad Mahrez penalty looked to have saved a 2-2 draw for City. Liverpool's 3-1 win over Norwich moved them to six points behind City. Chelsea beat Crystal Palace 1-0, Watford won 1-0 at Aston Villa while Burnley rose off the bottom by beating Brighton 3-0.

February 20

Late goals from Fred and Anthony Elanga ensured Manchester United came away from a frantic game against Leeds with a 4-2 victory. Daniel Podence scored the winner for Wolves as they beat Leicester 2-1. England Women drew 0-0 with Spain in the Arnold Clark Cup. Jack Wilshere signed for Danish club Aarhus until the end of the season, having been without a club since the summer.

February 21

The clamour for temporary concussion substitutions became louder after Leeds insisted they had followed the correct protocols when defender Robin Koch sustained a head injury during their defeat to Manchester United. Koch was allowed to play on for 15 minutes after clashing heads with Scott McTominay, but eventually sat down on the turf, unable to continue.

February 22

Kai Havertz and Christian Pulisic scored for Chelsea as they beat Lille 2-0 in the first leg of their Champions League last-16 tie, as it emerged that the final, scheduled to be held in St Petersburg, could be moved due to Russian president Vladimir Putin sending troops into Ukraine. The night's other game saw Villarreal salvage a 1-1 draw with Juventus after Dušan Vlahović scored in the first minute.

February 23

Manchester United saved a 1-1 draw in their Champions League first leg against Atlético Madrid, while Benfica and Ajax drew 2-2. In the Premier League, Liverpool thrashed Leeds 6-0, Crystal Palace beat Watford 4-1 and Antonio Conte hinted that he might leave Tottenham after they were beaten 1-0 at Burnley. England's Women won the Arnold Clark Cup by beating Germany 3-1.

February 24

Rangers completed their remarkable Europa League defeat of Borussia Dortmund by drawing the second leg at Ibrox, winning 6-4 on aggregate. Leicester went through in the Europa Conference League against Randers, but Bodø/Glimt knocked Celtic out. In the Premier League, two goals in the last eight minutes helped Arsenal beat Wolves 2-1.

February 25

UEFA confirmed the Champions League final would be moved from St Petersburg to the Stade de France in Paris, and entered discussions about their sponsorship agreements with Russian state energy firm Gazprom, after the escalation of Russia's military aggression in Ukraine. Oriel Romeu scored a thumper as Southampton completed a routine 2-0 win over Norwich.

February 26

Marcelo Bielsa was under pressure after Tottenham thrashed Leeds 4-0 at Elland Road. Phil Foden scored the only goal as Manchester City beat Everton 1-0, Manchester United had to settle for another drab draw, this time against Watford, while Christian Eriksen made his debut for Brentford, his first game since his cardiac arrest at Euro 2020, though they lost 2-0 to Newcastle.

February 27

Liverpool beat Chelsea in the Carabao Cup final after an extra-ordinary penalty shootout saw the sides share 21 successful penalties before Chelsea keeper Kepa Arrizabalaga missed. The unthinkable happened as Leeds confirmed the dismissal of manager Marcelo Bielsa, with former RB Leipzig coach Jesse Marsch lined up to replace him. West Ham beat Wolves 1-0.

February 28

Doubts were raised about Roman Abramovich's plans for Chelsea, after it emerged that the club's charitable foundation were not aware that he planned to transfer the 'stewardship' of the club to them in the face of potential sanctions over his involvement with the Russian government. Russia were suspended from all men's and women's FIFA and UEFA competitions over the Ukraine crisis.

March 1

Middlesbrough claimed their second Premier League scalp in the FA Cup after teenager Josh Coburn scored the only goal to beat Tottenham 1-0. Manchester City eventually broke Peterborough down to win 2-0 while Crystal Palace beat Stoke 2-1. In the Premier League, James Maddison and Jamie Vardy scored a couple of late goals as Leicester beat Burnley 2-0.

March 2

Roman Abramovich confirmed that he would be selling Chelsea after 19 years of ownership, claiming any proceeds would be used 'for the benefit of all victims of the war in Ukraine'. On the pitch, Chelsea survived a scare against Luton in the FA Cup, coming back from 1-0 then 2-1 down to win 3-2. Liverpool beat Norwich 2-1 and Southampton defeated West Ham 3-1.

March 3

Clyde's women's team left the club en masse in protest against the loan signing of David Goodwillie, the striker who a civil court had found to have raped a woman in 2011. Goodwillie had re-joined the club on loan from Raith Rovers, who had signed Goodwillie in January. In the FA Cup, Salomón Rondón scored both as Everton beat Boreham Wood 2-0 to reach the quarter-finals.

March 4

The queue of prospective buyers of Chelsea was growing, after Roman Abramovich had announced he would be selling the club. A consortium featuring US businessman Todd Boehly — who part-owns the LA Dodgers — and Swiss billionaire Hansjörg Wyss was considered the front-runner, but Turkish entrepreneur Muhsin Bayrak also threw his hat into the ring.

March 5

Caroline Weir scored twice as Manchester City beat Chelsea 3-1 in the Women's League Cup final. Liverpool laboured over their 1-0 win against West Ham, Chelsea beat Burnley 4-0 but Thomas Tuchel criticised fans after some chanted Roman Abramovich's name during a minute of appreciation for Ukraine, while Leicester beat Leeds 1-0 in Jesse Marsch's first game in charge.

March 6

Kevin De Bruyne and Riyad Mahrez scored two each as Manchester City made short work of Manchester United, winning the derby 4-1. Arsenal held on to beat Watford 3-2, thanks to goals from Gabriel Martinelli, Martin Ødegaard and Bukayo Saka. Arsenal extended their lead at the top of the WSL to eight points after they beat Birmingham City 4-2, Beth Mead among the scorers.

March 7

Harry Kane scored two of Tottenham's goals as they absolutely destroyed Everton 5-0, the scoring finished by the 55th minute. Nottingham Forest made it through to the FA Cup quarter-finals to face Liverpool after beating Huddersfield 2-1. Frank O'Farrell, who managed Manchester United in the 1970s and took Leicester to the FA Cup final in 1969, died at the age of 94.

March 8

Liverpool made it through to the Champions League quarter-finals despite losing the second leg of their tie 1-0 to Inter, hanging on for a 2-1 aggregate win. Robert Lewandowski scored a hat-trick in 11 minutes as Bayern Munich hammered RB Salzburg 7-1. The World Cup qualifying play-off between Ukraine and Scotland, scheduled for later in March, was postponed until June.

March 9

An extraordinary performance by Karim Benzema, in which he scored a hat-trick inside 17 second-half minutes, span Real Madrid's Champions League tie against PSG around as they went through 3-2 on aggregate. Manchester City drew 0-0 with Sporting, which wasn't too much of a problem as they leant on their 5-0 victory in the first leg to cruise through to the quarter-finals.

March 10

Roman Abramovich had his assets frozen by the UK government over his links to Vladimir Putin. The sanctions meant that Chelsea were unable to sell tickets or merchandise, and their spending on match-day expenses was limited. On the pitch they beat Norwich 3-1, Wolves beat Watford 4-0, Newcastle beat Southampton 2-1, while West Ham lost 1-0 to Sevilla in the Europa League.

March 11

Prospective buyers of Chelsea were instructed to present takeover proposals to the UK government, after the sanctions placed on Roman Abramovich threw the process into uncertainty. Mobile phone operators and Chelsea kit sponsors 3 announced they had requested that their logo be removed from the front of the team's shirts for the remainder of the season.

March 12

Luis Díaz and Mo Salah were the goalscorers as Liverpool beat Brighton 2-0. Cristiano Ronaldo scored a hat-trick, including an 81st-minute winner, as Manchester United beat Tottenham 3-2, while Ivan Toney grabbed a late brace as Brentford finally broke down Burnley to win 2-0. Roman Abramovich was officially disqualified as a director of Chelsea by the Premier League.

March 13

Kai Havertz got a late winner for Chelsea against Newcastle, Ukrainian Andriy Yarmolenko scored an emotional goal as West Ham beat Aston Villa 2-1 and Everton slipped further towards the bottom three after a Conor Coady goal gave Wolves a 1-0 win at Goodison Park. In the WSL, Manchester City beat Tottenham 1-0 while Sam Kerr scored to give Chelsea a 1-0 victory over Aston Villa.

March 14

Manchester City dropped what could be a crucial two points as they failed to break Crystal Palace down, having to settle for a 0-0 draw at Selhurst Park that gave Liverpool a sniff of chasing Pep Guardiola's City team. The FA confirmed that the prize money for the Women's FA Cup would dramatically increase in 2022-23, from just £428,000 to £3 million.

March 15

Manchester United were knocked out of the Champions League by Atlético Madrid, who won 1-0 in the second leg of their last-16 tie at Old Trafford, securing a 2-1 aggregate victory. In the other game, Benfica pulled off a surprise 3-2 aggregate win over Ajax. Christian Eriksen received his first call-up to the Denmark squad since his cardiac arrest at Euro 2020.

March 16

Liverpool cut the gap at the top of the Premier League to a single point as goals from Diogo Jota and Roberto Firmino were enough to beat Arsenal 2-0. In the Champions League, Chelsea put aside the chaos of their ownership situation to beat Lille 2-1 on the night, 4-1 on aggregate. The other game saw a big shock as Villarreal pulled off an extraordinary 3-0 win away to Juventus.

March 17

West Ham went through to the Europa League quarter-finals by beating Sevilla, Andriy Yarmolenko scoring the crucial extra-time goal that gave them a 2-1 aggregate victory. Leicester were through to the Europa Conference League quarters with a 3-2 aggregate win over Rennes. In the Premier League, 10-man Everton kept their survival hopes alive by beating Newcastle 1-0.

March 18

Leeds won a madcap game at Molineux as they came back from 2-0 down to win 3-2 against Wolves, Luke Ayling grabbing the winner in the 91st minute. The Champions League quarter-final draw saw Chelsea and Manchester City heading to Madrid, paired with Real and Atlético respectively, while Liverpool would face Benfica and Bayern Munich against Villarreal.

March 19

Bukayo Saka scored the only goal as Arsenal beat Aston Villa 1-0 in the Premier League, after which Ashley Young mocked the Gunners for celebrating 'like they'd won the league'. In the FA Cup, Romelu Lukaku and Hakim Ziyech strikes saw Chelsea beat Middlesbrough and make it through to the semi-finals, with Thomas Tuchel praising their 'team spirit' in the victory.

March 20

Liverpool were made to work hard for their FA Cup quarter-final win over Nottingham Forest, Diogo Jota scoring the only goal in the closing stages. Manchester City beat Southampton 4-1 and Crystal Palace made short work of Everton, winning 4-0. In the Premier League, Spurs beat West Ham 3-1 and Leicester beat Brentford 2-1. In Spain, Barcelona beat Real Madrid 4-0.

March 21

Tyrick Mitchell and Kyle Walker-Peters won their first ever England call-ups for the national team's friendlies against Ivory Coast and Switzerland. Belgian club Royal Antwerp attracted some criticism for appointing Marc Overmars as their technical director, who had left Ajax a month earlier after sending 'lewd' and unwelcome pictures to female members of staff.

March 22

Alexia Putellas scored twice for Barcelona in the first leg of their Women's Champions League quarter-final against Real Madrid, as the favourites ran out 3-1 winners. Marie-Antoinette Katoto bagged both goals for PSG as they beat Bayern Munich 2-1. The coast seemed clear for the UK and Ireland's bid to host Euro 2028 after no other country submitted a bid.

March 23

Lotte Wubben-Moy salvaged a 1-1 draw for Arsenal in the first leg of their Women's Champions League quarter-final against Wolfsburg. Juventus took a 2-1 lead into the second leg of their tie against Lyon. In the WSL, Ellen White scored as Manchester City thrashed Everton 4-0. Restrictions on Chelsea were loosened as they were permitted to sell tickets to their fans for away games.

March 24

Italy were sensationally knocked out of the World Cup qualifying play-off semi-finals by a late North Macedonia goal. Gareth Bale rolled back the years to score both for Wales as they beat Austria, while Portugal beat Turkey and Sweden bested the Czech Republic. Ada Hegerberg returned to the Norway squad after a five-year absence, having quit the national team in 2017.

March 25

A dramatic repeat of the Africa Cup of Nations final, this time in the World Cup qualifying play-offs, saw Egypt beat Senegal 1-0 in their first leg, while the Ghana v Nigeria grudge match ended 0-0, Algeria and Tunisia beat Cameroon and Mali respectively 1-0 and DR Congo v Morocco ended 1-1. In South America, Ecuador and Uruguay joined Brazil and Argentina in securing their spots in Qatar.

March 26

Christian Eriksen revealed a fondness for 'on the nose' narrative, as he scored on his comeback for Denmark in their friendly defeat to the Netherlands. Harry Kane's penalty capped a 2-1 victory for England against Switzerland, as Gareth Southgate's team came back from 1-0 down at Wembley. Chelsea pair Timo Werner and Kai Havertz scored for Germany as they beat Israel 2-0.

March 27

Chelsea went top of the WSL after hammering Leicester 9-0, taking advantage of Arsenal's game against Spurs being postponed due to COVID-19. A club-record crowd of over 20,000 at Old Trafford saw Manchester United beat Everton 3-1. Canada's men reached their first World Cup since 1986 with a 4-0 win over Jamaica, while the USA all but sealed their spot by beating Panama 5-1.

March 28

Former Manchester United manager Louis van Gaal had some words of advice for the man many expected to be their next boss. Netherlands coach Van Gaal advised Erik ten Hag, the favourite to take over in the summer, against leaving Ajax for Old Trafford, saying: 'United are a commercial club, so it's a difficult choice for a coach. He would be better going to a football club.'

March 29

Senegal once again beat Egypt on penalties, this time in the second leg of their World Cup qualifying play-offs. In the other African play-offs, Ghana beat Nigeria, Cameroon went through ahead of Algeria, Morocco beat DR Congo and Tunisia beat Mali. In Europe, Portugal beat North Macedonia to qualify for Qatar while Poland beat Sweden. England beat Ivory Coast 3-0 in a friendly.

March 30

A world record crowd for a women's club game of 91,553 at the Camp Nou watched an absolutely sensational spectacle in the Champions League, as Barcelona beat Real Madrid 5-2, 8-3 on aggregate. PSG went through in the night's other quarter-final, a 2-2 draw with Bayern enough for a 4-3 aggregate win. Ruud van Nistelrooy was named as new manager of PSV.

March 31

Arsenal were out of the Women's Champions League after they lost 2-0 to Wolfsburg in the second leg of their quarter-final. Lyon beat Juventus 4-3 on aggregate. The USA men's team qualified for the World Cup despite losing 2-0 to Costa Rica: their place was secure unless they lost by six goals. Premier League clubs agreed to increase substitutions from three to five from the 2022-23 season.

April 1

The draw for the 2022 World Cup took place in Qatar. England were drawn with Iran, the USA and the winner of the Wales/Scotland/Ukraine play-off, while the spiciest group was probably Portugal, Ghana, Uruguay and South Korea. Bruno Fernandes signed a new contract at Manchester United, agreeing a deal that would keep him at Old Trafford until 2026, with the option of a further year.

April 2

Brentford stunned Chelsea at Stamford Bridge as Christian Eriksen scored in and inspired an extraordinary 4-1 victory. Liverpool won their tenth Premier League game in a row when they beat Watford 2-0, but Manchester City's 2-0 victory at Burnley kept them top. Wolves beat Aston Villa 2-1, while Manchester United drew 1-1 with Leicester, VAR disallowing a late Foxes goal.

April 3

Tottenham moved ahead in the race to qualify for the Champions League as they beat Newcastle 5-1, but at the bottom of the table Everton had a player sent off for the third game in a row as they lost 2-1 to West Ham. Rotherham won the Papa John's Trophy at Wembley, beating Sutton in extra time. In the WSL, Arsenal and Chelsea thrashed Leicester and Reading 5-0 respectively.

April 4

Mikel Arteta called Arsenal's performance 'unacceptable' as they lost 3-0 to Crystal Palace, with Wilfried Zaha among the scorers. To make things worse for Arsenal, Thomas Partey was forced off with injury. Netherlands manager Louis van Gaal revealed that he had been undergoing treatment for an 'aggressive' form of prostate cancer, but he planned to lead the team at the World Cup.

April 5

Kevin De Bruyne scored the only goal as Manchester City won a spicy Champions League quarter-final first leg against Atlético Madrid 1-0. Liverpool had one foot in the semis after beating Benfica 3-1 in their equivalent game. Leah Williamson was named England Women captain with Steph Houghton's injury putting her in doubt for the summer's European Championships.

April 6

A Karim Benzema hat-trick gave Real Madrid a 3-1 win in their Champions League quarter-final against Chelsea, while in the night's other game Villarreal shocked Bayern Munich 1-0, Arnaut Danjuma scoring the only goal. In the Premier League, Burnley moved to within just a point of Everton as they beat the Toffees in the big relegation clash at Turf Moor.

April 7

West Ham managed to hang on to a 1-1 draw against Lyon in the Europa League quarter-final, despite having Aaron Cresswell sent off. Rangers lost 1-0 to Braga, Ferran Torres saved Barcelona in their 1-1 draw with Eintracht Frankfurt, while RB Leipzig and Atalanta drew 1-1. In the Europa Conference League, Leicester drew 0-0 with PSV Eindhoven in their quarter-final first leg.

April 8

Newcastle pulled further clear of relegation trouble after a Chris Wood penalty was enough for them to beat Wolves 1-0 in the Premier League, moving them (temporarily) into 14th. England Women were involved in another World Cup qualifying mismatch, as Beth Mead scored four in their 10-0 victory over North Macedonia, with Ellen White scoring her 50th international goal.

April 9

David de Gea lifted Manchester United's spirits by calling their performance in their 1-0 defeat to Everton a 'disgrace'. Mikel Arteta was similarly irked after Arsenal lost 2-1 to Brighton, Son Heung-min scored a hat-trick as Tottenham beat Aston Villa 4-0, Chelsea hammered Southampton 6-0, while Leeds staved off the threat of relegation by beating Watford 3-0.

April 10

Manchester City and Liverpool played out an extraordinarily thrilling 2-2 draw in the big top of the table clash, Diogo Jota and Sadio Mané twice equalising goals from Kevin De Bruyne and Gabriel Jesus. Norwich kicked a hole in Burnley's survival hopes with a 2-0 win, Leicester beat Crystal Palace 2-1 at the King Power Stadium, while Brentford beat West Ham 2-0.

April 11

UEFA ordered Atlético Madrid to partially close their Wanda Metropolitano stadium for their Champions League quarter-final second leg against Manchester City, after some of their fans appeared to make Nazi salutes in the first leg. Neil Warnock announced his retirement from management, four months after leaving his job as Middlesbrough manager.

April 12

Chelsea were 3-0 up and 10 minutes away from an incredible comeback win over Real Madrid, until Rodrygo then Karim Benzema scored to give Real a 5-4 aggregate victory. Villarreal completed a sensational shock victory over Bayern Munich, as Samuel Chukwueze scored to give them a 2-1 aggregate win. England's Women beat Northern Ireland 5-0 in World Cup qualifying.

April 13

In what turned out to be a full stadium, Manchester City went through to the Champions League semi-final after a 0-0 draw with Atlético Madrid secured a 1-0 aggregate victory in their quarter-final, with Felipe sent off for Atlético in a spicy encounter. Liverpool's passage was slightly bumpier than expected, as they drew 3-3 with Benfica on the night, winning 6-4 over the two legs.

April 14

Eintracht Frankfurt defeated Barcelona in the Europa League quarter-finals, winning 3-2 in the Camp Nou and 4-3 on aggregate. They were joined in the semi-finals by West Ham, who beat Lyon, and Rangers, who defeated Braga. Leicester made the Europa Conference League semis after beating PSV 2-1. Colombia great Freddy Rincón died aged 55, following a car crash.

April 15

Burnley surprised everyone by sacking Sean Dyche, their manager for almost a decade, despite him signing a new four-year contract only eight months earlier. Burnley were in the bottom three and four points from safety with eight games remaining, the recent defeat to doomed Norwich seemingly the final straw. Under-23s coach Mike Jackson was put in temporary charge.

April 16

Liverpool held off Manchester City to win their FA Cup semi-final 3-2, despite a late City goal making what had looked like a straightforward win look a little closer. In the Women's FA Cup semi-final, City beat West Ham 4-1. In the Premier League, Brighton beat Spurs 1-0, Arsenal lost 1-0 at Southampton and Cristiano Ronaldo scored a hat-trick as Manchester United beat Norwich 3-2.

April 17

Chelsea joined Liverpool in the men's FA Cup final after they eventually broke Crystal Palace down in their semi, winning 2-0 thanks to goals from Ruben Loftus-Cheek and Mason Mount. Chelsea Women beat Arsenal 2-0 in their semi-final, goals from Guro Reiten and Ji So-yun seeing them through to face Manchester City. Newcastle beat Leicester 2-1 in the Premier League.

April 18

Cristiano Ronaldo and his partner Georgina Rodríguez announced the death of one of their newborn twins. 'It is the greatest pain that any parents can feel,' they said in a statement. 'Only the birth of our baby girl gives us the strength to live this moment with some hope and happiness. We are all devastated at this loss and we kindly ask for privacy at this very difficult time.'

April 19

Mo Salah scored twice as Liverpool humiliated Manchester United at Anfield, the 4-0 scoreline somehow flattering Ralf Rangnick's side. The victory took Liverpool two points clear at the top of the Premier League. They would be joined in the top tier by Fulham, who emphatically confirmed their immediate promotion with a 3-0 win over Preston, Aleksandar Mitrović scoring twice.

April 20

Manchester City retook top spot in the Premier League by beating Brighton 3-0, with goals from Riyad Mahrez, Phil Foden and Bernardo Silva. Eddie Nketiah bagged two as Arsenal capitalised on some big Chelsea mistakes to win 4-2 at Stamford Bridge. Newcastle all but sealed their safety with a 1-0 win over Crystal Palace, while Everton salvaged a late draw with Leicester.

April 21

Manchester United confirmed that Ajax head coach Erik ten Hag would be their new manager, from the 2022-23 season. The Dutchman agreed a three-year contract, calling the appointment 'a great honour'. Burnley increased their survival chances in their first game of the post-Sean Dyche era as they beat Southampton 2-0 at Turf Moor, with Connor Roberts and Nathan Collins scoring.

April 22

Ralf Rangnick suggested that Paul Pogba would be unlikely to play again before the end of the season, so with his contract set to expire and little sign of him agreeing a new one, his time at Manchester United looked to be over. In the Women's Champions League semi-final first leg, another world record crowd saw Barcelona hammer Wolfsburg, winning 5-1 at the Camp Nou.

April 23

Granit Xhaka scored a thumping goal to secure Arsenal's 3-1 win over Manchester United, at a point in their Premier League game where the result was in the balance. Gabriel Jesus scored four as Manchester City beat Watford 5-1, Newcastle beat Norwich 3-0 and Spurs drew 0-0 with Brentford. In Germany, Bayern sealed their tenth straight title by beating Borussia Dortmund 3-1.

April 24

Everton held out for longer than expected in the Merseyside derby, but goals from Andrew Robertson and Divock Origi still gave Liverpool a 2-0 win. Burnley moved out of the bottom three after beating Wolves 1-0, while Chelsea defeated West Ham and Southampton drew 2-2 with Brighton. Lyon beat PSG 3-2 in the first leg of their Women's Champions League semi-final.

April 25

Antonio Rüdiger looked to be heading for Real Madrid, after he confirmed to Chelsea manager Thomas Tuchel that he would be leaving the club when his contract expired at the end of the season. Leeds gained a point as they looked to clamber away from relegation trouble, a scrappy 0-0 draw away to Crystal Palace doing the job for Jesse Marsch's side.

April 26

Manchester City were somehow left slightly disappointed after winning the first leg of their Champions League semi-final against Real Madrid 4-3. City were so dominant for long spells that they arguably should have scored more, but goals from Karim Benzema and Vinícius Júnior kept Real in the tie. Kevin De Bruyne, Phil Foden, Gabriel Jesus and Bernardo Silva scored for City.

April 27

Liverpool were in a commanding position going into the second leg of their Champions League semi-final, after Sadio Mané and an own goal from Pervis Estupiñán ensured they beat Villarreal 2-0 at Anfield. 'It is a dangerous scoreline,' said Jürgen Klopp after the game. 'How much work is left to do? The full work. Nothing has happened yet. It's 2-0 at half-time.'

April 28

Jürgen Klopp agreed a contract extension that would keep him at Liverpool until 2026. West Ham lost the first leg of their Europa League semi-final 2-1 to Eintracht Frankfurt, while Leicester drew with Roma in the first leg of their Europa Conference League semi. In the Premier League, Manchester United and Chelsea drew 1-1. In the WSL, Chelsea beat Spurs 2-1.

April 29

Ralf Rangnick caused some raised eyebrows after he was confirmed as the new manager of the Austria national team, despite theoretically remaining at Manchester United as an advisor beyond his stint as head coach. The group led by LA Dodgers part-owner Todd Boehly was confirmed as the 'preferred bidder' to buy Chelsea, despite a late offer from billionaire Jim Ratcliffe.

April 30

Liverpool and Manchester City maintained their relentless pace, beating Newcastle and Leeds 1-0 and 4-0 respectively. Norwich were relegated after losing to Aston Villa. Real Madrid were confirmed as Spanish champions following a win over Espanyol. Barcelona would play Lyon in the Women's Champions League final after holding off Wolfsburg and PSG. Agent Mino Raiola died aged 54.

May 1

Everton took a big step towards Premier League survival when a goal from Richarlison and a stunning performance by Jordan Pickford gave them a 1-0 win over Chelsea. Arsenal beat West Ham 2-1 thanks to goals from Rob Holding and Gabriel. Son Heung-min hit two as Tottenham beat Leicester 3-1. Vivianne Miedema scored twice as Arsenal thrashed Aston Villa 7-0 in the WSL.

May 2

Cristiano Ronaldo was among the scorers as Manchester United beat Brentford 3-0 at Old Trafford. Aleksandar Mitrović broke the second tier scoring record with his two goals as Fulham hammered Luton 7-0. UEFA finally confirmed that Russia would be banned from the Women's European Championships in the summer, and they would be replaced by Portugal.

May 3

Liverpool survived a scare to come from behind against Villarreal in their Champions League semi-final, winning 3-2 on the night and 5-2 on aggregate. Bournemouth secured promotion to the Premier League after a Kieffer Moore goal beat Nottingham Forest 1-0. Earlier that day their midfielder David Brooks announced he had been given the all-clear after suffering from cancer.

May 4

Real Madrid produced another extraordinary comeback with two injury-time goals by Rodrygo and another in extra time from Karim Benzema to beat Manchester City in their Champions League semi-final. The shirt that Diego Maradona wore when he scored his 'Hand of God' goal against England in 1986 sold for a record £7.1 million. Roy Hodgson announced his retirement.

May 5

The Europa League final would be between Rangers and Eintracht Frankfurt: Rangers pulled off a surprise to beat RB Leipzig, while Frankfurt eased past West Ham after Aaron Cresswell was sent off. Roma would face Feyenoord in the Europa Conference League final after Tammy Abraham scored in their semi-final second leg against Leicester, while the Dutch side beat Marseille.

May 6

The takeover of Chelsea inched forward after the consortium featuring LA Dodgers part-owner and the private equity firm Clearlake Capital signed a contract to buy the club, subject to Premier League and government approval. Both Arsenal managers signed new contracts, with Mikel Arteta agreeing a deal until 2025 and Jonas Eidevall until 2024.

May 7

Liverpool's chances of winning the Premier League took a significant hit as they could only draw 1-1 with Tottenham. Manchester United's dignity suffered a major blow after they were thrashed 4-0 by Brighton. Watford's relegation was confirmed after they lost to Crystal Palace, while Burnley looked like joining them after they were beaten comfortably 3-1 by Aston Villa.

May 8

Chelsea were crowned WSL champions after Sam Kerr scored twice as they beat Manchester United 4-2, pipping Arsenal to the title. Manchester City took a step towards the Premier League title after they thrashed Newcastle 5-0, while Everton claimed another colossal three points with a 2-1 victory at Leicester. They were further helped when Arsenal beat Leeds 2-1.

May 9

Erling Haaland moved closer to joining Manchester City from Borussia Dortmund after passing a medical ahead of his transfer. Sunderland reached the League One play-off final after Patrick Roberts' stoppage-time goal was enough to earn a 1-1 draw on the night against Sheffield Wednesday, seeing them through to Wembley 2-1 on aggregate. There they would face Wycombe Wanderers, who edged past MK Dons the day before, also winning 2-1 on aggregate.

May 10

Liverpool stayed in touch with Manchester City at the top of the Premier League after goals from Joel Matip and Sadio Mané earned them a 2-1 win over Steven Gerrard's Aston Villa. Manchester City confirmed the signing of Erling Haaland for around £51 million. The Premier League looked set to be awarded a fifth Champions League place after UEFA announced reform of its competitions.

May 11

Kevin De Bruyne scored four times in an extraordinary performance as they hammered Wolves 5-1 at Molineux to maintain their three-point advantage over Liverpool. Leeds were firmly in the bottom three after they lost 3-0 to Chelsea, while Everton inched towards safety after a 0-0 draw with Watford, who appointed Forest Green Rovers manager Rob Edwards as their new boss.

May 12

Tottenham moved ahead of Arsenal in the race to qualify for the Champions League after a 3-0 home win over their rivals. Harry Kane scored twice and Son Heung-min got the other, while Arsenal's Rob Holding was sent off in the first half of a game that was effectively over by the break. Aston Villa confirmed the permanent signing of Philippe Coutinho from Barcelona.

May 13
Amnesty International said that a rumoured Newcastle away kit design, which bore a striking resemblance to the Saudi Arabian national team shirt, would represent 'clear evidence of the regime using Newcastle to portray a positive image'. The first leg of Luton and Huddersfield Town's Championship play-off final ended 1-1, Sonny Bradley and Danel Sinani with the goals.

May 14
Liverpool won the second trophy of their potential quadruple as they beat Chelsea on penalties in the FA Cup final. Cesar Azpilicueta and Mason Mount missed in the shootout, and while Édouard Mendy saved from Sadio Mané, Kostas Tsimikas scored the winning kick. Nottingham Forest took a 2-1 lead into the second leg of their Championship play-off semi-final against Sheffield United.

May 15
Chelsea's Women completed the double when they beat Manchester City in the FA Cup final, with Sam Kerr once again starring by scoring twice. Manchester City opened the door to Liverpool at the top of the Premier League after drawing with West Ham. At the bottom, Burnley lost to Spurs and Leeds drew with Brighton while Everton were still in it after they were beaten by Brentford.

May 16
Jake Daniels, a 17-year-old Blackpool forward, became the first male professional footballer in the UK since Justin Fashanu to come out as gay. Bruno Guimarães scored in Newcastle's 2-0 win over Arsenal, essentially killing the Gunners' Champions League

chances. Jordan Rhodes scored the winner for Huddersfield as they beat Luton in the Championship play-off semi-final.

May 17

Liverpool took the Premier League title race to the last day of the season after a much-changed team beat Southampton 2-1, with goals from Joel Matip and Takumi Minamino. Nottingham Forest reached Wembley for the first time in 30 years after they beat Sheffield United on penalties in the Championship play-off semi-final: goalkeeper Brice Samba saved three spot kicks.

May 18

Eintracht Frankfurt won the Europa League, beating Rangers on penalties in Seville. The game ended 1-1 after extra time: Joe Aribo gave Rangers the lead, but Rafael Borré equalised, then in the shootout Aaron Ramsey missed giving Borré the chance to score the clincher. A Nottingham Forest fan was arrested after he barged over Sheffield United's Billy Sharp after the play-off semi-final.

May 19

Everton confirmed their Premier League survival in hugely dramatic circumstances after they came from 2-0 down to beat Crystal Palace 3-2, the winner scored by Dominic Calvert-Lewin in the 85th minute. Burnley climbed out of the bottom three with a 1-1 draw against Aston Villa, thanks to an Ashley Barnes goal. Marcos Alonso scored to give Chelsea a 1-1 draw with Leicester.

May 20

Merseyside police announced they were investigating Crystal Palace manager Patrick Vieira, after he appeared to aim a kick at some Everton fans who had invaded the pitch following their victory the previous evening. They ultimately pressed no charges.

In an echo of 'Lasagnegate', a stomach bug went through the Tottenham squad ahead of their last game of the season.

May 21
Lyon won their eighth Women's Champions League title after beating Barcelona 3-1 in the final, Ada Hegerberg among the scorers. Sunderland finally won promotion back to League One after a dominant 2-0 victory over Wycombe in the play-off final. Kylian Mbappé dramatically decided to sign a new three-year contract at PSG, turning down the chance to move to Real Madrid.

May 22
Manchester City won their fourth Premier League title in five years on a dramatic final day. At one point they were 2-0 down to Aston Villa, but came back with three goals in five minutes to win 3-2 and pip Liverpool, who beat Wolves 3-1. Burnley were relegated after they lost to Newcastle and Leeds beat Brentford 2-1, while Tottenham confirmed fourth place by thrashing Norwich 5-0.

May 23
Erik ten Hag was officially unveiled as Manchester United manager, saying that it was his aim to challenge Liverpool and Manchester City at the top of the Premier League. Liverpool announced the signing of Fulham midfielder Fabio Carvalho, but a bigger concern for them was the fitness of Thiago Alcântara and Fabinho, who were both doubts for the Champions League final.

May 24
The Premier League approved Chelsea's £4.25 billion takeover by the Todd Boehly and Clearlake Capital consortium: only the nod from the government was required after that. Jarrod Bowen and James Justin won their first England call-ups for Nations League

games against Hungary, Germany and Italy. Jürgen Klopp was named the LMA's manager of the year.

May 25
Roma won the first ever Europa Conference League final and their first major trophy since 2008 after they beat Feyenoord in the final held in Tirana. Nicolò Zaniolo scored the only goal in a classic José Mourinho performance, as the Italian side shut down the game in the second half. Mo Salah announced that he would definitely stay at Liverpool for at least the 2022-23 season.

May 26
Aston Villa agreed a deal to sign Sevilla central defender Diego Carlos a few days after snapping up Marseille midfielder Boubacar Kamara, while Leeds announced they were to sign Red Bull Salzburg midfielder Brenden Aaronson. Lucy Bronze became the latest high-profile player to leave Manchester City Women, joining Georgia Stanway and Caroline Weir in departing.

May 27
Tottenham were given a significant boost after Antonio Conte agreed to remain at the club following talks with sporting director Fabio Paratici. His first signing looked to be a former player of his, Ivan Perišić, who agreed a two-year contract to sign for the club on a free transfer from Inter. Liverpool and Real Madrid prepared to face each other in the Champions League final.

May 28
Real Madrid won their 14th Champions League title after a Vinícius Júnior goal was enough to beat Liverpool 1-0 in the Stade de France. However the game was disrupted and arguably overshadowed after organisational chaos outside the stadium prevented thousands of Liverpool fans from gaining entry to the ground, forcing kick-off to be delayed by half an hour.

May 29

Nottingham Forest ended their 23-year absence from the top flight after they beat Huddersfield Town 1-0 in the Championship play-off final at Wembley, with the only goal coming in the form of an own goal by Chelsea loanee Levi Colwill. Ralf Rangnick announced that he would not in fact take up his consultancy role at Manchester United after he stepped down as interim manager.

May 30

The takeover of Chelsea by the Todd Boehly and Clearlake Capital consortium was finalised when the government approved the sale. 'Our plan of action is to invest in the club for the long term and build on Chelsea's remarkable history of success,' said Boehly. Robert Lewandowski announced his time at Bayern Munich was 'over' as he pushed to leave the Bavarian giants.

May 31

Liverpool demanded answers from UEFA about the chaos outside the Champions League final — more than 5,000 fans provided details about the situation at the Stade de France, most of whom contradicted the French government's story that the issues were caused by fans turning up late, and with fake tickets. Tottenham confirmed the signing of Ivan Perišić on a free transfer.

Anna Ivanova, Ukraine, the war and football

by Daniel Storey

Before Russia invaded Ukraine in February 2022, Anna Ivanova was *just* a footballer. After she was forced to flee her home, she dreams of just being a footballer again . . .

It was supposed to be the best season of Anna Ivanova's short career. In July 2021, FC Kryvbas Kryvyi Rih signed an agreement with financially creaking club Nika Mykolaiv to replace them in the Vyshcha Liha, the top tier of Ukrainian women's football. The club appointed Moldovan Alina Stetsenko as the new coach, signed three Brazilian players and built a young squad. Ivanova was named its captain.

'The atmosphere in the team is great,' Ivanova said after an excellent start to the season. 'This makes our team very friendly and cohesive. Our successful start is not a surprise; it is the result of quality work. Victories do not fall from the sky — they come only through hard work.' When the league split into its championship and relegation groups, Kryvbas were third.

On 24 February, the FC Kryvbas squad climbed aboard a coach and headed towards the airport. They were due to fly to Belek in Turkey for a training camp ahead of the winter break in Ukrainian football. They would meet several members of the group who had been away with the country's national age-group teams. Coach Stetsenko was excited about how a warm-weather camp could make a real difference to the second half of the season. She spoke of arranging three matches to focus on game patterns with and without the ball.

On 24 February, Russia invaded Ukraine. It was early morning and the players remember vividly being on the coach and hearing three loud explosions, understandably causing mass panic. Russian forces had struck two military installations in Kryvyi Rih with missiles. After frantic phone calls, it was agreed that the coach would redirect to a hotel in the city that was also owned by FC Kryvbas' owner.

The players had only the luggage they were taking to Turkey, but they would at least be in comparative safety. The hotel provided beds, meals and electricity. The players were able to communicate with family members, easing their concerns. It would be their home for the next two weeks.

Now Kryvyi Rih, the largest city in central Ukraine, is famous as the birthplace of the country's most famous modern son. Volodymyr Zelensky was born in Kryvyi Rih, where his father was a professor at the University of Economics and Technology and his mother worked as an engineer. His comedy group and film production company were named after the Kvartal 95 housing block in which he lived as a child. His parents still own an apartment in the complex, although they were moved on the eve of war.

The squad's escape came via Artur Podkopayev, a twenty-something Hamburg resident who had played in FC Kryvbas' youth teams as a child, winning a national championship before he moved to live in Germany. When the invasion began, he phoned his old coach Evhenii Arbuzov who was now the club's technical director and asked him about the club's situation. Arbuzov told him the news of the women's team, and the pair worked on a plan to get the squad to Germany. At that point, Podkopayev says, everything was decided. The team had to move to further safety.

Podkopayev reached out to FC Köln, who deserve huge praise for the haste and extent of their welcome. The three parties — Köln, Podkopayev and Arbuzov — worked together and it was agreed that if Arbuzov and Podkopayev could work on finding spaces on a plane out of Ukraine, FC Köln would work with charitable foundations to provide accommodation in the city, supply the squad with food, clothing and supplies. The club would welcome FC Kryvbas under their own umbrella, allowing them to use the training facility when required and making them guests of honour at home games of both the men's and women's teams.

It's impossible to imagine how much the instant shift from normal life, putting your career on hold through no fault of your own, can change a person. When speaking to several Kryvbas players in March, they spoke of the 'shitty feeling' of leaving your city not because you want to but through necessity. They are incredibly grateful to the city and football club of Köln, whose magnificent gesture will create gratitude that lasts a lifetime.

But nowhere else can ever truly feel like home. One player, Violetta Ta, spoke at length of how much she misses walking along streets in half-thought and missing seeing buildings that you have never entered but that provide a familiarity that reinforce normality. She thinks constantly of the specifics of her own home.

'I'm looking forward to seeing my family, firstly; that's obvious,' Ivanova said. 'But beyond that it's the ability to do normal things without planning them first or worrying if they are even possible, like sitting outside in the sunshine with a plate of food. More than anything, I want to talk about meaningless subjects that have nothing to do with war.'

For Ivanova, captaincy took on a new role. She was used to organising young team-mates on the pitch and offering support away from it, but without matches, and with fear pervading the squad, she became a vital pillar for those around her. That's an awful lot for a young woman to deal with when she has her own worries to cope with. How could it not change her?

'Everything changed overnight and it changes you emotionally too,' Ivanova told me. 'You come to value different things in different ways. Before the war, material possessions appeared important and now they are meaningless. And the things that used to seem unimportant, everyday things, now have a greater importance than we could ever have known.'

Training on an almost daily basis helps. So too have the other elements of a footballer's normality: attending matches, having team meetings, spending time with team-mates who inevitably become friends through the amount of time they now spend together and the situation into which all have been submerged. But the notion of football as escape cannot last forever. It is a sugary epithet that fails to stick around.

'When we are training, it's a wonderful distraction,' Ivanova said. 'We can laugh and smile and when we are training we only think about football. But as soon as we get back on the bus and we read the news, it all comes back to us. We are back in reality again.'

Hundreds of miles now separate FC Kryvbas from conflict, of the news of bombings in Kryvyi Rih, Mariupol, Kharkiv and beyond. But they are simultaneously far away from war and right next to it. Despite regular updates from family and friends that they are safe and surviving, their city stands at the epicentre of a war that their compatriots are fighting desperately to win against all the odds.

Having managed to find refuge, thoughts inevitably turn to those who could not escape. Some of the squad are also dogged by guilt because they are a few of the few while many others remain at home. When those others include your closest family and friends with whom you have shared at least half a lifetime, guilt mixes with angst and is multiplied. Players have spoken of a second-hand insomnia, the inability to sleep because you know the explosions and sirens are stopping millions of others sleeping too. Again, Ivanova and the coaching team are offering help and love to those who need it. Again, she is going far beyond the job description of her role.

One thing that stood out when talking to Ivanova and her team-mates was the manner in which they have educated themselves on the conflict back home. We have grown used to footballers understandably choosing to exist in their own bubbles, focusing on the day job rather than offering opinions on geopolitics. This group, partly because of the severity of their own experience, are different. Ivanova asked me specifically to publish a line in our original interview calling for a no-fly zone over Ukraine that she said would stop more innocent people dying.

If anything, leaving home only reinforced their national pride. They watched news reports, followed accounts on social media, spoke to those back home when they could. The idea that this group left Ukraine and escaped war is only true in a physical sense. Emotionally, it made them more determined to spread a message of peace.

'We are extremely proud of the Ukrainian army and the Ukrainian people, because I think they have become something unique: at one together,' said Ivanova. 'With this mentality we believe that we can win this war. That is the same mentality that we have in our team, that everyone is a unit and looks after each other and nobody is left behind. That spirit of the country has brought us closer as a group.'

Kryvyi Rih is a mining city, the second biggest in Ukraine by area. It initially became a crucial location in Russia's invasion because it provides the only viable entry point to Dnipro, one of the country's foremost industrial hubs. Kryvyi Rih took on extra importance after the shelling of factories in Kharkiv and Mariupol. In peacetime, its industry accounted for 10 per cent of Ukraine's GDP; that rose given the destruction elsewhere.

On 30 April, Kryvyi Rih prepared to repel Russia's attacks as they advanced closer to their city. Just as crucial was the mass migration towards the city from those fleeing their homes in the south and east of the country. The deputy mayor, Sergiy Miliutin, estimated that 1,000 people a day came to Kryvyi Rih from Kherson alone and that the city was doing all it could to provide shelter — it was seen as a symbolic haven because it is Zelensky's hometown. One refugee, who escaped to Bolton from Kryvyi Rih in March, spoke of hiding in a cellar to escape the bombing. Her husband, left behind to help fight for the cause, is one of many who had, until late May, kept the city out of Russian hands.

Russia's advances were blocked far more effectively than anyone could have dreamed, but the comparative frivolities of normal life were never likely to last. On 12 May, the Ukrainian Football Association announced that FC Kryvbas' league season was over. The campaign was officially abandoned, although it was clear for some time that no other conclusion was likely. Football, that great escape from the relentlessness of everyday life, can easily be trampled by extraordinary events. English football learnt that in 2020. Nobody would be named champion, the 2021-22 season instead left empty in the record books. That somehow feels apt.

In any other circumstance, finishing third in their debut top-flight season would be a cause for great celebration. Ivanova would be lauded as a difference-maker on the pitch for helping to smooth the acclimatisation of many new players and an emphatically young team. She and I would never have spoken. The story of FC Kryvbas would have been just another football club in an ocean of good news stories and hard-luck sporting tales.

Instead, Ivanova has made a far greater difference. She was a role model and a crutch for those around her. She became one of many emblems of the social impacts of war. She decided that she must become a spokesperson for peace and for national pride.

She and her team-mates dream of training on a familiar pitch, celebrating and cursing football's myriad soap operas. They will invite their families to their first games back. Twelve months ago, Anna Ivanova was *just* a footballer. Now all she dreams of is just being a footballer again.

Roman Abramovich and the damage done to football

by Nick Miller

Roman Abramovich was forced out of Chelsea in 2022, and while the damage he did to football has been done we should at least celebrate the symbolism of his departure . . .

If you search through the archives of *The Guardian* newspaper, one of the earliest mentions of Roman Abramovich comes in a feature titled 'The hard men behind Putin' from March 2000. Some 22 years later, it would be Abramovich's links with Vladimir Putin that led to him being forced to sell Chelsea, having done nothing more than completely change football, probably forever.

The sanctions placed upon Abramovich by the British government, which effectively forced him to divest himself of Chelsea in the spring of 2022, were in the wider scheme of things one of the less consequential knock-on effects of Russia's invasion of Ukraine.

But they brought to an end one of the most extraordinary eras of English football, for better or worse — read: better for Chelsea, worse for everyone else — and the closing of the chapter that changed football entirely.

Because this was the first time that a football club had been backed by limitless financial resources. Before Abramovich, we had clubs owned by wealthy benefactors, from the 'local boy done good' types like Jack Walker at Blackburn, to media moguls like Silvio Berlusconi and Milan. We had clubs owned by those who conjured money from somewhere and it turned out to be a mirage that harmed them in the long-term, like Leeds United or Parma. We had clubs backed, officially or otherwise, by states, like Real Madrid under Franco or Honved in Hungary.

But nobody before with a bottomless, seemingly consequence-free, Scrooge McDuck-esque pit of money.

When Abramovich bought Chelsea in 2003, he paid something in the region of £140 million, which included debts of around £80 million, meaning the club was valued at £60 million. That's less than they spent on Kepa Arrizabalaga 15 years later. It's a handy illustration of both general inflation in the football world, and how different the Chelsea of 2003 was to the Chelsea of 2022, that Todd Boehly's consortium paid about 70 times that to take control.

It is worth returning to those pre-Abramovich days to remember what sort of state Chelsea were in back then. A common misconception that has grown over the years is that the club was in danger of going out of existence without his investment. First, they had qualified for the Champions League before he arrived, so the money from that alone would have kept the wolf from the door. But even if they hadn't beaten Liverpool in that colossal match in May 2003, their peril was not existential.

They probably would've had to sell a few of their better players, and the likes of John Terry, William Gallas, Eiður Guðjohnsen and Frank Lampard would have raised a few quid. 'It wasn't as dramatic as people were saying,' director Mark Taylor told *The Athletic* in 2020. 'We weren't on the verge of bankruptcy, as everyone seemed to think we were.'

Nevertheless, in the time between the end of the 2002-03 season and Abramovich's arrival, their transfer activity had extended to signing two reserve goalkeepers — Jürgen Macho and Marco Ambrosio — on free transfers. Most of their energy was directed at trying to keep Gianfranco Zola, whose contract was up, rather than scouring the world for expensive new additions.

Ken Bates, at the time chairman and owner, had been seeking investment for about 18 months. A few months before the take-over he had proposed a new share issue that would create a further £10 million of equity. Chelsea Village, the company that owned the football club and the hotel that Bates built behind the Shed End, had lost £11 million in the six months from July 2002 to December 2003. Players have spoken of pre-takeover cost-savings, like sharing rooms on away trips rather than having their own. They needed a new source of cash.

Then on a Tuesday in late June 2003, chief executive Trevor Birch took a phone call from the influential agent Pini Zahavi, telling him that an unnamed businessman was keen. Not just on investing, but buying the club. Birch met Zahavi on the Wednesday, then on the Thursday Bates, Birch and some others met Abramovich.

'It was very, very swift,' Taylor told *The Athletic*. 'We'd never heard of him. So actually, on the Friday morning, his lawyers brought in *Forbes* magazine from America and he was No 15 on the list, with billions of dollars, which seemed to be quite a good starting point.'

Then on a sunny Wednesday morning at the start of July, the takeover was announced. Just as when Sheikh Mansour bought Manchester City five years later, there was little to no warning, no speculation in the press, no rumours. We all just woke up one day and football was different.

Chelsea fans rejoiced. Everyone else . . . did not. 'Roman Abramovich has parked his Russian tank in our front garden and is firing £50 notes at us,' said David Dein, vice-chairman of Arsenal.

Chelsea signed 11 players that summer for a total of about £111 million, adding Scott Parker the following January for a further £10 million, just for yucks. One of those original 11 was Damien Duff, a £17 million signing from Blackburn and the first of nine times Chelsea broke their transfer record under Abramovich's ownership.

After that came Didier Drogba (£24 million), Michael Essien (£24.4 million), Andriy Shevchenko (£30.8 million), Fernando Torres (£50 million), Álvaro Morata (£60 million), Kepa Arrizabalaga (£71.6 million), Kai Havertz (£90 million) and Romelu Lukaku (£97.5 million). In the end Chelsea spent something in the region of £2 billion on players under Abramovich, from those early days pumping up the price of players everywhere.

Those that defend the likes of Abramovich and Sheikh Mansour usually present two arguments: first that other teams spend plenty of money too (sometimes more than those owned by these fabulously wealthy benefactors) and second that 'investment' like theirs allow other clubs to challenge the traditional, legacy giants of the game, and theoretically create more competition.

The second point has some merit, but only in isolation. Yes, Liverpool spent £75 million on Virgil van Dijk and Manchester United bought Paul Pogba for £89 million and Arsenal spent £72 million on Nicolas Pépé, but what unlimited wealth brings is not just the ability to buy incredibly expensive stars, but the ability to basically make as many mistakes as you like and still be fine.

City, for example, went through a phase of chucking £40-50 million on a string of different full-backs, safe in the knowledge that if they didn't work out (which many of them didn't) they would simply be able to buy another.

It's a similar story with Abramovich's Chelsea and managers; they could easily afford to churn through as many as they wanted, André Villas-Boas being perhaps the most pertinent example. They spent £13 million on prising him from Porto in 2011 — an unheard of sum for a manager then — knowing full well that if he turned out to be crap, they could happily pay him off and move to the next one. Which, as it turned out, is exactly what happened.

As for the competition argument, what has actually happened is that the identity of the dominant teams has just been flipped. At the time of this book being published, six teams have won the Premier League since Abramovich arrived: two of them are Chelsea and City, who have 11 of the 19 titles between them. Manchester United account for another five, all won under a generational genius manager who had built his club up to be a behemoth. Arsenal have one — a season in which they went unbeaten and was the first of the Abramovich era, so the money hadn't really had time to properly impact the title race. Leicester City have one, an astonishing, freak event unlikely ever to occur again — essentially the football equivalent, in terms of odds, of being hit by a comet while doing your gardening.

Which leaves Liverpool, who are, at the time of writing, City's most plausible competitors — something they have only achieved by a) having another generational genius as a manager and b) getting absolutely every decision right. Yes, huge sums have been spent on players, but until the end of the 2021-22 season at least, the closest they have come to a big-money dud has been Naby Keïta, and he's not exactly been a spectacular failure.

Imagine a post-Alex Ferguson world without teams backed by unlimited wealth. Imagine the free-for-all it might have inspired. Sure, the Premier League would still probably be dominated by the wealthiest clubs, but there would at least be a chance of a bit more variety.

And none of that takes into account all the knock-on effects of such wealth, or indeed the moral questions of where that wealth came from. It may have created more challengers, but at what cost?

Abramovich was the first, but many followed. At City, Sheikh Mansour's wealth, a ruthless football structure and the brilliance of

Pep Guardiola have allowed them to dominate English football. In 2011, the Qatari state bought PSG, and won eight of the next 10 French titles. Then in 2021, the Saudi Public Investment Fund took over Newcastle, with the aim of doing similar.

The arms race that can be traced back to that first Chelsea spending spree has inflated transfer fees and wages as everyone else tries to keep up. Abramovich wasn't the first owner to spend colossal sums of cash in an attempt to make his club competitive or dominant, but he was the first to be able to spend so heavily and so consistently. For everyone else, eventually the money ran out, but even with UEFA's attempts to curb things with Financial Fair Play rules and Chelsea eventually becoming something close to a self-sustaining club and business, that never happened under Abramovich.

Others have taken up the baton. As of 2022, the two most expensive players in the world — Neymar and Kylian Mbappé — were bought by PSG, and the third was Philippe Coutinho who was bought with proceeds from the Neymar sale. The most expensive goalkeeper of all time was bought by Chelsea. The most expensive player ever bought by an English club was Jack Grealish, signed by Manchester City.

But the transfer fees are arguably not the most damaging part. It's true that most Chelsea fans will not have known much about Abramovich when he arrived. But anyone with half a brain who saw the arrival of this 36-year-old, who had gathered billions through energy markets in Russia, will have known that trouble was afoot in some way. Did they think of the provenance of his money? Did they wonder what Abramovich had to do to acquire this wealth?

Almost certainly not. And there's a decent argument to say that they are not the ones that should have to make those judgements or think about those things. But the fact that they don't care is damaging and has given people an excuse not to worry about future takeovers.

The problem is that allowing football fans and the football business not to be concerned about where the money comes from has led to the situation where Abu Dhabi owns Manchester City, Qatar owns PSG and Saudi Arabia owns Newcastle. And sizeable chunks, if not almost all, of those clubs' fans don't care about the well-documented human rights problems in those countries.

They don't care because the money has made or will make those clubs successful — or, more to the point, it has made or will make those clubs compete with clubs like Chelsea and owners like Abramovich. He created an environment where clubs were so desperate to compete with his club and his wealth that they would accept anyone who looked like they could do similar things, regardless of who they were.

In the football world of 2022, success must happen at all costs and the quickest way to success is having money. That's not just a problem started by Abramovich, but his involvement has taken it to extremes.

Abramovich is gone, and while the damage has been done, at the very least the symbolism of his departure should be welcomed.

Frank Lampard: football manager – a concept explored

by Adam Hurrey

Frank Lampard is on his third job and has thus far taken each club to . . . exactly where he found them. So is he any good? What is 'any good'? And why does he bother?

If we wanted to condense the first act of Frank Lampard: Football Manager into its most subtly representative few seconds, one sunny April afternoon at Goodison Park may have provided them.

Knee-deep in his first relegation battle, and about to face the media to franklampard his way through some questions about a draining Merseyside derby defeat and the upcoming visit of his former club Chelsea, Everton's manager went back to his particular basics.

All alone on the Goodison pitch, save for a groundsman carefully trimming the grass nearby, Lampard embarked on a series of slightly laboured shuttle runs, from one penalty area to the other. The perception of Lampard's hard yards here, as with much of what he does, wasn't just about quiet determination but also a keenness to be *seen* to be quietly determined.

Subsequently secured on that same turf with a roof-raising comeback win over Crystal Palace, Everton's Premier League survival in 2021-22 surely constitutes the end of the prologue to Lampard's post-playing career. It's been a chaotic four years already: a mad dash to the Championship play-off final with Derby County, via the riveting managerial culture clash of Spygate feat. Marcelo Bielsa; his Chelsea homecoming in the shadow of their transfer ban, which unravelled into the worst defensive record in the top half and a not-entirely-unprecedented boardroom schism; a year of simply pulling out of the running for jobs that didn't quite suit him (or vice versa); and, finally, the unfathomable ballache of being parachuted mid-season into Everton, who were stumbling Championship-ward despite spending half a billion pounds since 2016.

But, that febrile night, as he embraced the Everton hierarchy and posed for selfies on the roof of some corporate boxes halfway up the Main Stand, some coordinated Twitter snark was being smugly unleashed. The gist was essentially that — despite a lot of frowning — Lampard had steered Derby, Chelsea and Everton to . . . exactly the same league positions in which he'd been handed them.

There is unquestionably more to football management than that, most of which remains (in)conveniently tricky to quantify, but one of the more neutral subtexts to the well-actuallying posed a very timely question: *do we know if Frank Lampard is any good at being a football manager?*

How, unless they're being gleefully thrown into the air by their trophy-winning squads while being gently seasoned with confetti, can we know if *anyone* is a good manager? That might be a futile pursuit but it doesn't stop us examining the very curious ways they go about one of the most draining-looking jobs in sport and entertainment. And, right at the intersection of the draining/ curious axes — squinting 50 yards or so into the distance — is Frank Lampard.

It's tricky to place the former Latin GCSE ace's mannerisms in the current managerial landscape. Lampard can be affable in his press conferences, but will never charm a room like a post-victory Jürgen Klopp. He can be brow-furrowingly intense in his post-match assessments, but without the convincing menace of Pep Guardiola. As a former elite player, he talks a very earnest game, but somehow without the rigid steel of Steven Gerrard, his theoretical managerial peer. Brendan Rodgers, you sense, would out-philosophy him, while the unflappable Eddie Howe and Graham Potter have a few extra years' experience of downplaying the praise and straight-batting the speculation.

In fact, as much as it sometimes sounds like younger head coaches are reading from a telemarketing script, Lampard has already begun to cultivate his own managerial personality. At its core is the concept of the Lampardian Transition — essentially, his habit of twitchily switching from a light-hearted point to a deadly serious point in the space of a near-subliminal 'but, yeah, no'. This has spiralled from its origin in a 2014 observation from one respected scholar of the footballing vernacular, to its nadir of a meme tweeted from Sevilla's English-language account in 2022 about qualifying for the Champions League. Whatever the trajectory of his managerial development from here, Lampard has at least made a true cultural impression, just perhaps not the one he's aiming for.

To draw one semi-serious conclusion from his now-trademark verbal tic, it suggests a manager wrestling with his own self-awareness, having spent 20 years playing under managers not shy of expressing themselves (kicking off with Harry Redknapp's truly legendary defence of his nephew's prospects at a West Ham fans forum in 1996 and peaking under José Mourinho v1.0 at Chelsea). Now faced with a press pack whose threshold for being impressed by a football manager's oration remains bewilderingly low, Lampard has quickly got to grips with his script.

The fact that modern, young (and invariably British) managers find it so overwhelmingly necessary to pepper their press conferences with the phrases 'football club' and 'football matches' — the absolute cornerstones of earnest managerial chatter — perhaps explains why Lampard took so long to get back into the game. After all, Norwich City, Crystal Palace and Aston Villa simply cannot compete with the extremely football-clubbable 'Everton'.

(Dean Smith's unveiling at Carrow Road in November pre-tested this theory to breaking point, however: he managed to squeeze in the phrase 'football club' 14 times in less than 22 minutes, or once every 93 seconds. Lampard's Everton introduction was less spectacular, but he nevertheless maintained a tireless rhythm of 'Everton Football Club' over the last four months of the season.)

Lampard's carefully chosen words make for a perilous emotional tightrope and, while the idea of him sharing a training-ground joke with his players is quite a plausible vision, it's hard to imagine him *absolutely losing it* in the dressing room, proverbial teacups flying and the likes of Seamus Coleman cowering in the corner. His celebratory air-punches during Everton's intermittent late-season revivals made him look like an angry dad of three trying to get Sellotape off his hands in the midst of a panicked Christmas Eve wrapping marathon.

As an arm-around-the-shoulder type, Lampard is naturally aware of the benefits of keeping the punters happy, too: his very deliberate choice of phrase after the Palace barnstormer — 'My feeling was "Get one goal and the Gwladys Street would suck the ball into the net," as the old saying goes' — was a well-timed echo of the great Howard Kendall. From a distance, these sentiments can look basic, telegraphed; in the moment, they feel like everything.

And while he continues to iron out his managerial profile, there are some mini-contradictions. To his credit, Lampard is a solid fronter-up, and Everton's see-sawing form gave him plenty of practice: a 5-0 obliteration at Tottenham, a lamentable FA Cup exit at Crystal Palace, what could have been a mortal 3-2 defeat at Burnley in April, and another at home to Brentford.

On the other hand, when faced with mild criticism from the outside, he stills seems stuck in elite-player mode, bristling at any suggestions that he's come up short. The last days of his Chelsea reign were punctuated by thin-skinned retaliations at pieces he had read in the media, culminating in this response to the suggestion that confidence was perhaps low in a team that had lost five of its last nine.

'I think their confidence would be shot if they read some of the pieces you are writing at the minute. I read some of them and some of the confirmation bias that you always reflect on games with . . . so, for a journalist to be objective would be a big start.'

It's easy to leap on any flashes of defensiveness from managers, whose modern role seems to revolve disproportionately around deflecting criticism of themselves or their players in precisely the right direction, but there has to be some sympathy too. Why do former world-class footballers do this to themselves? While the top table of tactical thinkers and man-managers is not entirely dominated by those with humble playing CVs or born coaches who hung up their boots in their twenties to write PhDs on pressing triggers, their motivation for the 14-hour days and video-analysis sessions is at least more explicable.

But there is one often-cited reason for these wealthy, decorated retirees deciding to reach for the UEFA Pro Licence, the laminated set-piece folders and the shoulder of the nearest fourth official: 'the day-to-day buzz'.

The components of the day-to-day buzz have never been officially defined, but are generally understood to include 'being in and around the lads', being 'out on the grass' and being hard-coded to crave the entirely understandable adrenaline rush of 'match day'. These things are clearly hard to let go for a career in property management or after-dinner speaking, and manifest themselves in things like 'kicking every ball' (the physical comedy of a manager 'heading' their own team's goals in at a virtual back post within their technical area which, once spotted, is a spectacle you can never ignore) or, more viscerally, in moments of genuine comradeship with players under their wing. Once those post-Palace celebrations had finally reached the home dressing room at Goodison, the floor strewn with the usual post-match detritus of bandages, flip-flops and Lucozade bottles, Lampard hauled Everton's sheepish-looking captain Seamus Coleman to his feet for an intimate — and yet inevitably viral — tribute:

'This fella (loud cheers) — nah, nah, nah, nah, nah, nah, no — this ... this fella ... this fella is, like, pfff — to say (looks to camera) in front of everyone — one of the bes- THE BEST people I've ever met, as a man ... as a man and what you are ... and as a player.'

Everton's Premier League survival had been confirmed, a mathematical fact, but this was a fleeting example of those intangibles that football managers ought to be defined by. It's often quipped how dramatically the job ages people but, to be blunt, Lampard has looked *absolutely knackered, all the time.*

The fruits of those 108 days of labour — 'it's constant, you take it home, you work every hour of the day to find gains' — extended beyond simply finishing 16th in the league table. Lampard has done well to win over some sceptical, fatigued Evertonians after Carlo Ancelotti jumped ship for Real Madrid, after Rafa Benítez's torturous six months and after his own poor start of seven league defeats in nine. The fanbase — to borrow a Love Islandism — 'had their barriers up'; to be sharing joyous moments with them, whatever the context, feels like an achievement in itself.

But Lampard's managerial career so far — a collection of paragraphs, really, rather than chapters — raises the rather loaded question of: what next? The aggressive camaraderie of that Everton dressing room suggests management is unquestionably for him (and that the door to TV punditry, a seemingly day-to-day-buzz-less world, is now closed by choice) but those moments will be so easily forgotten if Everton limp out of the traps. Where could he go then?

If another Premier League club can't be convinced, you can picture a brief Steve McClaren-esque breakthrough on the Continent, away from the UK media glare, or — equally vividly — a return to MLS to steer a glamorously located franchise to brave play-offs failure.

In any case, you hope that Lampard eventually becomes a manager comfortable in his own skin — able to repel the slings and arrows casually and absorb the strain rather than letting it corrode him in real time, but without becoming too philosophical about it all like Mick McCarthy or just transforming into one big human sigh like Steve Bruce.

The challenge for Frank Lampard, then — a man so accustomed to being scrutinised as he toils away — is to achieve the near-impossible: to manage like nobody's watching.

Hayes v Eidevall: the birth of beef in the Women's Super League

by Katie Whyatt

The Women's Super League has never really had rivals in personality, but in 2022 the managers of Chelsea and Arsenal changed that . . .

In the abiding image of the season, Jonas Eidevall roars. He embeds his toes in the grass at the Emirates, drops to his knees and, hands pulled into fists, roars. In the photos, he is frozen at an impossible angle, his legs primed to fold in on themselves. Then he twists and blasts towards Beth Mead, roaring louder still. The relief unspools from him in numberless waves, as though from an unstopped bottle.

The shots are beamed around the world — not only because of what they represent but because of how forcefully, how unapologetically, they do it. Eidevall's Arsenal have defeated Chelsea 3-2 in their first game of the season — the first time they have beaten Chelsea in close to three years — and Eidevall has scorched the touchline in his own fire and ice to match his side's relentless invention on the field.

In those hazy September days, the season bulges with promise, and Eidevall, soon to be crowned manager of the month, has arrived to dismantle the established order. Arsenal, after a choppy few years, could be back where they belong, and Eidevall will do it with his heart on his sleeve, with Mead bewitching beleaguered back lines, with 2021's Champions League finalists chasing vanishing shadows.

Increased levels of visibility have granted women's football a new kind of permanence. With larger fanbases, the ephemeral becomes the iconic: moments that previously passed unobserved and undocumented are now shown live on Sky and Eidevall roars from televisions and tablets and phones and laptops and profile pictures across the country. That he does so in shorts and a white T-shirt, like a kid on school sports day poking at the parameters of sportsmanship, lends the whole thing a comical, unforgettable air. This is what Eidevall will be remembered for, regardless of the rest. His public lapped it up.

Nine months later, Millie Bright and Erin Cuthbert reprise the image. Chelsea are champions, on a day when the title swung between them and Arsenal five times, and either side of the trophy Bright and Cuthbert emulate Eidevall's pose. Cuthbert posts the photo to Instagram and at least its caption – 'if you know you know' – does not purport to be anything other than what it is.

This Chelsea team that always seem to find infinite ways to hurt you – Sam Kerr in the billiard room with the dagger; Guro Reiten in the library with the lead pipe – have found another and, while gleeful, it is not entirely without bite. Bright adds: '245 days ago', with a train of shushing emojis. The former Chelsea goalkeeper Carly Telford notes that she has 'seen that celly somewhere before', and one fan says: 'Not sure what's better – that celebration or Erin liking every salty reply.'

A penny for what Eidevall might have put were he the kind to have scores of burner accounts. Not that he needs anonymity to speak his mind. A point separated Chelsea and Arsenal on the final day but perhaps none should have — what else could Eidevall have been hinting at when, with three league games left, he accused Chelsea of manipulating the fixture list, rescheduling games around the absence of Sam Kerr? Officially COVID-19 cases and injuries put paid to Chelsea's matches against Spurs and Everton, the latter postponement happening at Everton's request, but Eidevall appeared decidedly unconvinced.

'I didn't focus on Chelsea when they were rearranging their fixtures in January so that Sam Kerr didn't have to miss games because of the Asia Cup,' he said, of the period in which Arsenal were without four players due to the same competition but fulfilled — and lost — their game against Birmingham. 'We were one of the few teams that chose to play that weekend whereas other teams got their games rescheduled.'

Was he cracking? Was this the moment that Chelsea reassured themselves that they had the mental edge? Did he hope that the FA would investigate, or dock points? Would Hayes, as Sir Alex Ferguson had reportedly done when Rafa Benítez unfolded that A4 piece of paper and plunged into his infamous 'facts' speech with the confidence of a set of schoolchildren who had pulled together a group presentation on Henry VIII and didn't know who was going to read which line, be watching and cackling away? For her part, she said that she 'didn't care'.

In its earlier years, the Premier League sold itself globally on the force and charisma of its personalities as much as its on-field product: seagulls followed trawlers, and Ferguson and Arsène Wenger traded insults between flying pizza slices while José Mourinho set about composing his own mental burn book on Wenger.

Some have unfolded over years, often with the kind of venom that suggested one might have been prophesied to destroy the other, and even decades later the cultural obsession with those relationships remains. Nottingham Forest welcomed Leeds United to the City Ground in 2017 with a programme cover featuring Brian Clough and the words: 'I wanted to have a crack at the European Cup. I wanted to win it. I wanted to win the league but I wanted to win it better.'

How spicy did the 2021-22 WSL get? In the build-up to the FA Cup final between the two sides, Eidevall revealed that he was superstitious — 'I don't let any black cats cross my way, ever', to the point of 'rerouting a couple of miles' if he sees one while driving. After the game Hayes, basking in a 3-0 win, reflected that Chelsea 'purred from start to finish' and meowed at the cameras; Chelsea players posted images to social media with the trophy surrounded with black cat emojis.

It might not seem like much by comparison, but this is new territory for the WSL, where disagreements may simmer privately but are rarely aired publicly. There have been a few moments of what the internet might call needling, but very rarely has it meta-morphosed into what the internet might call beef.

There was a little milk spilt by her rivals when Alex Morgan sipped her tea, pinkie extended, in the 2019 World Cup semi-final, but not in the way it soaked the halls of Old Trafford in 2017, when José Mourinho had a bottle of semi-skimmed thrown over him in the aftermath of a Manchester derby. Piers Morgan posted a photo of his namesake with the words 'make these cocky yanks choke on it' and the former England footballer Lianne Sanderson said that she found the celebration 'disrespectful', but generally the discourse around the USWNT and their celebrations resisted a unified tone.

Some verged on the political — whether they were right to cheer every goal scored in the vastly under-resourced Thailand 13-0 or whether silence was patronising — and others incorpo-rated the equality campaigning for which the USWNT has become renowned. 'I feel like we have to be humble in our successes and have to celebrate, but not too much or in a limited fashion,' Morgan said of her critics.

Mostly, though, women's football fans just seemed happy to have another GIF to add to the collection: delighted that one of the all-time greats had produced this moment, on one of the biggest stages, and that they had been there to witness it in real time. Fans harbour loyalties in women's football, but respect for other teams feels far less grudging than it does in other sports. There is often admiration for what these players have achieved against the odds, and their role in helping to push the sport onwards. Managers, aware of the financial constraints in which their counterparts are often working, have come out in support of each other more than they have with grievances to air. Unsupportive boards and chairmen are more routine targets.

Beef, then? The response to Morgan stretches the definition. At Euro 2017, the former England head coach Mark Sampson called the France coach Olivier Echouafni 'wet behind the ears', all because Echouafni, then 44 and 10 years older than Sampson, had had the temerity to suggest that England 'would not want to play France'. Sampson's speech carried some of the hallmarks of conference-enacted rivalry – 'he's played three won one, I've played 11 won nine, (and) he'll learn who to talk about and not to' – but never became much more.

Why? It will doubtless come as a surprise to fans of the men's game to learn that most clubs did not host regular press conferences until 2019. Chelsea held only a handful in 2018-19, the year they reached the Champions League semi-final against Lyon, and Hayes' press conference in France on the eve of the fixture saw two English newspaper journalists – I was one – try to fill a cavernous lecture hall. Away from the biggest clashes, too many WSL games are still sparsely attended by journalists and post-match press conferences may only have two attendees, one of whom is the manager. To get a point across in those situations may be like starting a fire with wet kindling – only periodically does it catch. And how invested will fans be if they hear from these managers about as much as they hear from estranged relatives?

The WSL is a league that has in equal parts relied on and resisted — or maybe not always had the fans for — using the men's game as its template. There has always been a tension between those two points, borne out in myriad ways: in the financial reliance on men's clubs to fund attached women's teams; in the wish to capture the interest of those who grew up exclusively following the men's game without all the attendant problems, distilled so virulently in the Euro 2020 final.

There has been an influx of fans originally raised with the men's game, and their presence has not always been unwelcome. The introduction of Manchester United Women into the Championship heralded, too, the arrival of the pyramid's most partisan fans, eager to stoke rivalries in a sport in which those fixtures do not come laden with the same weight of history as they do in the men's game. How can they, when players have always bounced between the London clubs and many clubs do not operate separate home and away ends? The decision to do so at the 2021-22 FA Cup final was widely lauded, either end an undulating mass of lifting and falling flags.

But there have been uncomfortable moments — ones that, for a game that has prided itself on its inclusivity, have offered uneasy reckonings. The former Manchester United player Alex Greenwood spoke of the vitriol that flooded her inbox following her move to City, tainting her first few months back in the WSL. That would not have happened five years earlier, and to paint it as inevitable feels lazy. In this period of fledgling professionalism, women's football has some semblance of control over its identity but the growth of the game will tip that autonomy away. Is this what the game wants to be?

That has been the most pertinent question for the women's game as it has grown in the shadow of the men's. The Premier League offers the most obvious comparison — always helpfully, given the difference in wealth — but it is a counterpoint, too. Forging an identity comes with scores of questions — we have not even touched upon the debate around the usefulness of games in a club's main stadia — and some of them are not always comfortable or answered easily.

Yet there will be firsts, too, and the rivalry between Hayes and Eidevall — however genuine, however helpful, however dangerous or harmless — is one of those.

Giorgio Chiellini: the last great pure defender?

by James Horncastle

Giorgio Chiellini planned to stay on for the World Cup and hoped to leave Juventus with a Scudetto. Neither happened, but he still leaves Italy as a champion . . .

Giorgio Chiellini reached the stage where he just couldn't take it anymore. It wasn't the football. It was the grieving process his Juventus team-mates were going through as his final appearance for the club approached.

'Locatelli's been crying for days,' Chiellini laughed. 'At a certain point I just had to say: "Come on, Manu. Enough's enough".'

Locatelli was one of the first to hug Chiellini when his number came up in Juventus's last home game against Lazio. Withdrawn in the 17th minute, Chiellini wasn't injured. His knee hadn't buckled again. Juventus were simply making a gesture.

'It was one minute for every year I've spent at the club,' Chiellini specified.

He would have liked this one to end better. 'It's been a difficult year,' he said. The first trophy-less one since 2011 when Andrea

Agnelli was still new to the role of chairman. Every time Agnelli and the executive team flashed up on the big screen at the Allianz, sections of the crowd whistled on a night of mixed and heightened emotions.

Before trudging off to be replaced by Matthijs de Ligt with a smile every bit as wide as the one he wore during the Euros, Chiellini tied the captain's armband around Paulo Dybala's bicep. Leonardo Bonucci will skipper Juventus next season, but the mid-life crisis of a year he spent at AC Milan has kept him a rank below Dybala ever since his return to Turin.

By seniority the Argentine is Chiellini's deputy after seven uninterrupted seasons. But there was an added poignancy as Chiellini latched up the velcro and embraced him one last time as Dybala was also on his way out. Unlike Chiellini he did not depart on his own terms and sobbed uncontrollably after the final whistle.

The trauma and disruption, the highs and lows of this year in Italian football hung like a cloud over the Allianz Stadium that night. Chiellini's original intention was to play another season in Turin. After captaining Italy to their first European Championship win since 1968, an achievement he movingly dedicated to the memory of Davide Astori, the veteran centre-back wanted to have another go at winning the World Cup. Qatar was always supposed to be the goal for Roberto Mancini's national team.

As it turned out Italy were beaten, improbably, by North Macedonia in the World Cup play-offs. Afterwards a tearful Chiellini, whose stoppage-time introduction was the 37-year-old's last competitive appearance in Savoy blue, described himself and Italy as 'tired and destroyed'.

'We're gutted, heartbroken,' Chiellini said. 'There's going to be a huge void deep inside of us and I hope that in the future the energy we need to come back can be drawn from this void, as was the case over the last years. I hope Italy do it together with Mancini, who I consider essential to the national team. I remain proud of this side and my team-mates.'

The Azzurri did not expect to come out on top last summer, viewing it initially as a stop on the journey rather than the destination itself. Alas, Jorginho's missed penalties and Domenico Berardi's wayward finishing meant Switzerland qualified at their expense and an undefeated Italy went into the play-offs where they lost in the semi-finals to North Macedonia.

Just when the ghosts of missing out on the 2018 World Cup had been laid to rest, a haunting was reported in Palermo. The plain, uncooked pasta Bonucci said England fans would have to eat after assuming the Euros were coming home was now a dish served too close to home.

'Of course I wanted to go to the World Cup,' Chiellini said. 'It was a little dream I had after the Euros. Inevitably I wasn't going to play all the games but I wanted to be part of the squad. It didn't go as we would have wanted and that accelerated my decision. I'm leaving the national team and Juventus in good hands.'

The shock defeat to North Macedonia was not 'apocalyptic' in the same way as losing to Sweden was four years ago. For all the calls for Roberto Mancini to resign, winning the Euros was still too fresh in everyone's minds.

The game in Palermo was the first played in front of a full house since the pandemic began. Life moved on and what was once normal and taken for granted became special and assumed a hyper-real dimension. Crowds returned in their droves to Serie A stadia. Chiellini got the send-off he deserved — one he perhaps would have been denied had he retired after the serious knee injury he suffered in 2019. UEFA's decision to reschedule the Euros and postpone it for a year gave him a renewed sense of purpose.

And what purpose. Italy's quarter-final against Belgium in Munich was the high point. Up in the gantry at the Allianz Stadium, Fabio Caressa must have felt an exhilarating sense of déjà vu.

In Dortmund, 15 years earlier, Sky Italia's excitable lead commentator shouted 'Cannavaro! CAN-NA-VARO!

CAN-NA-VA-RO!' as the Italy captain headed away one Germany cross, then dashed out of his back four, won another header and started a counter-attack that culminated in Alessandro Del Piero's unforgettable breakaway goal to make it 2-0 late in extra time. Fabio Cannavaro won the Ballon d'Or a few months later on the back of that display and will forever be known as the Berlin Wall for his heroics in that World Cup semi-final.

In Munich, Caressa was at it again. 'Chiellini! CHI-EL-LINI! CHI-EL-LINI!' he cried as Italy's skipper transformed into the rocks along the coastline of his hometown Livorno. Wave upon wave of Belgium attacks crashed against him and that sinking feeling consumed Roberto Martínez on the sideline. No one was getting past Chiellini.

On the eve of the game, Chiellini said he would have no trouble sleeping that night. All the preparation he does puts his mind at rest. Chiellini watches clips of the striker he's up against for 45 minutes. It's a habit he started when Claudio Ranieri was his manager at Juventus.

'It helps me form a connection with them,' Chiellini explained. 'I need to know what they like most, which runs they make. It's my way of getting on their wavelength and syncing up with them. I watch every goal a team has scored that season, too. If we're playing Barcelona, that means watching 80 or 90 of them, but you get an understanding of how they play from how they score and how you might be able to guess their intentions.'

Rather than take notes and record voice notes to prompt him, Chiellini tries to memorise everything he's seen so he can take it on the pitch with him. 'Great defenders have to have a database,' he wrote in his book *I, Giorgio* — an instant recall of all they've seen from studying someone like Lukaku every bit as hard as he studied for his degree.

Where Chiellini wants to be is in his opponent's nightmares instead. He tries to get into their heads. 'It's a subtle psychological game, reading a striker's mind,' he explained. 'It's the most important side to my game. We're talking about moments, feelings. A top defender has to be almost clairvoyant.'

'I've got a big collection on my head,' Chiellini said. 'They must have given me at least 100 stitches. Blood doesn't bother me, especially not my own. For me, defending is joy. Getting a decisive block in is pure joy. Those last-gasp tackles and unthinkable goal-line clearances give me so much more satisfaction than scoring a goal. Scoring's nice, but it isn't my life. Stopping one from going in is.'

You can see it in the way Chiellini celebrates shutting down a striker and killing a chance dead. Often he looks like Muhammad Ali stood over a knocked-out Sonny Liston in that iconic John Rooney photo shouting: 'Get up and fight, sucker.' 'If you don't concede, you demoralise your opponent,' Chiellini believes.

On the eve of the tournament, some pundits looked at his age and pace and thought he might be a weak link in this Italy side. Social media called for Inter Milan wunderkind Alessandro Bastoni to play after helping winning last season's Scudetto, which was also a slight on Francesco Acerbi, who deputised for Chiellini during his rehab and was the best centre-back in Serie A during the centurion's absence last year.

The debate offered a reminder of the game's fickleness, to say nothing of the lack of recognition Chiellini is due abroad and how skewed our analysis of centre-backs is towards build-up play and passing rather than defending. On Friday in Munich, Chiellini once again showed he is the best defender's defender and his interpretation of his role is an art form.

'Destruction,' he likes to say, 'is also a creative operation.'

On the eve of the season, Juventus were considered the favourites to take the Scudetto back from Inter. The return of a serial winner like Massimiliano Allegri was supposed to be enough on its own for normal service to resume. Antonio Conte had walked out on Inter and the club needed to sell Romelu Lukaku and Achraf Hakimi. Christian Eriksen could no longer play in Italy after he was fitted with an ICD (implantable cardioverter defibrillator).

Pessimists believed the champions would face a fight just to qualify for the Champions League. Instead it was Juventus who struggled. Cristiano Ronaldo abandoned them at the last minute. 'He left on August 28,' Chiellini said. 'It definitely would have been better if he'd gone earlier. That way we would have been better prepared. It cost us.'

Juventus spent the first month of the season in the relegation zone before stabilising and putting a long unbeaten run together. The €70 million signing of Dušan Vlahović from Fiorentina in January was intended to bridge the gap between Juventus and the top four. Not only did it do that, it fleetingly made people believe they could even gatecrash the title race.

But Inter put a stop to that by beating them at the Allianz in April. They would come between them and any silverware this season. Inter got the better of their fiercest rivals in the Super Cup with a last minute Alexis Sánchez goal in extra time and came back from behind to defeat them in the Coppa Italia final too. Simone Inzaghi was poised for a domestic treble but a mistake by back-up goalkeeper Ionuţ Radu in Bologna caused destiny to slip from Inter's hands.

Milan caught it and won the league for the first time since 2011, an achievement that could act as a paradigm shift in Italy. Winning the Scudetto is in keeping with a club of Milan's history and tradition (even if this was only the third since the turn of the Millennium) but doing it this way — cutting costs while increasing performance, applying data and analytics, building one of the youngest teams in Europe — feels new within a Serie A context.

Juventus could learn from it. This season has little defence from criticism and yet how Italy defend in the future will be a source of interest going forward.

Chiellini is an all-time great, a sportsman who loved a battle, celebrating blocks and clearances as if they were goals. After graduating with a first class honours degree in business, the expectation is that it won't be long before he becomes an executive. And yet Chiellini's way of defending — which is defending per se — is a dying art. The skills are being lost as more and more midfield playmakers masquerade as centre-backs without having a clue about positioning, posture, when to step up and when to drop.

'They should send a video of Chiellini to (the national team's training base) in Coverciano to show the next generation how to defend,' Allegri said. 'It should be sent to all the academies too.'

Sections of this piece have previously appeared on The Athletic.

Gareth Bale: Madrid, Wales, love and hate

by Tom Williams

Gareth Bale's departure from Real Madrid was greeted with barely disguised glee, but to every Welsh fan who has watched him, he will always be a hero . . .

The sky glowed pink over Canton as kick-off neared in Wales' World Cup play-off semi-final against Austria at the end of March. From the pubs and restaurants that line Cowbridge Road East, a mile west of Cardiff city centre, fans in replica shirts and trademark red, green and yellow bucket hats spilled out into the fading sunshine and set off on the short walk south to the Cardiff City Stadium.

It had been a warm spring day in the Welsh capital; a day for leisurely al fresco boozing, for counting down the hours until kick-off, for setting out starting XIs, predicting scorelines and nonchalantly sharing the fruits of the hard yards put in on the Austria national football team Wikipedia page. Now, as the game drew closer, the nerves began to creep in — but so too did those curious feelings to which Welsh supporters have slowly and warily become accustomed over the last seven or eight years. Expectation. Optimism. Belief.

Victory would take Wales to within one match of qualifying for the World Cup for the first time since 1958. The fairytale run to the semi-finals at Euro 2016 and progress to the knockout phase at Euro 2020 had, belatedly, put Wales on the footballing map, but World Cup qualification remained a chimera; the unsuccessful campaign to qualify for the 2018 tournament the one bum note in an otherwise melodious symphony.

Austria represented doughty opposition. They had taken eventual champions Italy to extra time in the last 16 at Euro 2020 and had reached the World Cup qualifying play-offs by dint of achieving promotion to the top tier of countries in the UEFA Nations League. Their line-up in Cardiff included the unflappable David Alaba, the mercurial Marko Arnautović and the talented Marcel Sabitzer, who is predominantly a central midfielder but also plays in a multitude of roles including attacking midfielder, second striker, winger and defensive midfielder.

Wales, for their part, could call upon both Gareth Bale and Aaron Ramsey, although the pair's physical readiness was a source of concern. Ramsey had made only one league start for Rangers since his January loan switch from Juventus, while the sum total of Bale's contribution to Real Madrid's La Liga campaign over the previous seven months had been a solitary 74-minute run-out at Villarreal six weeks previously. He had made only five appearances since the start of the season and had not scored a goal in club football since August.

Yet when Wales won a free kick mid-way through the first half, 25 yards from goal towards the right-hand side of the penalty area, there was little doubt as to who would take it. Bale paced out his run-up, took a deep breath and slammed an inch-perfect strike into Heinz Lindner's top-left corner via the underside of the crossbar. The collective howl that shook the stadium was equal parts delight at the importance of the goal and disbelief at the outrageous quality of the strike.

'You know when there's that couple of minutes of just: "Did that just happen?",' says Wales fan Hales Evans, who watched the game with a group of family and friends at the top of the Canton Stand. 'It was just shock really. And then it was like: "Did I just imagine that?". It was out of this world. Absolutely out of this world. He's had so many great moments for Wales, but this was right up there.'

Bale added another goal early in the second half, brilliantly arrowing a shot past Lindner after Ben Davies had touched Daniel James's cross into his path following a short corner, and although Sabitzer replied for Austria, it proved enough to take Rob Page's side through.

In a now wearily familiar routine, the days preceding the game had been dogged by sniping from the Madrid press about Bale's very presence in the squad. Amid reports of a back problem, he had missed Madrid's chastening 4-0 defeat by Barcelona the previous weekend, with head coach Carlo Ancelotti explaining that the former Tottenham man 'didn't feel right'. When he was pictured in training for Wales the very next day, *Marca* went to town.

On the day before the Wales-Austria match, the paper's front page carried a picture of a beaming Bale training alongside Joe Rodon, accompanied by the mocking headline: 'IT DOESN'T HURT ANYMORE'. On the morning of the game itself, *Marca* went even further, branding him a 'parasite' in an editorial and hammering home the insult with a crude cartoon image of an insect with Bale's face sucking blood from the Madrid crest.

Bale's celebration of his first goal had seemed tellingly effusive. After a trademark belly slide towards the corner flag, he had leapt to his feet, punched the air and was belligerently bellowing 'What! What!' into the ether as he disappeared inside a scrum of jubilant team-mates. Although he grinned his way through a post-match interview alongside Ramsey on Sky Sports, his words betrayed his frustrations. 'I don't need to send a message,' Bale said when he was asked if his display had been one in the eye for his detractors. 'I don't need to say anything — it's a waste of my time. It's disgusting. They should be ashamed of themselves. I'm not fussed — end of.'

If Bale is obliged to display a degree of restraint in his comments on Madrid and the Madrid media, Wales fans do not have to proceed with quite so much caution. '*Marca* is a weird publication,' says Evans, who has been attending Wales games since 2000. 'And Madrid fans are a very weird bunch — they are so fickle. It's like they don't appreciate him. They criticise him for not playing — he doesn't pick the team. What's he supposed to do? They're not even putting him in the squad half the time.'

For those who follow Wales, one of the hardest things to fathom is the contrast between the portrayal of Bale in the Madrid media as some kind of cold, scheming con artist and the carefree image that he conveys whenever he is representing his country. Whether addressing the media, messing around in training or going for a pre-match stroll with the squad, when the camera alights on Bale while he is away on international duty, he is invariably smiling from ear to ear.

'I've had the pleasure of watching him train a couple of times and he just giggles,' says Russell Todd, founder of Podcast Pêl-droed, a podcast dedicated to the Welsh national team. 'He's just always, always laughing, giggling, taking the mickey. He's not aloof; he's not above all of that. There's even a little bit of immaturity. I think that's reflective of just how comfortable he is in that environment and how comfortable everybody is with him. People seem to forget that these players were all playing with one another at 14, 15, 16 and that he's just one of the lads.'

Welsh fans have taken genuine pride in Bale's achievements with Real Madrid — the five Champions League titles, the 100+ goals, the touchline-sprint solo goal in the 2014 Copa del Rey final, the incredible overhead kick against Liverpool in the 2018 Champions League final — but as his relationship with the club and its cheerleaders soured, so the support he received while on international duty took on a more protective and provocative edge. Former Madrid striker Predrag Mijatović's infamous 2019 comments about Bale's supposed priorities spawned the notorious 'Wales, Golf, Madrid' chant and the knowledge that his commitment to the Welsh cause had become such a source of irritation in the Spanish capital only served to make Wales fans savour it even more.

'He's played in Wales friendly games that he had really no need to play in,' says Todd. 'No need to be on the pitch for Wayne Hennessey's 100th cap (against the Czech Republic in March), but he does it because him and Wayne Hennessey are huge mates. He doesn't need to come on for Chris Gunter's 100th cap (against Mexico in March 2021) and he came on for a substitute appearance. If that grinds the gears of people in Madrid, then there is a certain pleasure taken about that. If he isn't bothered by it, why should any of us be? It doesn't seem to affect him at all. If it was affecting his availability for Wales, his performances for Wales, his influence, then I guess I'd probably give more of a shit. But it doesn't.'

Bale had not been a regular starter at Madrid since the early weeks of the 2019-20 season, but during the intervening period he has led Wales into the knockout rounds at Euro 2020, helped them to achieve qualification to Nations League A (Wales are the smallest nation, in terms of population, to have reached the top tier) and turned in match-winning displays such as his hat-trick performance in a crucial World Cup qualifying win away to Belarus in September 2021. That he has continually risen to the occasion for Wales despite injuries, insults and rising levels of inactivity in Madrid has only enhanced the esteem in which he is held by the Welsh support.

'I feel terribly disappointed for Gareth that some of the Real Madrid fans and a lot of the press have turned against him,' says 62-year-old Wales fan Tim Hartley from Llandaff. 'It's just not fair and it's ungrateful. But the way he came back against Austria suggests that this has actually galvanised him. It makes him a harder, better player, a more resilient player, and I do think we've been very privileged to see the best of him.'

Want to feel old? The Austria match was nearly 16 years since Bale made his Wales debut as a gangly 16-year-old substitute in a May 2006 friendly match against Trinidad and Tobago in the Austrian city of Graz. He turned 33 in July 2022 and although he has remained as pivotal as ever on the pitch, when he lined up against Austria it was as one of the team's elder statesmen. For the next generation of players coming through the ranks, being able to train alongside the country's greatest ever footballer has been an education in itself.

'We've had little conversations here and there,' 23-year-old Huddersfield Town winger Sorba Thomas, who made his Wales debut in October, told Wales Online. 'I was talking to him about his time playing with (Cristiano) Ronaldo and all that. He's a top guy and everything I aspire to be. I watched him in training and I'm just trying to take bits from his game and trying to add it to mine.'

On top of all the vital goals and the virtuoso performances, it is Bale's unwavering commitment to the national team that has set the strongest example. 'It's not just about his ability,' says Hartley. 'It's what he's done off the pitch as well. You hear from the Welsh camp how great it is that young players — you know, Sorba Thomas, Ruben Colwill — will be greeted at the entrance by Gareth Bale, who'll have heard of them, will know them and will talk to them. And he will turn up even when he knows he can't play a part in a match.

'He's turned up for international camps knowing he's injured. He's not going to play a minute of competitive football, but he's there to help the younger players get on with it and they must look at that and think: "Yeah, playing for Wales is a big deal, it's a privilege and this guy wants to be here even if he's not kicking a ball in anger". So he's doing as much for the Wales team off the pitch as he's doing on it.'

At the start of June, what everyone previously knew was confirmed with the announcement that he was leaving Real. There were few tears shed in Madrid but a few days after that he forced the goal in the play-off final against Ukraine that took Wales to their first World Cup since 1958. Back home, from Barry to Bangor, they know exactly how lucky they have been.

Mbappé and how the boy who loves Madrid stayed in Paris

by Julien Laurens

Absolutely everyone expected Kylian Mbappé to leave Paris St Germain and join Real Madrid. He didn't, and by some way that was the highlight of a flat season in Paris . . .

In 10 or 20 years' time, it is already easy to see that only one thing will be remembered from this 2021-22 season in Ligue 1, and it won't be PSG winning the title again.

For years to come, it is guaranteed that Kylian Mbappé deciding to stay in Paris instead of going to Real Madrid will be the only thing that will stick in the football consciousness when the history books are written.

Mbappé was meant to go to Madrid. It was his destiny; his dream. The famous white shirt, the Bernabéu stadium, the 14 Champions League trophies, the legacy, the Galacticos — all of this drew the French prodigy to Spain.

He was going to leave PSG on a free and was going to conquer Spain and Europe alongside Karim Benzema. He was going to be the future of the Spanish giants. Or not.

The day before the last game of the season, Mbappé finally announced he had decided to stay, which took everyone — including PSG — by surprise. No transfer, no big move, no change of scenery. It shook the whole football world like never before. This was the most incredible transfer saga in the history of the game with the most incredible twist right at the end.

For years — actually since he was 11 — Real Madrid have tried to recruit him. He snubbed them when he was 11 and 12 and 14, and back in 2016 and in 2017 too. And again in 2022. It was suddenly very cold in Madrid. The air conditioning was on full blast while in Paris, it was sunny and warm.

But what a deal it took to keep him. It was something never seen before. The numbers are mind-boggling enough — over €50 million net a year, plus the huge signing-on bonuses — but the real centrepiece of the deal was the power that Mbappé was given. PSG president Nasser Al-Khelaifi was ready to give up anything he wanted, and he did. On top of the money, they agreed that Mbappé will be consulted for pretty much everything. He didn't want to work with sporting director Leonardo anymore so the club sacked the Brazilian. He wanted to be reunited with Luis Campos, close to Mbappé's dad since Campos looked after Kylian at Monaco, and Campos was hired. Kylian Mbappé was the new boss of the club. The new King of Paris.

To name the end of the Mbappé transfer saga as the main thing to remember from the 2021-22 season might look a bit harsh, but it is the reality. The announcement and the fact that he chose to stay in Ligue 1 did more for the French league than anything we saw during the domestic campaign.

Mbappé was pretty clear in the interviews he gave around his new contract: 'I have done it for Paris but also for France,' he said many times. He wanted to have the credit of not just helping his current club, but also helping his country. In fairness to the striker, who is Paris born and bred, he chose the best time to make a huge announcement like this. He did it on the back of his best season as a professional. His figures were incredible: 28 goals and 19 assists in 35 league matches. He finished top goalscorer and top assister — and won the player of the year award, of course.

But apart from all that, perhaps the most fascinating thing was to see how he developed his game outside of the goals. The influence of Benzema is clear for all to see. It used to be all about goals for Mbappé. Instead he has become a more complete player, with assists, chances created: more altruism and less self-ishness. A couple of years earlier, he only wanted to play centre-forward and to score as many goals as possible. Now, he is happy to also play wide — much like when he started his career — to get more involved in the game and create more. Mbappé walked on water and walked on Ligue 1 all season long. He was unplayable and unstoppable at times. He scored almost a third of PSG's goals in the league on his own and took his team to a record 10th French title.

Maybe playing alongside Lionel Messi also had an impact on the Parisian. Because as big as Mbappé was, for all the above reasons, let's not forget that this was also Messi's first ever professional season outside of Barcelona and outside of Spain. It was crazy, back in August 2021, when PSG confirmed the arrival of the Argentinian. It will stay forever as one of the biggest trans-fers of all time. It was impossible for him to leave the Camp Nou, but once it was clear that he would not stay there was just one destination for him: PSG.

He needed time to adapt to his new life. He did wonder, pretty early on, what he was doing there. Everything was so different: the life, the language, the food, the weather, the people, the atmosphere. At 33, it is not easy to change everything. Messi was sad, his wife Antonela was sad, their three sons were sad and even Hulk, the dog, was sad.

His difficulties on the pitch didn't help, of course. It took him a while to get going. His first goal came in the Champions League, at the Parc des Princes, against Manchester City to seal a famous 2-0 win. It was a perfect counter-attack, a perfect one-two with Mbappé and a perfect finish.

He learnt a lot and we learnt a lot about him too. He is not the incredible finisher that he was before. His game evolved into more of a creative role, putting assisting ahead of scoring more than before. His 15 assists in 26 league appearances are pretty good. He only scored six times but he hit the woodwork 14 times. It was better in the Champions League, until the last 16 second-leg in Madrid where, like the rest of his team, he sank at the Bernabéu. The GOAT said that next season will be better — I guess you'll have to wait for the next book to find out exactly what was better, why it was better and exactly how it was better.

The problem for Messi, Mbappé and PSG is that, overall, the season was disappointing. Or underwhelming, to say the least. We expected fireworks, sparkles and bubbles. And we got none of it. They won the Ligue 1 title of course, which is good. But that's about it.

Mauricio Pochettino's PSG lacked so many things that we would need a whole book to do it justice. That's the reason he departed at the end of the season. What he did for 18 months at the club was just not good enough, in terms of results and of style of play. When the Qataris took over PSG in the summer 2011, they were really clear on what they wanted: trophies, big stars and great football. In their 11 years in charge, the football has not always been amazing but, most of the time, it has been entertaining. Not in 2021-22.

For Paris not to win away from home against any top nine team was a disgrace. They lost at Rennes (2-0), Nice (1-0), Nantes (3-1) and Monaco (3-0), drew in Marseille (0-0), in Strasbourg (3-3), in Lens (1-1) and in Lyon (1-1). On top of that, they also could not win away from home in the Champions League (draws in Brugge and in Leipzig, losses at Manchester City and Real Madrid). That is the worst away form in a decade.

Pochettino's inability to get things right away from the Parc des Princes showed his limitations. His passivity during the remontada at the Bernabéu in the Champions League last 16 second-leg, where he didn't do anything to stop the team crumbling, was a huge low. He never really got the confidence of his dressing room. The leading players were disappointed by some of his drills and lack of tactical work. The underwhelming season was not all his fault, because PSG is clearly a very difficult club to manage, but he was still mostly to blame. His cold relationship with then-sporting director Leonardo didn't help. Neither did the fact that he could not discipline the players who needed to be disciplined in the way he would have wanted.

Which takes us nicely to Neymar. In the years since his amazing arrival at the club for a world-record fee of €222 million in August 2017, the Brazilian superstar had been the biggest name, the biggest player, the darling of the owners and of the president. That changed in 2022. Despite giving him a new contract in 2021, tying him to the club until June 2025, PSG grew tired of the former Barcelona man.

The 2021-22 season was his most disappointing. Only 28 appearances in all competitions, 13 goals and six assists but, most damningly, not many moments of brilliance either. He finished the campaign well (nine goals and three assists in his last nine Ligue 1 games), but it was too little too late, and there were too many moments where he let himself and the team down.

The club opened the door to letting him go, but who will sign him? Who will be able to sign him? He turned 30 in February 2022 and, as a sign of times, even his birthday party was nowhere near as luxurious and extravagant as in previous years. Will Neymar be in Paris for much longer? Will he be able to get back to his best? Would PSG be better without him? So many questions need answering.

The club has taken a new direction with a new manager and a new sporting director but also big changes to the squad with more French players, more young players and fewer average ones. It was a huge rebuilding job and it will take some time. It is clearly the plan that Mbappé agreed to when he decided to extend his contract and stay at the club for a bit longer.

The rest of Ligue 1 will look on with curiosity, hoping that the PSG reboot takes a while to get going and to work. They will have the ambition to do what only Montpellier (2012), Monaco (2017) and Lille (2021) have been able to do since the Qataris took over: beat PSG to the title. The likes of Marseille (2nd in 2022) with Jorge Sampaoli and an intelligent recruitment strategy, Monaco (3rd) and Philippe Clement who were the best team in 2022, then there's Lyon, Nice, who want to keep growing, Rennes, Strasbourg and Lens.

But the most important thing for PSG, and French football, is that Mbappé is still there.

The education of Wayne Rooney, manager

by Elias Burke

Wayne Rooney was given a thankless task at Derby County, heading inexorably to relegation with a 21-point penalty. This is the story of his first full season as a manager.

The defeat away to Queens Park Rangers that confirmed relegation to League One was a sad denouement to a season that will live long in the memory of Derby County supporters for its euphoric highs and the agonising lows.

Despite victories against Bournemouth, Fulham and Sheffield United, Derby narrowly missed out on one of the greatest escapes in English football history as the 21 points deducted for entering administration and breaches of EFL Profit and Sustainability (P&S) regulations proved insurmountable for Wayne Rooney's gang of misfits. But, as the players left the pitch with their fate decided, 3,000 travelling supporters made it clear that it was not their fault. When these players return to Pride Park — whether in the black and white of Derby or another capacity — the supporters will greet them with a hero's ovation.

Plagued by former chairman Mel Morris's misdealings, the club had spent the season in and out of legal battles with the EFL and rival clubs. Unsurprisingly, with impending legal cases and Derby losing more than £1 million a month, Morris had been trying to sell or find new investors in the club since they lost in the Championship play-off final to Aston Villa in 2019.

Fast forward to the summer of 2021, with Spanish businessman Erik Alonso's proposed takeover having fallen through, the club was in limbo. Fourteen players returned to Moor Farm, Derby's training ground, on 1 July to begin preparations for the new season. Of that number, there were no senior centre-backs and only one striker — Colin Kazim-Richards, who was about to turn 35. Derby's embargo meant they could only sign free agents on one-year contracts. Curtis Davies joined without assurances of a contract, along with Richard Stearman and Phil Jagielka. Davies and Stearman signed year-long deals alongside Ravel Morrison — his eighth club in five years — while Jagielka signed an emergency contract until January.

Hamstrung by a transfer embargo, Rooney looked to his current squad and identified areas for internal improvement. Tom Lawrence was undoubtedly the most gifted senior attacker still contracted to the club, but had spent much of the season before on the sidelines through injury. If the club were to upset the bookies' odds and beat the drop, Lawrence would need to turn inconsistent moments of brilliance into a reliable source of creativity and goals. So the manager asked whether he thought he was ready to become the captain, hoping that the added responsibility would encourage him to take the next step.

Handing the armband to the club's most talented attacker is hardly controversial, but Lawrence was a character who split opinions. Sections of the fanbase were concerned that Rooney had granted such responsibility to someone convicted of drink-driving 18 months earlier, who also had a penchant for collecting needless bookings. Davies was the people's choice, but Rooney had learnt from the best in management, and the best trust their instincts. Rooney maintained his belief in his captain throughout the season, who went on to score a career-best 11 goals and finish as the club's top goalscorer.

Educated by scars of a 19-year playing career spent under intense media scrutiny, his experience in the limelight has informed his player-welfare-first management style. 'We'll be eating lunch, and he'll be looking over at a player, he'll say, "I need to speak to him. Something's up. The way he's eating his food — he doesn't normally eat like that". That's the level of detail he'll go into,' Liam Rosenior, Derby's then assistant manager, said. 'He can just smell it in people. It's a gift. There's an empathy, a soft side to him that I don't think has been reflected. And actually, that has been his greatest strength.'

At 16 years old, Rooney was anointed as the new face of English football when he became the youngest goalscorer in Premier League history. Following that goal, a 25-yard curling effort into the top corner against Arsenal, Arsène Wenger described him as 'the biggest English talent I've seen since I've been in England' but noted that he hoped that 'mentally he will be able to cope with what's happening to him'. A few months later, he became the highest-paid youngster in Everton's history and one of the richest teenagers in European football. As Wenger alluded to, Rooney sometimes struggled to manage the intense pressure.

Still, after five Premier League titles, an FA Cup, a Champions League, a Club World Cup, highly publicised claims of extra-marital affairs and fallouts with Sir Alex Ferguson — not to mention a drink-driving case of his own — Rooney hung up his boots aged 35, retiring as one of his era's true greats. He did not leave a closing legacy in Everton blue as he might have initially planned, nor did he call it a day in the United States like England team-mates Steven Gerrard and Frank Lampard. Ole Gunnar Solskjær did not ask him to return to United for one final hurrah, à la Thierry Henry with Arsenal or Didier Drogba with Chelsea. Instead,

Rooney's curtain call came in the second tier of English football after Phillip Cocu — the manager who signed him — was sacked and the club could not afford to look elsewhere. For Rooney, however, this was years in the making.

Though nostalgia played a part in Rooney's return to Goodison Park, he took all of his late-career decisions intending to coach in the future. He inherited the tricks of man management from Sir Alex Ferguson, who he described as 'by far the best' in that respect, and keenly listened to insights from Louis van Gaal and José Mourinho, who he revered as elite tacticians. Then he played under Ronald Koeman until he was sacked and replaced by Sam Allardyce, whose disciplined and defensive brand of football was the polar opposite of anything he had played under previously. Then came MLS, where he had a substantial commercial impact on D.C. United for 18 months until he was tempted by a player-coach role with Derby in late 2019.

By the time he arrived at Derby, Rooney was a far cry from the world-class talent he once was. The pace was not there, and the searing 25-yard strikes were few and far between. Mentally, though, he was still as determined as ever, and that was clear as soon as he walked through the door at Moor Farm, where he assumed a role in the leadership team, acting as a mentor for the once-in-a-generation academy class that had just won the Under-18 Premier League title. 'First and foremost, you notice that he was a great player, obviously, but he was an even better person around the place,' says Derby midfielder Jason Knight, a crucial part of that title-winning side. 'Especially for us young lads, he's helped us all the way through.'

As manager, Rooney looked inward to a prolific academy that he could promote and mould in his image. As well as already established first-teamers Knight, Max Bird and Lee Buchanan, the manager set his sights on young Republic of Ireland international Festy Ebosele, who had spent most of the season before with the Under-23s.

Relying on academy graduates for consistency is difficult

enough in ideal circumstances, so it was a minor miracle that Rooney kept his players' eyes firmly on the job at hand when the points deductions arrived. In the three matches after entering administration in September – and with that a deduction of -12 – they claimed six points from a possible nine.

While the penalty dropped them to the foot of the table, Rooney set monthly targets and pinned a table on the dressing room wall without their points deductions that showed Derby in the top half. 'It (Rooney's alternative table) is a good thing,' said Derby defender Craig Forsyth, 'because you can sometimes get distracted if you are getting results and you are still in negative points or seven, eight points behind people when realistically we'd be near the play-offs on this form. It's important we keep that going and keep climbing the table.'

But Rooney did not just shoulder the responsibility on the pitch; he stood up to the role as the face of the club. With Derby's chief executive Stephen Pearce silent, and Quantuma, the club's admin-istrators, only fleetingly available, Rooney assured the club's staff, and the 20 made redundant, that he would do all he could to fight for them. He maintained this message throughout the season and invited every staff member to the training ground after relegation was confirmed to extend his gratitude for their help in retaining some normalcy in light of the circumstances. Never mind having to turn a ragtag squad that was both very old and extremely young into a competitive Championship side, or galvanise a group of players to overcome the highest points deficit in second-tier history, Rooney had to shoulder the responsibility of providing hope to a city that relies on its football club.

While the dream of achieving the impossible spurred on Derby, particularly following the added nine-point deduction in November, the possibility of liquidation lingered around uncomfortably on the terraces of Pride Park. Worse, false hope came on Thursday, January 13, when Rooney sat before local journalists – over Zoom as the stricter pandemic restrictions were still in place

— and confidently said that the long-awaited announcement of a preferred bidder to buy the club would come within 24 hours.

Derby supporters erupted with excitement on social media at the prospect of using the final fortnight of the winter transfer window to strengthen a squad that had picked up 10 points from the previous four matches to push towards Championship survival over the season's final four months. However, hours later, Quantuma had a meeting with the EFL, who disapproved of their plan.

The following morning, in an emotional meeting at the training ground, Rooney told out-of-contract dressing room leader Jagielka that he could not extend his contract. Rooney and Jagielka had worked closely and productively along with Davies and Stearman to create a senior leadership team that acted as a lighthouse for the youngsters in uncertain times. It was a substantial blow to the squad's dynamic and survival aspirations, and the playing staff were worried.

For fans and players alike, the anxiety around the club's future was at its zenith. Then, with Derby set to host a Sheffield United side on a four-match winning streak and bound for the play-offs the next day, Quantuma sold experienced midfielder Graeme Shinnie, who had started 21 of the 25 league games up to that point, to League One promotion-chasers Wigan Athletic — for less than £30,000.

With the crumbling foundations of a club built by Steve Bloomer, Brian Clough and Peter Taylor threatening to collapse totally, Rooney somehow galvanised his players to deliver an unforgettable 2-0 win in front of an emotional crowd. Lawrence, Rooney's controversially appointed captain, scored a spectacular second-half double so good both were later among the 10 nominees for Derby's goal of the season. If ever there was a day to encapsulate the undying spirit that Rooney created at Derby, that was it.

Over the season, Rooney demonstrated all of the required

qualities to have a long career in management. Of course, he knows how to win football matches, but he is multi-layered, with a deep understanding of man-management and developing young players' talent and character. With Morrison's chequered history, other managers may have passed on the opportunity to sign him. But, under Rooney, he reinvented himself as a reliable and hard-working team player, making 36 league appearances — the first time he had reached 30 league appearances for a club in his career.

Yes, Derby were relegated to the third tier for the first time in almost four decades. But without a genuine understanding of what it takes to succeed, Rooney would not have come close to achieving the impossible. In his first job in management, he dutifully served as the face of a football club on the verge of liquidation, tying the fans and players closer than they have been since the glory days under Clough and Taylor. He is over-achieving, hardworking and empathetic, and he has designs to reach the same heights in management as he did as a player. Even after leaving Derby, write him off at your peril.

The Great Clasico and the making of Barcelona Femení

by Charlotte Harpur

In March 2022 91,553 people watched a Clasico between Barcelona and Real Madrid, a record for a women's game. This is how it all happened.

With her left hand behind her back, Alexia Putellas, the captain of Barcelona Women, twirled her right hand in an extravagant gesture and bowed like a matador.

The Camp Nou — filled with 91,553 adulating fans, a world-record attendance for a women's match — chanted her name as their queen celebrated Barcelona's fourth goal on a historic night for her team and women's football.

An hour before kick-off, there was just a sprinkling of fans dotted around the iconic amphitheatre. Those dots became lines and lines became blocks as the drums banged and the 'Barca!' chants rang out.

In the opening minutes, every Barcelona pass was met with applause and every tackle was cheered. Equally loud were the cicada-sounding whistles as soon as Real Madrid committed a foul.

When the crowd waited for free kicks, the thunderclap began, increasing in tempo. 'Oohs' and 'aahs' followed after any close chance.

Then Maria León's left-footed 20-yard curling strike triggered a deafening wall of euphoria. Goosebumps.

Boos filled the stadium when referee Stéphanie Frappart pointed to the penalty spot. So high-pitched were the whistles when Real Madrid's Olga Carmona stepped up that some fans tried in vain to block them out by putting their fingers to their ears.

Penalty scored. Silence. But only for a matter of seconds. Then the drums restarted and the applause echoed.

Claudia Zornoza's 40-yard strike sailing over Barcelona goal-keeper Sandra Paños shocked the crowd but again, only momentarily. When nothing was given for a suspected foul in the box on Caroline Graham Hansen, the eventual player of the match, the screeching noise, like an army of angry crickets, lasted for minutes.

Then Barcelona turned the screw, showing that killer instinct, scoring three goals inside 10 minutes. Rebounding chants pinged back and forth from opposite stands as the Catalan club pulled clear.

Playing in front of fans at the men's team's ground for the first time in March 2022, Barcelona beat rivals Real Madrid 8-3 on aggregate.

Putellas, the Ballon d'Or winner whose replica trophy sits in the club museum, struggled to sum up her emotions.

'I'm almost speechless, honestly,' she said after the game. 'This has been utterly magical. When the match finished, the fans simply didn't want to go home!'

This was not a one-off, this electrifying performance did not come out of the blue. You can't sell 85,000 tickets in three days without a sustainable fanbase. When the women's team used to play in the now-demolished Miniestadi, a stone's throw from the

Camp Nou in the city centre, the average attendance was between 500 and 1,000. Further out of the city at the Johan Cruyff Stadium, which was constructed for the women's side in 2019, between 3,000 and 4,000 fans attend.

In January, Barcelona trounced Atlético Madrid 7-0 in the Super Cup, rounding off 2021 when they won every title possible – the Champions League, the league and the League Cup, named the Copa de la Reina.

They clinched the 2022 title with six matches to spare. They won all 30 of their league games, scoring 159 goals and conceding just 11.

But it wasn't always this way. Their success is a far cry from 21 years ago. The freshly-branded Spanish Superliga didn't even accept Barcelona as members because of their poor results in the 2000-01 season. The women's team were only incorporated into FC Barcelona as their own official sector a year later.

After three years in the top flight from 2004 to 2007, they were relegated, and there were concerns about the future of the women's side. They returned to the top flight at the first time of asking in 2008 though, and won their first league title in 2012 to qualify for the Champions League the following season, albeit losing to Arsenal 7-0 on aggregate in the first round.

The club went professional in the summer of 2015 – a turning point according to sporting director Markel Zubizarreta, who joined that year.

'There was a mindset change seven years ago,' says Zubizarreta. 'The club was not building a women's football project but a professional football project in women's football. To invest in the same way, to build the same project.

'It's really simple to say but to change the mentality in all the club's departments, that was the work.'

From 2015 to 2022, Barcelona transformed the structure of their women's teams. The number of first-team staff has grown to include roles such as an additional assistant manager, a goalkeepers coach, an analyst, a team delegate, a kit manager, doctors, psychologists and nutritionists.

The academy was revamped to allocate two coaches per youth team from the under-10s up to the B team, as well as physios, doctors, psychologists, physical trainers and methodologists.

The women's section also has a dedicated regional and international scouting department as well as a sports science team.

The football management, scouting, playing methodology, sports science and academy departments replicate the men's model, with the same facilities.

In 2015, Barcelona did not want to invest a lot of money in the world's best signings. Instead, their philosophy was to invest in their first-team and academy players.

They believe the future lies in the success of their academy and are giving opportunities to the players it produces.

The squad that faced Real featured ten players who came through the Barcelona academy system, and eight of the starting XI joined the first team after 2017.

It was apt that on such a historic night, it was Barcelona academy products Aitana Bonmatí and Clàudia Pina who turned the tide. At 2-1 down, Bonmatí finished her darting run with an arrowed shot that nestled into the bottom corner, and this was shortly followed by Pina's delightful chip.

Since 2018, Barcelona's under-10, under-12 and under-14 girls' teams have played in boys' leagues — the only club in Spain to do this. Even their under-18s girls' team consists solely of under-16s, the theory being if they play in tough conditions now, they will benefit in the future.

The focus is not on winning, but on understanding the Barcelona style and training at a high level — three to four sessions per week, increasing to five or six as players get older.

But that does not mean winning is not a part of the academy. The girls' team has won the boys' league and their under-14s side is on course to top the table again this season.

'The academy players have a lot of talent — maybe more talent than the first-team players, because they have played in a professional academy since they were 11,' explains Zubizarreta.

By comparison Putellas, the FIFA women's player of the year, didn't start playing professionally until she was 21 years old.

'It's different and we need to keep this difference because everyone is investing in women's football. If we stop, the clubs behind us may reach our level.'

Barcelona's serious investment in the women's side was shown when, for the first time since its founding in 1979, La Masia welcomed female residents in August 2021.

The academy teenagers who play for the Barcelona B team combine their training with their studies. They are the only female athletes living on-site, with their bedroom view looking across to the Johan Cruyff Stadium.

The building houses athletes from Barcelona's football, basketball, handball, futsal and roller hockey teams. They are educated in classrooms on the ground floor — the auditorium hosts seminars on what the club calls 'invisible training', broaching topics from diet to social media.

Club nutritionists advise the kitchen on the meals offered in the dining room and players' food intake can be tracked every week.

There is a deep-rooted, relentless desire to improve among the women's team and that stems from the challenges they have faced.

From 2015 to 2019, Barcelona could only finish as runners-up in the league. They were losing.

'To keep that investment, to keep that focus on our players at that moment was a huge step,' says Zubizarreta.

In 2019, Barcelona reached their first Champions League final but suffered a chastening 4-1 defeat against Lyon, who were then the dominant force of European women's football.

The team realised they had to improve their fitness and physical strength. 'We have the best version in terms of the physicality of all our players,' Zubizarreta says. 'The players who have experienced this progression are conscious that they need to make the most of their time here.

'When I see the players coming every morning to the training centre, they are still hungry.'

Characterised by short passes and movement, the Barcelona style is unique to the club and encompasses every team, whether male or female. The methodology is the same for both, and some of the men's coaches have joined the women's side.

'When I talk with players signing for Barca academy and the first team, I talk about football in a way that is completely different to what they have heard,' says Zubizarreta.

'We're talking about understanding, not doing. The language is about possession, not attacking or defending, but positioning, timing and space.

'The game is the same. If there's a Barca fan that puts on the TV and they cannot recognise if they're women or men, they'll say, "That's a Barca team". That is important.'

Former head coach Lluís Cortés left in 2021 and, within three days, they had appointed then-29-year-old assistant coach Jonatan Giráldez despite receiving CVs from 100 coaches around the world. Having spent two and a half years at the club already, Giráldez understood the Barcelona DNA.

Of course, performances are not perfect and the club are constantly reviewing but not making dramatic changes. There is no knee-jerk reaction. Their core method remains, with the focus on playing the game their way.

'We think it is the correct way, it is not under discussion,' says Zubizarreta.

'Right now, it's easy, because we are winning more than losing. But four years ago, we were losing. We had (Patri) Guijarro, Bonmatí and Putellas in the team. So at that moment, OK, we need to invest more in them. Now they play our style and are the best midfielders we can find.'

Part of Barcelona's style is the need to adapt to different situations quickly and an in-depth understanding of the tactics.

When Arsenal hosted Barcelona at the Emirates in December, two hours before kick-off, Guijarro tested positive for COVID-19 so the match plan had to change. Putellas switched to a holding midfield role, a position she rarely plays, and yet the team didn't look out of sync at all. They won 8-1 over two group-stage games.

Barcelona don't just win, they win in style, and the quality of their football has caught the eye of male players past and present.

Academy boys who, previously, would bypass the women training without batting an eyelid, now wait 20 minutes for a photo with them. Carles Puyol has been a huge advocate for the women's team, posting support from his Instagram account, with a casual 11.1 million followers.

'We are not a product of women's football, we are a product of football,' says Zubizarreta.

Granddaughters and grandsons took their long-supporting grandparents to the Real game, while parents wanted their sons and daughters to witness the momentous occasion. Supporters from as far as Mexico and South Korea flooded through the stadium gates, waving flags and flares, chanting as the Barcelona team bus arrived.

Fiorella D'Angelo, a 26-year-old Catalonian, has supported the team since that first Champions League final in 2019 and goes to every game at the Johan Cruyff Stadium.

'I felt let down by the men's team,' she says. 'I saw a poster of Alexia in the city and I started watching the women's team.'

Tickets started at €9 (£7.60) and around 30,000 of Barcelona's socios — club members — signed up during the first 24-hour window of exclusive access. They were able to purchase up to four tickets. The Camp Nou was sold out within three days, setting up the possibility of a world-record attendance.

Putellas said: 'I couldn't picture myself at Camp Nou when I was a girl, because I could only see men. I knew I could play but I never imagined I would play here,' she said.

'It's a starting point. We can open so many doors for so many girls. I feel very proud that Barca makes it possible.

'It will be a turning point in women's football in Barcelona, Catalonia, Spain and hopefully all around the world, because Barca is an international team. We will broadcast an important message.'

A version of this article first appeared on The Athletic.

The wasted second act of Paul Pogba

by Nick Miller

Many thought Paul Pogba was the man to bring balance to Manchester United, but six years after his return he left with only the faint memory of hope to show for it . . .

In 1970 the German director Hellmuth Costard gathered a bunch of 16mm cameras, headed to Manchester and made an experimental film about George Best which simply involved filming him, and only him, during a game against Coventry City.

Douglas Gordon and Philippe Parreno did a similar thing with 2006's Zidane: A 21st Century Portrait, following the great man around the pitch as he played for Real Madrid against Villarreal. This, paired with an atmospheric Mogwai soundtrack, then qualified as an arty documentary.

It's a preposterous concept really, and one that those of us who watched a lot of Sky Sports in the late '90s and early 2000s will simply recognise as the ditched feature 'Player Cam'. There is usually so much going on during a high-level football game that it seems pointless and needlessly obtuse to limit yourself to just one player.

There are a few players you can make an exception for, though. If you ever get the chance to attend a game in which Paul Pogba plays, try — even if it's just for a short while — to ignore everyone else and just watch him.

Watch the way Pogba sweeps around the pitch, running with an elegance that seems incongruous for someone of his size. Watch him whip passes across the turf, addressing the ball with a combination of delicacy and power. Watch him gather the ball and scoop it close to him, keeping it in his orbit as if held by magnets.

It's a truly wonderful sight and would be a terrific use of 90 minutes. The problem is that if you had done that for the majority of Pogba's second spell at Manchester United, it would have been the footballing equivalent of watching one of those films. Nice to look at, but what are you left with at the end, of any practical use?

If you wanted to cause Manchester United fans some angst in the time between Pogba's two spells at the club, you would just have to encourage them to watch a Juventus match. There he was, inspiring the Italian giants to league titles, the glorious promise of his youth at United seemingly realised. This was the player United let slip through their fingers, either because of disagreements with his agent, the late Mino Raiola, or his impatience at being given a first-team place.

The game, in his last season, against Blackburn Rovers when United's primary central midfield options were unavailable but Sir Alex Ferguson chose Rafael, a right-back, and Park Ji-sung, a winger, instead of Pogba was the last straw. 'I was disgusted,' Pogba said in 2014.

For the four seasons he spent in Italy, it felt like that game could have represented the biggest mistake in United's modern history. Pogba could have been the player to guide United out of their post-Ferguson funk.

And then they made right that mistake. Making it right was an expensive business, United spending nearly £90 million on a player they had lost for free four years earlier, but it was just money. They had plenty of it — so why not spend it on a generational talent like Pogba? Hope infused the air, a new dawn, a flashy introduction video featuring Pogba dabbing and Stormzy rapping. This was United in 4K.

Six years later, Pogba left again having won a few trophies but achieving little of note, other than causing three managers to scratch their heads, his only real legacy being a trail of increasingly circular debates between those who thought he was a waste of space and those who thought he was the great misunderstood footballer of his time.

As ever with these things, the truth probably lies somewhere in the middle, but there's one thing that can't be up for too much debate: if anything sums up post-Ferguson Manchester United — a club who have bumbled from one ill-informed decision to the next with £50 notes falling out of their pockets with every step and who have drastically underperformed considering the resources available to them — it's Pogba.

It simultaneously feels like such a waste, and also inevitable. How could they not get the best from this graceful sensation, a player with Patrick Vieira's physique and Cesc Fàbregas's touch? And at the same time, how could we have thought anything different? The phrase 'this is Manchester United' used to mean unrelenting high standards — expectations of only the best — but since Ferguson retired it has gradually become shorthand for an organisation that consistently gets things wrong.

As with many of United's transfer decisions, the motivation behind bringing Pogba back in 2016 seemed to be 'he's there, and we can'. There seemed little thought as to what they would actually do when they signed him; it was the signing that was the important bit, the ability to say they could still attract the most coveted stars in the game, even as they steadily fell behind Manchester City, Chelsea and, increasingly, Liverpool.

It was as if the club was just buying an asset that they hoped would either appreciate in value, make them look good or both. The actual business of playing football they would leave to the manager to sort out, regardless of whether Pogba actually fitted with the manager's plans or not.

The manager at the time was José Mourinho, someone who you would never put together with a player like Pogba, his increasingly conservative style not suiting a player who prefers to be a free spirit. ESPN's Wright Thompson described Pogba playing under Mourinho as akin to 'a sequinned jacket in a hit man's closet.'

Maybe we should have known from the start. United signed Pogba without realising he would be suspended for their first game of the season, and things went patchily from there, the first two years passing in a stream of inconsistent performances and arch interviews from both sides.

Then there was the curious episode in September 2018, when Mourinho was furious with Pogba because of an Instagram post, of all things. Pogba had been rested and was watching United's League Cup defeat to Derby, and he posted a clip of him, Luke Shaw and Andreas Pereira laughing and having a nice time in the stands. The trouble was, due to Old Trafford's famously ropey WiFi, the clip didn't actually go up until after full-time, which gave the impression that Pogba was laughing at his defeated team-mates. A terse exchange on the training ground followed, in full view of the TV cameras, and everything got a little bit silly.

The next manager was Ole Gunnar Solskjær, a coach who occasionally got things right in the same way that a blindfolded person throwing darts at a board would occasionally hit treble 20. There was much talk at the start of his reign that he had brought back the 'real' Pogba. 'Before the coach arrived I was in the shadows, on the bench, and I accepted that,' he said in January 2019. 'It is a pleasure to play again. Now I am always smiling.'

But eventually that faded as United did, and by June that year he was talking of a 'new challenge somewhere else.' And then there was Ralf Rangnick, a bizarre appointment who wasn't there long enough to do much of anything really.

There never seemed to be a manager who quite knew what to do with Pogba, or to get the best out of him in the way that Max Allegri did during his first spell with Juventus, or Didier Deschamps did at times with France. Was this a collective failure of imagination? A collective failure of tactical understanding?

We were repeatedly told that Pogba was at his best with Juve on the left side of a three-man midfield, so why did that happen so infrequently at United? Was it because they were Manchester United, a club who still regard themselves as an august institution that cannot be dictated to by one man?

You are tempted to think, though, that when you've paid £89 million for that man, you should put the institutional ego to one side for a bit and do whatever you can to get the best from them.

The other side of the argument is that, while it is better to use a player in his preferred position, it's not ideal when that player can't perform to his expected standards if he's playing five yards further to the right than he wants. You're sometimes tempted to adopt an old-fashioned parent role with Pogba, and say, 'Oh will you just get on with it?'

Indeed, when three United managers can't quite figure out how to get the best from a player, the instinct is to look for the common factor in the whole thing: perhaps Pogba's defenders might wonder if he's the issue, rather than the multiple coaches.

There's also the question of injuries. A perception built of Pogba as a player who was cautious about his own fitness, and wouldn't play unless he was 100 per cent. Logically, there's not much wrong with that position, but in a world still dominated by a form of masculinity that views that sort of caution as a weakness, he was always going to struggle for approval.

Then again, the injuries were an increasing source of frustration. He missed 89 games in his time back at Old Trafford through various ailments, an average of 15 games a season which was back-loaded — 72 of those games came in the second three years. From that perspective it was apt that his final appearance would end early, limping off in the early stages of a 4-0 defeat to Liverpool that flattered United greatly, and served as an illustration of just how emphatically their old rivals had overtaken them.

There was also the persistent fridge buzz of rumour suggesting that he wasn't happy at Old Trafford. Admittedly, the source of that tended to be his agent, and asking Raiola to keep his thoughts to himself was easier said than done. But Pogba didn't help himself on occasion.

None of this would really have mattered if his performances on the pitch had been consistently stellar, but maybe even those have been misjudged. Carl Anka, who you'll find elsewhere in this book, was fond of saying that we would judge Pogba very differently if he was a few inches shorter. His skillset doesn't really tally with his size, or at least received ideas of how a player of his size should play. General ideas of how tall, black footballers should play are wrapped in lazy and often racially coded preconceptions: powerful, strong, athletic. Racism — non-direct in this case and direct in the form of social media abuse suffered by Pogba — is a part of his story that cannot be ignored.

Pogba is strong, but that's not what should leap out at first when you watch him. What should leap out is his extraordinary touch, his sweeping grace, his passing ability. His physical size doesn't usually manifest itself in the power to knock someone else off the ball, more the aesthetics of how he manipulates his long limbs.

It leads to the quandary of what we could have reasonably expected from Pogba. It's almost certainly true that he was judged by a different standard to everyone else: there is an old-school element to the football commentariat that disapproves of Pogba's extra-curricular activities, when in reality that only actually extends to some dancing, some brand deals and an active presence on social media. Those detractors judged Pogba's performance on the pitch through the prism of things off the pitch that were harmless, but that they didn't understand.

Perhaps because of the fee, the fact he was 'coming home' and his undoubted talent, fans, the media and everyone else wanted him to be some sort of saviour, the man to bring balance to Manchester United, when in reality he is just a very good footballer performing in a flawed system. Maybe he delivered all that could be reasonably expected of him.

So we come back to the central question: was Manchester United's Paul Pogba greatly misunderstood, or a colossal disappointment? Was he a man who didn't live up to his own talent or one let down by a failing institution? Whose fault was it that things didn't work out: his or United's?

The sweeping answer to all of those questions is: yes. Paul Pogba's second act at Manchester United was, ultimately, a waste. A waste for both him and the club. It could have been so much more.

Liverpool v Manchester City: is our greatest rivalry actually a rivalry?

by Sasha Goryunov

What really makes a great rivalry? Is it only about two brilliant teams challenging each other, or does it need something more than that?

Manchester City had just beaten Newcastle United 5-0 to go three points clear of Liverpool with three games of the 2021-22 season to play, and Pep Guardiola was speaking to an international broadcaster: 'Everyone in this country supports Liverpool,' he said. 'The media and everyone.'

Taken in isolation this sounds baffling, but Manchester City's insistence on being the underdog story is just one aspect of a rivalry that has dominated English football over the last few seasons. Jürgen Klopp had the chance to respond the following day. 'I live in Liverpool so yes, here, a lot of people want us to win the league,' he said with a smile. 'That's true but even here it's probably only 50%.'

Growing up on Merseyside in the mid-'90s, matches against Manchester City generally provided light relief for Liverpool fans, away from miserable scrappy derbies against Everton and the unwelcome sight of Manchester United disappearing over the horizon.

Now though, it's all much more serious. Liverpool and City have been the dominant forces in English domestic football since around 2018, when Guardiola and Klopp's work really started to take hold.

But in 2021-22, when both teams were sweeping all aside, the question was raised about what sort of rivalry this really was. Is it enough just to be dominant? What actually makes a good rivalry?

To understand what makes a rivalry great I turned to fellow contributors to *The Totally Football Show*. The first key factor is balance, be it in size or in fortune. Dom Fifield observes: 'It's no good if it's a complete mismatch — if one club is in the top division and the other is floundering lower down the pyramid, with very little chance to compete against each other.' Indeed, 'If clubs do not play against each other a few times per decade then the rivalry tends to dilute,' chips in Alvaro Romeo, but, as per Dom, this can 'breed contempt over time so that, when the inevitable happens and they are flung against each other in a cup competition, there is a dramatic outpouring of passion (or aggression)'.

When the teams do play each other regularly, Tom Williams points out that 'rivalries are no fun when they're one-sided'. In that case, can a rivalry stop and start again or is there simply a spell when, as Alvaro points out, 'rivalry only matters for the lesser side'? For example, take the 20-year period post-1992 when Atlético only beat Real Madrid twice and the Madrid derby became a bit of a joke to most and a ritual humiliation for the *colchoneros*.

Yet Carl Anka makes a beautiful argument that 'a rivalry is never completed because it has an emotional narrative to it', which can cut through the technical aspects. Perhaps this is not limitless, but can make a difference when teams of comparable standard meet. Liverpool against Manchester United is often held up as England's ultimate contest, yet they went up against each for the title on only a handful of occasions (most recently in 2009). The rest of the time was spent with one team in the shadow of the neighbour trying to spoil some of that success. Adrian Clarke adds: 'History tends to breed grudging respect and perhaps most importantly, historical "beef"! A rivalry without beef is weak.'

This brings us to the next definitive factor: animosity, or simply hatred — rational or not. For Nick Miller it should be all-encompassing: 'Between the fans, the players, the managers, whoever, because the football is only half the point.' And, as Matt Davies-Adams points out, it needs time to emerge: 'A rivalry can only exist when the teams in question have an established dislike of one another dating back no less than five years, preferably far longer.' It helps 'if there is some sort of high-profile falling out, like poaching a manager, signing a player or a serious injury in a meeting of the sides.'

Benji Lanyado, though, does not even need a real cause to set it all off. 'You need to hate your rival for a not particularly good or rational reason. You just feel it deep within you that you don't like these people; they annoy you, you want them to fail.' It is left to Charlie Eccleshare to concisely sum up: 'Drama is conflict — you want that needle.'

While it was already discussed what happens when teams face each other too infrequently, Nick Miller actually points out that 'less is more with these things. For example, Liverpool against Chelsea got a bit boring in the late 2000s because they just seemed to be playing each other every month.' Carl Anka puts it diplomatically: 'You want to have it structured in a way that you can face each other quite often but not too often.'

The Old Firm seems immune to this, but then again that is driven by powerful ideology. It is one of the many derbies Dom Fifield covered and he found that 'the level of hostility truly takes the breath, and not in a particularly comfortable way'. Alvaro Romeo points to the 'ongoing political narrative' underpinning Real Madrid versus Barcelona. The political element of one club's support can find it at odds with another, or even most of the country, as is the case with the left-leaning Livorno ultras in Italy.

And finally, the managers. They can take a rivalry beyond all others but it feels that everything has to peak at the same time as them.

It all came together in England in the late 1990s, when Arsenal and Manchester United delivered a rivalry for the ages. They were closely matched and pretty consistent. Arsenal finished in the top two for seven successive seasons. Manchester United did not drop below third. Arsenal won three Premier League titles and four FA cups, including two doubles and went an entire season unbeaten. Manchester United won four Premier League titles (including three in a row), two FA Cups and one Champions League, completing a treble.

And how they hated each other. Dom Fifield immediately thinks of Roy Keane against Patrick Vieira. 'You can't have a rivalry without a bit of pantomime hatred. Or real hatred.' For Flo Lloyd-Hughes 'it felt authentic — you definitely believed that Roy Keane hated all the Arsenal players and Arsène Wenger, and if he could he probably would've beaten the shit out of them.'

Two great managers at their peak oversaw it all. Adrian Clarke certainly enjoyed it: 'Wenger v Ferguson was the pinnacle. The two best slugging it out, sharing the wins, and putting on some amazing games brimming with spite. When two bosses, the symbols of their teams genuinely dislike/fear one another it can take a rivalry to the next level.'

Duncan Alexander sums it up brilliantly: 'It threw up just the right combination of violence and beauty, of success and petti-ness. From pizza, to Keown, to the tunnel fight, to that Henry goal at Highbury, to Rooney ending the 49-game run. Arguably, rivalry perfection. United won more trophies but then Arsenal would do something incredibly stylised like score in every game (2002) or go unbeaten (2004) and you knew it wound up Ferguson.'

In hindsight, the fact that the Invincibles season came after Abramovich landed at Chelsea made it an even more beautiful swansong. The end of the affair, the 2005 FA Cup final, was forgettable and, indeed, immediately forgotten as Liverpool mounted their incredible comeback in Istanbul only a few days later. Arsenal, financially constrained by their owners and the building of their new stadium, have not challenged for a title since. Despite the Glazers' arrival Manchester United still had enough money and vision to re-adjust and defeat Chelsea, before hammering Arsenal 8-2 in 2011. The rivalry was definitely no more.

And so, to City v Liverpool. To everyone's surprise, Liverpool under Brendan Rodgers mounted a real title challenge in 2014. For a while, it was a three-horse race and, if anything, it looked like José Mourinho's Chelsea were the team to beat. Chelsea bottled it, Liverpool beat Manchester City and the title was theirs to lose . . . which they did in that match against Chelsea.

The calamity of Gerrard's slip was such that it obscured everything else about that title run-in. It seemed like no one cared about who actually won the title — it was all about how it was lost.

The arrival of Klopp in 2015 and Guardiola in 2016 changed everything. Klopp always felt like the perfect cultural fit for Liverpool — an ideal leader for a fanbase that loves to idolise a manager. Guardiola was perfect for the City project. One component was in place.

Within two years one component became two. While Manchester City steamed towards their 100-point season in 2017-18, Liverpool managed to deliver warnings of what was to come. A devastating three-goal 10-minute spell at Anfield in January 2018 left Guardiola and his players visibly shaken as they suffered their first defeat of the season. In April 2018 Manchester

City visited again in the Champions League. A bottle of cider hit their bus, they again conceded three quick-fire goals and had an away goal chalked off for a very tight offside. Seething with the injustice of it all, City delivered a furious opening 45 minutes in the return leg, yet Liverpool held on and eventually went through.

In 2018-19 Liverpool went for it, reaching levels never seen before. Their astonishing run, which started in March 2019, would take them to the title in 2020. They didn't win the league in 2019 but they reached City's level, and they didn't break under the tremendous pressure of having to win every game. Liverpool won the Champions League but it genuinely felt they could do more the following season. They won the Club World Cup and the Premier League, only for City to fight back in 2020-21, while Liverpool physically broke down. Then Liverpool were back again with their third 90+ point season in four years and . . . it was not enough.

Tom Williams says: 'In terms of comparable sporting ability, you could not find two teams who are more perfectly matched. Plus there's the fact that their respective coaches have such different visions of the game, which adds an additional layer of intrigue.' 'In sports terms it is the best rivalry you can find now,' agrees Alvaro Romeo. For Adrian Clarke 'from a football perspective it's a rivalry I enjoy watching because neither team plays with fear. They slug it out and try to outscore each other without worrying about negating the other's strengths. It's refreshing and entertaining.' But . . . they all want more.

Colin Millar thinks 'it is an ideal rivalry for neutrals more than fans'. Adrian finds that 'there is a lack of edge. In that sense it's a very modern, clean-cut rivalry.' Matt Davies-Adams is also after more emotional drama: 'It's all just a bit too perfect and polite. There needs to be some genuine rancour between the teams to really stoke the rivalry.'

Fundamentally, there is simply not enough hatred to go around. The managers speak well of each other, are competitive but without much open resentment. The players . . . Kevin De Bruyne's children go to school with Virgil van Dijk's. The clubs' Brazilians hang out at Fernandinho's place. And the fans . . . Liverpool's simply don't care or, at worst, make fun of empty seats amid City's great success.

Duncan Alexander feels that 'technically this is the best rivalry English football has ever seen, but it needs a little bit more edge'. 'I can completely see why the two teams, and even their managers, might become sick of the sight of the other,' mused Dom Fifield hopefully. 'Maybe the back story is being cultivated now. Perhaps it will stick.'

Duncan goes all *Lord of the Rings*: 'If Liverpool and City are Gandalf and Saruman or vice versa, then United are Sauron, a huge malevolent force that hovers over both sides, watching – always watching.' Colin Millar thinks that 'secretly, both sides wish the other was Manchester United because that would add the "personal" aspect and a club who they broadly identify as the polar opposite.'

And, yet, maybe, something is brewing. The relief among Liverpool fans that greeted Real Madrid's unexpected last-minute comeback against City in the Champions League semi-final felt genuine. The build-up to a final against City would have been unbearable, the pressure to win too great. For the first time, it felt like there was an emotional narrative, which made this game one 'we could not afford to lose' against 'them'.

I'll leave you with Dom Fifield's conclusion. 'Perhaps in time, and if they remain the dominant forces in five or ten years . . . by then, that level of animosity might have developed because they will be so familiar with competing against each other at the top of the league, and for the same honours. But it is a work in progress.'

Megan Rapinoe, the USWNT and the lessons to be learned

by Flo Lloyd-Hughes

The US Women's National Team have been pioneers in standing up for equal pay and many other social causes: it's time for those in England to do the same . . .

'Our society has one way that lets you know that you're valued, and that's how much you're paid,' Megan Rapinoe told the *LA Times* in June 2021. 'In male sports, that's the peacocking — all the salaries and endorsements are out there. It's kind of interesting how women are the only ones who feel they have to keep quiet or feel like it's not polite to share their salary. I think that's just stupid. Without transparency, you just keep money in the hands of people who have it.'

Rapinoe, an Olympic gold medallist and two-time World Cup winner, is never one to shy away from saying what she really thinks. The Californian is outspoken, blunt and often damning. When she speaks the world listens.

That quote is from an interview she did just before the release of LFG (Let's Fucking Go), a documentary about the US Women's

National teams lengthy fight for equal pay. It was released before the US Women's National Team's Players Association (USWNTPA), alongside the men's equivalent, agreed to a new collective bargaining agreement with the US Soccer Federation in May 2022. The agreement finally brought equality to the men's and women's teams across pretty much every benchmark that was up for grabs.

From then until the end of 2028, there will be an equal split of World Cup prize money, with the men's and women's teams pooling prize totals. There will be an equal split of commercial revenue, ticket sales, fees for camp, bonuses and game-appearance fees.

At the time it was revealed, Walker Zimmerman, a US men's player and member of the leadership group for the men's union, the US National Soccer Team Players Association (USNSTPA), told *The Athletic*: 'This is the first time that we have sat down together, and we accomplished something historic.'

Historic is the perfect way to describe the agreement, because the foundations for its formation had been laid by generations of USWNT players.

Rapinoe and the US Women's National Team have been setting the tone in women's football since the 1990s. The iconic '99ers', who won the 1999 Women's World Cup on home soil, transformed the status of women's football in the US and around the world. The team and its big stars like Mia Hamm, Brandi Chastain and Julie Foudy became celebrities, featuring on late night talk shows, ringing up tons of endorsements and becoming household names.

The win in 1999 was the start of a women's football dynasty for the US. Winning trophies became expected and almost guaranteed. They have since won the Olympic title multiple times, taken three more World Cups and dominated the Concacaf region.

Some of the iconic 99ers group have now gone on to become owners of Los Angeles side Angel City FC and continued their legacy in the NWSL, the US women's league.

With all the success, the USWNT took on an arrogance and swagger. Everywhere they went, fans welcomed them like The Beatles. In 2019, at the World Cup in France, thousands of young girls sang forward Alex Morgan a happy birthday in the middle of the team's semi-final against England. There was a screeching hysteria that awaited their every move; it was like following a One Direction tour. That same tournament fans chanted 'equal pay' as the USWNT lifted a fourth World Cup.

Every USWNT match is like a party, except you're invited to sit and witness their greatness, not participate. Some may interpret this as arrogance, and Morgan's sipping of tea celebration after scoring the second goal in the US's 2-1 victory over England certainly ruffled a few feathers, but that arrogance has categorically led to fundamental change that could impact women's sport around the world, not just football.

In March 2019, the USWNT filed a lawsuit against US Soccer, alleging discrimination and asking for compensation for years of unequal reward. Although the lawsuit was only filed a few months before they won that fourth World Cup, it had been brewing for some time. Three years earlier, five players filed a complaint with the Equal Employment Opportunity Commission, taking the first step towards discrimination litigation. That complaint got stuck in the system while presidents changed and governments switched, eventually, after years of waiting, the team were allowed to bypass the EEOC and take a lawsuit to their employers.

Over the next few years the battle with the national federation would be ugly and embarrassing, especially for the federation's hierarchy. But the success of the team, the profiles of the stars within it and the activists at the heart of it eventually led to success for everyone, from the elite squad to the grassroots game.

That legal dispute with US Soccer was settled in February 2022, with the federation agreeing to pay the USWNT $24 million, but the bigger prize at stake was equal pay.

The USWNT have been an example to every athlete and their personality and outspokenness has influenced and should shape the behaviour of others around the world.

In 2016, Rapinoe took a knee as the American national anthem played during a NWSL fixture in a moment of solidarity with NFL star Colin Kaepernick, a move that would lead her to be ostracised by her own coach and some team-mates. She was one of the first athletes to support the NFL player and many others followed suit. It hasn't been the only time Rapinoe has used her voice. She has stood up for trans rights, publicly challenged former US president Donald Trump and supported anti-racism work across the US.

She is just one of the many activists in the USWNT set up. Morgan led the charge for the introduction of the NWSL's first anti-discrimination policy and supported whistleblowers in the league who spoke out against alleged sexual coercion from former high-profile coach Paul Riley. Riley denies the allegations.

At so many points over the last few years, when the world has become polarised, toxic and dark, and fans have looked to athletes to speak out for a cause, players within the USWNT have delivered.

But in England, we rarely see our women's footballers speak out. Anita Asante recently announced her retirement from the sport after a 20-year career, several trophies and over 70 caps for England. She has been one of the few players to use her platform to speak up and out.

When Eni Aluko took on the Football Association, one of the most powerful football institutions in the world, over alleged bullying and discriminatory comments by former England manager Mark Sampson, Asante was one of the few to support her. Team-mate Nikita Parris famously ran over to Sampson in a public show of support after scoring in a game against Russia in 2017. Parris later apologised to Aluko, admitting the celebration was 'thoughtless'.

There was little-to-no public support for Aluko from any of her white team-mates and, at the time, she said she was 'disappointed and surprised' by the lack of support.

Aluko told BBC Sport: 'I've had a lot of support from other countries: Norway, Sweden, France, particularly the United States girls.'

In 2020, following the murder of George Floyd and the protests inspired by the Black Lives Matter Movement, a movement many leagues showed solidarity and support for, it took the English Women's Super League months to follow suit.

For many reasons, English women's football has not found itself at the forefront of the fight for equality on and off the pitch. In many ways it's cultural: the English aren't outspoken, often afraid to rock the boat or stick their head above the parapet and aren't naturally — and somewhat unfortunately — an activist culture.

The women's game is also fragile; players are on small salaries, afraid to lose their status, power and value. If something happens in the English women's game, players often close ranks. It's not easy being the outlier and putting yourself at risk by challenging a coach, a captain or an entire system. The fact they are women in a sport still dominated by men, still run by men and still broadly sexist, also makes it difficult for women to speak out and be listened to.

The most blunt reason for this could be that some players plainly don't care about things outside of their bubble, but that's probably unfair on the vast majority who would speak up if they felt more empowered.

The 'transparency' Rapinoe referenced in her interview in 2021 is vitally missing in English women's football. Everything feels like a closed shop. Issues are swept under the rug, people don't speak out or speak up; they follow along and maintain the status quo.

Rarely do we see a player feel confident enough to speak up. Chelsea captain Magdalena Eriksson was brave in her condemnation of the Qatar World Cup in a newspaper column, and along with her partner and team-mate Pernille Harder has campaigned for LGBTQ+ rights for years. But they're a rare find in the WSL.

USWNT players don t-shirts calling for the protection of trans-gender youths every week, they hold signs calling to end gun violence in the US. They go on Black Lives Matter marches.

In the men's game, Manchester United and England's Marcus Rashford has used his platform to take on the British government and helped feed children in need. Aston Villa defender Tyrone Mings joined Black Lives Matter marches in England and criticised home secretary Priti Patel for 'pretending to be disgusted' over racist abuse that England players suffered after defeat to Italy in the Euro 2020 Final. These two players do have the luxury of wealth and status, but they still have a lot to lose by taking the stances they have.

There's so much the English women's game can learn from its US equivalent and it should look to the transformational success of the recent collective bargaining agreement as a moment to stand up, take notice and fight for their futures and those coming after them.

They should look to the success of the USWNT players, who are activists and icons at the same time, as role models and examples. Those players have truly left a legacy.

Upon agreement of the USWNT's settlement with US Soccer in February 2022, Rapinoe said: 'Obviously, we have been in this for a long time, and coming from a long history of women who have fought to put this sport in a better place. I mean, I think pride comes to mind, just incredibly proud of the women on this team and all the women who this lawsuit represents. The thing I look forward to and am really proud of is that, you know, the justice comes in the next generation never having to go through what we went through. It's equal pay from here on out.'

It's time for English women's football to do the same.

Pérez, Real and audiotape: another strange year in La Liga

by Alvaro Romeo

The 2021-22 La Liga season provided us with more examples of how the powerful bend things to their will. Step forward Florentino Pérez, and Gerard Pique.

The use of words gave rise to human civilisation, but it was silence that made human coexistence possible.

Florentino Pérez might wish he had stayed quiet the times he hit out brutally at Real Madrid's *sancta sanctorum*. Or perhaps not. After all, he might not give a toss.

Take some time to consider the names Pérez has lobbed vicious verbal attacks at: Iker Casillas, Luís Figo, Cristiano Ronaldo, José Mourinho, Vicente del Bosque, Guti, the golden boys of La Quinta del Buitre — the quintet of club heroes that dominated the 1980s — Raúl and Mesut Özil.

Without going into specifics, his opinions on them combined varying degrees of disdain for their professional, financial, personal and intellectual worth. And the names above are not just some names; all but three are listed on the football legends page of the club's website. Raúl, manager of Real Madrid Castilla (the club's reserve team), still works for Real and is expected to climb the ladder one day. Emilio Butragueño, La Quinta del Buitre's poster boy, acts as the club's institutional spokesman.

The leaked audio files of Pérez were published in July 2021 by a digital news outlet called *El Confidencial*, three months after the riot over the Super League plans. In a hurried statement, Real Madrid's president argued the audio was recorded secretly and without his knowledge, on various occasions over the years, by a well known radio personality called José Antonio Abellán. The leak happened due to Pérez's involvement as 'one of the driving forces behind the Super League', the statement added.

So far, no one from the aforementioned Real Madrid personalities has hit back at Pérez. From the lambasted lot that still work for Real Madrid in some capacity, Raúl was singularly vilified. 'Raúl uses Real Madrid in his benefit. He is the culprit of Real Madrid's bad moment. It's terrible how bad the guy is. Him and Casillas are Real Madrid's big frauds', Pérez said.

He was referring to Raúl the player, not the coach.

Whether Raúl the coach was hurt or went ballistic or felt rabid but never dared to lift the phone, remains unknown. There was not even a public glimmer of resignation from Raúl's side. Neither from Pérez. At the end of the day, nothing irremediable had occurred. Turning around Michael Corleone's reasoning to his brother Sonny, it was something strictly personal, not business.

Thanks to Raúl's silence, Pérez and Raúl still coexist peacefully.

Carlo Ancelotti hasn't been spared Pérez's scrutiny either. In 2014 Carletto received pressure from the top of the club's pyramid to start Gareth Bale, via an online website authorised and supervised by Pérez, in a decaffeinated Barçagate-like manoeuvre. It is likely that Ancelotti ended up knowing where the pressure was coming from.

Thanks to his silence, he and Pérez still coexist peacefully.

On the surface, Pérez didn't do much to stop Florentinogate, as the leakage was labelled. Coincidentally, the increasingly successful El Chiringuito (the show where Pérez presented the Super League to the world) never mentioned the case in the aftermath of the revelations.

Gerard Piqué was very vocal when El Chiringuito turned a blind eye to Florentinogate. The Catalan defender played an active role on Twitter reminding his 20 million followers of the show's editorial choices. Ironically, Piqué himself would be the subject of more leaked audio in spring 2022. More on that later.

It is not news that football club chairmen try to exert an influence on media agendas. Pérez is no exception. His determination to control things goes beyond the borders of Madrid's autonomous community. It invades the public sphere too, as revealed by one of his less resonant but definitely more controversial leaked clips. 'La 1 (Spanish public TV channel) director is one of us. La 1 will change completely now. Luis Fernández (the director) is a Real Madrid taliban. The sports show is going to be pro Real Madrid. Eduardo Inda is *Marca*'s director thanks to Antonio (Antonio García Ferreras, current star man for private channel La Sexta) and me. We have to take control of *Marca*.'

By the names of the protagonists it can be inferred these quotes from Pérez belong, roughly, to the start of last decade, or even before. Since then his power has not dimmed. He is Real Madrid's president and the chairman of ACS Group — one of the leading construction companies in the world. He runs two powerful enterprises in a big city like Madrid.

The majority of estate-wide TV and radio shows are produced in Madrid and broadcast from there to the rest of the country. Having most of the news desks, production crews and studios in Madrid, a capital city situated exactly in the centre of the Iberian peninsula, inevitably produces a predominance of central

Madrid-based narratives told by Madrid-based journalists whose stories get pumped towards the country's periphery.

Therefore, news about Real Madrid, also the most supported club in the country, is prevalent. Now, put that together with the adulation Pérez can receive — 'he is a superior being', Butragueño once said — and it results in the most bizarre amalgamation of ideas.

Radio Marca's host Raúl Varela wrote some unbeatable lines the day after Camp Nou hosted a record crowd of 91,553 for a women's game during El Clásico in the UEFA Women's Champions League.

Here we go. 'The fan number 91,554 name is Florentino and his surname is Pérez', Varela said. 'Barcelona needed, it couldn't be differently, Real Madrid as passenger 91,554 for this flight to the stratosphere to be a success. With more social responsibility than faith in the sport, Florentino has done it again.'

This was said by a radio host on a national radio station. A world record attendance was attributed to Florentino Pérez for having started a women's team. It certainly sounds like a parody sketch of a football club's official TV.

Three weeks later Camp Nou's own record was broken again (91,648 spectators this time) with VfL Wolfsburg (women's) as the opposition. 'With more social responsibility than faith in the sport, Wolfsburg did it again,' Varela would have concluded.

Kylian Mbappé's failed transfer is very paradigmatic too. A potential move from the Frenchman to Real Madrid dominated the main national sports media outlets from 2018 — four years of avid anticipation. His contract with PSG was due to expire in June 2022. As a result, Mbappé's name was ever-present in Spain's sports shows. The excitement for his arrival degenerated into the most bizarre takes, such as well known pro-Real Madrid media personalities supporting Mbappé's France over Spain in the 2021 Nations League final. They were not a majority, but the majority of them appeared on the shows the majority of people watch.

But there was one tiny problem: Mbappé was still playing for PSG as he had an ongoing contract with the French club. Despite Mbappé not actually playing at the Santiago Bernabéu, the media managed to craft a spiritual presence of the Frenchman throughout the season, like Harry Lime in *The Third Man*.

In a metaphorical way, Lime, the ambiguous and sinister character played by Orson Welles, hovers over the whole story, his eyes watching us from somewhere, his presence always felt. Lime is referenced endless times only to appear at the end of the story in one of the most memorable unveilings of a character in cinema history. Fast forward to 2021-22 and Mbappé was Harry Lime.

Except he never turned up.

Mbappé extended his contract with PSG. Unsurprisingly, those who chose the Frenchman over Luis Enrique's side reacted furiously to the news.

The day Mbappé announced he was staying in Paris he scored a hat-trick against Metz. Spanish football fans can watch Ligue 1 games on Twitch. When Mbappé found the net for the third time, the co-commentator, also a commentator for Real Madrid TV, shouted 'go and fuck yourself!' repeatedly. On the very platform owning Ligue 1's TV rights.

Not many have questioned Florentino's failed chase, perhaps because in spite of the pandemic Real Madrid were in the financial position to have Mbappé on the payroll. Pérez hasn't put Real Madrid on the brink of bankruptcy like Josép Maria Bartomeu did with Barcelona.

Which brings us to a discomforting point. 'It's the economy, stupid,' as American political consultant James Carville said. As terrible as it sounds, a great financial system combined with a lack of opposition has won the game for Florentino. His draconian rules have to be accepted because, as head of the club, he has deterred pretty much every person who aspires to his position. He is never challenged in an electoral campaign and the media have been benign, under the premise of good finances bringing good results — which is fair enough as long as you don't mind nasty takes on Real Madrid legends or selfish visions on public TV's neutrality.

Meanwhile, the multi-faceted Gerard Piqué proved that he knows how to play the business too. *El Confidencial* also revealed leaked audio of conversations held between Piqué and Spanish FA chairman Luis Rubiales. The Catalan defender appeared to display conflicts of interest. He urged Rubiales to draw his club, Andorra, in an easy league group. He begged to play for Spain in Tokyo 2020. As the organiser of the Spanish Supercopa via his company Kosmos Holding, he broke down with ice-cold ease how to share the tournament's money.

On the pitch, with the cameras and microphones turned on with the footballers' knowledge, La Liga 2021-22 showed Real Madrid's vast superiority over their rivals. Aware of Messi's departure and Atlético's struggles, Ancelotti understood the circumstances offered a chance to open a gigantic gap from the initial weeks. In January Real Madrid won the Supercopa. By mid-March they boasted a 15-point gap over an improving Barcelona. The title was merengue.

It was a phenomenal campaign for los blancos. Benzema's explosive minimalism translated into more than 40 goals in all competitions. Vinícius Júnior married his devilish speed with goals. Thibaut Courtois excelled. Luka Modrić performed (again) with his usual good taste for the ball. And the refreshing Eduardo Camavinga and Rodrygo proved that no scenario is too big for them. Besides, the Champions League reconnected the players and the fans after a year playing in Valdebebas. The remontadas against PSG and Manchester City will be passed down from parents to children as part of the club's sentimental legacy, and yes, they became European champions for the 14th time.

Betis won the Copa del Rey. Manuel Pellegrini, another man who suffered an unacceptable amount of aggro by the aforementioned *Marca* director Eduardo Inda, won his first accolade in Spanish football.

Barcelona swapped Ronald Koeman for Xavi. The team offered encouraging signs at the end of winter, scoring 4 goals against Atlético, Valencia, Napoli, Athletic Club, Osasuna and Real Madrid in the space of 6 weeks, only to return to the mediocre in May. It will take a while until Barcelona and financial struggles don't go together in a sentence.

Villarreal's Champions league dream was the fairytale story of the season. Unai Emery's men left behind Atalanta, Young Boys, Juventus and Bayern Munich in their run to the semi-finals. They also had Liverpool against the ropes for a short while in the tie's second leg. Let's not forget they did all this with Gerard Moreno, arguably their best player, suffering from muscular issues during the whole campaign.

And a further mention before pulling the curtain. Gareth Bale left Real Madrid. The Welshman's Spanish adventure is fascinating because he must be one of the few employees at Real Madrid who has somehow got his way with Florentino. He is some sort of high-octane, pony-tailed Bartleby — a man rising only to his own personal occasion, carefully saving his bullets for the battles he believes in.

Life can be hard, shit happens, bosses can be bosses and the system laughs at us every day. Isn't it comforting to see a truly talented man laughing back at the system? It was interesting to have you around, galés. Un abrazo. Adiós.

250 days to end 23 years of Nottingham Forest misery

by Nick Miller

Steve Cooper arrived at Nottingham Forest with the aim of just avoiding relegation. He ended up taking them back to the Premier League for the first time in a generation . . .

'The referee should blow his whistle . . . and call time on Forest's extended stay outside the top flight . . . that's it! Forest are Premier League! Nottingham Forest are . . . PREMIER . . . LEAGUE! 23 years they have waited to get back into the top flight . . .'

Colin Fray has been BBC Radio Nottingham's lead Forest commentator since 1993. His voice has been the soundtrack to a generation of mostly disappointments, of frustrations and failures — both operatic and mundane — as Forest spent over two decades away from the Premier League.

So on 29 May 2022, when Forest had beaten Huddersfield 1-0 in the play-off final, hearing him announce that those 23 years were over — that they had finally shaken off the shackles of incompetence and won one of the most improbable promotions in recent times — was a moment of profound catharsis for every Nottingham Forest fan around the world.

It doesn't feel dramatic or an exaggeration to say that it was all down to one man. Everything changed for Nottingham Forest 250 days before Fray voiced the moment of ecstatic release. That was when Steve Cooper arrived with Forest in the bottom three, fresh from their first win of the season in their eighth game.

Chris Hughton had overseen the first seven with just a single point to show for it, gained against local rivals Derby County. It was Forest's worst start to a season in 108 years. Then when he was sacked, caretaker Steven Reid took control for a 2-0 win over Huddersfield. Absolutely nobody, beyond the most committed fantasist, thought the sides would meet again at Wembley the following May.

The fact that not only did Forest reach the play-off final after that start, but that it was actually a consolation prize after narrowly failing to win automatic promotion, sounds like an absurd tale that any self-respecting fiction editor would send back for revisions. For a man to stroll into a club that 27 previous permanent and caretaker managers hadn't been able to make sense of since the last time they were in the top flight, and not even need a full season to completely turn things around . . . it ranks as one of the second tier's most extraordinary managerial feats ever.

Cooper drew his first game in charge, but won the next four: a thrilling counter-attacking display against Barnsley having gone behind, an efficient 3-0 dispatch of Birmingham, a tight 2-1 home success against Blackpool, and then came the trip to Bristol City. That was the game where the implausible was shown to be possible, and hinted that there might actually be something different to Cooper's Forest.

City were 1-0 up going into the 90th minute, before Lyle Taylor scored twice in the 91st and 92nd minutes to secure an extraordinary victory. The entire team jumped on top of each other.

Goalkeeper Brice Samba sprinted from his own goal to join the celebrations. Djed Spence got so excited he threw his GPS tracker into the crowd.

It's easy to look back on that game and apply undue retrospective significance to it. But even at the time it felt like something different was happening. Before Cooper arrived, Forest had only come from behind to win once in the previous 75 games. After this comeback, they'd done it twice in four games. 'All of the belief had been slowly drained from the dressing room,' said Taylor of the pre-Cooper days.

A few days later Forest lost 4-0 at home to Fulham, and while the scoreline was harsh, the temptation was to view that game as an expectation-tamer, a result to just calm everyone down a little bit and not expect miracles. But lo, miracles did occur.

It wasn't just the dire situation that Cooper found himself in that made promotion so unlikely. This was a club that seemed to pulse with misfortune and mismanagement, who had spent over two decades finding new and interesting ways to fail.

You can trace the mess back to the last time Forest were promoted to the top flight, in the summer of 1998. With a brilliant team that had sashayed to the second tier title and looked good to have a decent tilt at survival, they torpedoed their own chances by selling Colin Cooper, their key defender, and Kevin Campbell, one half of a strike force that had scored 57 goals between them. The other half, Pierre van Hooijdonk, irked at first those sales and then the club preventing him from following Cooper and Campbell, went on strike. From there they had no chance: they were relegated with three games to spare and thus began the 23 years of exile.

Those 23 seasons have carried assorted forms of calamity and indignity. There were the three Italian players – Gianluca Petrachi, Salvatore Matrecano and Moreno Mannini – signed at great expense by player-manager David Platt, but who went on to make just 33 starts between them.

After the Platt experiment came some optimism under Paul Hart who, like Cooper, built a team of thrilling young players, but unlike Cooper fell short in the play-offs. Little money was spent augmenting those youngsters afterwards, and when the following season ended in disappointment, Hart was gone, replaced by the twin indignities of Joe Kinnear then Gary Megson.

A combination of their management and the general decay of a football club saw Forest relegated to League One — the first former European champions to sink into the third tier of their domestic league. At the start of that relegation season, the club had launched an ill-advised season ticket marketing campaign with the slogan: 'We're serious about promotion — are you?'

Forest would stay in League One for three seasons, losing another play-off semi-final to Yeovil, before eventually sneaking up automatically on the final day of the 2007-08 season. Again, this was a young team, built around local talents like Julian Bennett, Lewis McGugan and Kris Commons.

Colin Calderwood, the manager behind that promotion, lasted until December 2008, replaced by Billy Davies, under whom results were good but life off the pitch not so great. One former colleague described him as 'the worst person I've ever worked with in football', and despite two more trips to the play-offs, he was sacked in 2011, only to return for another brief, less successful spell two years later.

By that time Forest were owned by Fawaz Al-Hasawi, a Kuwaiti fridge magnate whose reign was defined by big promises and chaos: managers came and went, players were signed in industrial quantities, and assorted slapstick stories were gathered along the way. The club official who asked a colleague how long a football match lasted summed things up neatly. Then there were the multiple times that late payments were blamed on Kuwaiti public holidays, of which there seemed to be rather a lot. And the transfer of George Boyd from Peterborough, cancelled at the last minute because he apparently failed an eye test as the results were inconclusive.

By 2017 Al-Hasawi had been replaced by Evangelos Marinakis, and while the early signs were good, the turnover of managers remained high and fans were left wondering whether things were actually improving at all. The calamitous end of the 2019-20 season was enough to make even the biggest fan lose faith: Forest went into the last two games requiring just a point to reach the play-offs, and even if they couldn't manage that they just had to avoid a five-goal swing on the final day. You don't need to be told what happened there.

Then, Cooper.

It feels strange to say after all that happened, but the reaction to his appointment wasn't universally positive. At his previous club Swansea, he wasn't as popular as you would think for a man who had taken them to two successive play-offs. Other candidates that were mentioned around the time of Hughton's sacking arguably felt more exciting: Chris Wilder and Eddie Howe both had promotions to their names, Arminia Bielefeld's Frank Kramer had the thrill of the unknown. Even John Terry was mentioned.

Cooper — this slightly unassuming Welshman, son of referee Keith Cooper, not immediately and outwardly charismatic — felt like a sensible if not massively exciting choice.

More than anything though, the apathy was created by the string of Cooper's predecessors, all of whom began to form one large amorphous mass — a single entity with a series of slightly different faces who had all either failed or had not been there long enough to do anything at all. It felt like Cooper was just the latest rube who would be sucked in the maw of ennui that is Nottingham Forest, never to be seen again.

But Forest just kept winning and, arguably more importantly for Cooper's popularity, kept creating great moments that the fans could feel warm about. There were late equalisers in successive games against QPR and Sheffield United. An emphatic 4-1 victory at Swansea. A win over local rivals Derby that was more dominant than the 2-1 scoreline suggests.

Then there was the run in the FA Cup. Forest beat the previous two winners of the competition, Arsenal and Leicester, with some ease, then were only defeated 1-0 in the quarter-final by Liverpool — who at that time had a good case to be classed as the best club side in the world.

He made likeable players good and good players likeable. Brennan Johnson, Ryan Yates and Joe Worrall were all local boys, products of the club's famed academy. James Garner, on loan from Manchester United, improved every week. Brice Samba was loved for his superb shot-stopping and commitment to winding opposition fans and players up. Spence, drummed out of Middlesbrough, became one of the best players in the division.

He not only got to know the players ('He might as well have a rotating door in his office, because there are players in and out so often', said Steve Cook in April), but their families too, calling parents of the younger squad members regularly to reassure them he was taking care of their boys.

With two games to go, astonishingly, automatic promotion was still possible. But defeat to Bournemouth sent the Cherries up and meant Forest had to suffer the crippling nerves of the play-offs. Ultimately, that would prove preferable, simply because it afforded this team the chance to give their fans another set of memories.

The semi-final against Sheffield United was a perfectly constructed tie, the sort of thing whoever invented the two-legged format presumably had in mind. In the first leg Forest were fluid, attacking and should have scored more than two goals; United were timid, intimidated, lacking in any sort of imagination and were lucky to escape with a 2-1 defeat. In the second leg Forest looked like 11 rabbits in the headlights, United were aggressive and forceful and were only denied by a sensational goalkeeping performance by Samba.

Then, penalties. Samba — who is sometimes capable of the most inexplicable errors, from your basic dropped crosses to cuffing an opponent around the head for no good reason, as he did in one game – was in his element here, giving the impression that he was actively enjoying this ludicrously tense scenario. Thanks to his alpha behaviour and some meticulous planning (he taped his research on where the United players would aim their penalties to his water bottle), he saved three, and Forest were going to Wembley for the first time in 30 years.

The whole of Nottingham seemed to decamp to north-west London. The west side of Wembley was a pulsing, trembling mass of red, 36,000 people simultaneously giddy at the prospect of being 90 minutes from the Premier League, and terrified about what those 90 minutes might hold.

Did it matter that the only goal went in off Huddersfield defender Levi Colwill's knee and Forest could easily have had two penalties given against them? Not in the slightest.

At the final whistle, the Forest fans exploded, the players ran in different directions, Cooper had to sit down on the bench for a few seconds, away from everyone else, as the enormity of what he had achieved hit him. In the end, it had only taken 250 days to make right 23 years of frustration and disappointment. Whatever the next 23 years hold, Forest will never forget it.

The redemption of the pioneer, Aliou Cissé

by Maher Mezahi

Aliou Cissé was haunted by failure in Africa Cup of Nations past. Then, with the help of Sadio Mané et al, he achieved redemption and sealed his legendary status . . .

Aliou Cissé is a man fulfilled.

After a long and arduous seven years at the head of the Senegalese national team, the 46-year-old coach finally reached the pinnacle of his career in early 2022.

Cissé won the 2021 Africa Cup of Nations in February and helped Senegal capture a 2022 World Cup berth one month later — a third appearance for the West African nation of just 16 million.

Football is fickle, however, and were it not for the Cup of Nations triumph, it is likely that the bespectacled caretaker would have now been out of work. In order to understand the complete 180 spin in public perception both at home and abroad, it is necessary to understand the importance of winning the continental title for Senegal.

'It haunted me for a long time.' Cissé told French newspaper *Le Monde*. 'I am finally at peace.'

To understand how personal winning the AFCON was for Cissé, you have to understand the two charges levied against his coaching record.

The first blemish was purely technical. Both domestically and internationally Cissé was seen as a talented but tactically limited young coach. 'Sometimes we don't really see the "Cissé touch" when his team plays,' explains Babacar Diarra, a journalist based in Dakar.

'Critics say that he just trots 11 players out there and the quality of the Senegalese squad does the rest.'

In addition to tactical deficiencies, there was a second, much more problematic, accusation directed towards Cissé and all of Senegalese football: for a long time, the conventional wisdom was that Senegal had an inability to win big matches under pressure.

For a country that has produced the footballing talent that the West African nation has, it was seen as impermissible that they still had not managed to win a single continental title. 1965 was Senegal's first AFCON and they were eliminated on a bizarre goal average rule to hosts Tunisia. Senegal hosted the tournament in 1992, but they were disappointingly bounced in the quarter-finals by Cameroon. In 2017, Senegal came out firing and looked like the most impressive group stage side until Sadio Mané missed a crucial penalty in the quarter-finals — again — against Cameroon.

And Cissé played a pivotal role for the two most heartbreaking chapters of Senegalese footballing lore. During the 2019 AFCON final, Cissé was out-coached by his Algerian counterpart and close friend, Djamel Belmadi, who established an intricate defensive shell and threatened on vertical counter-attacks. The Teranga Lions seemed perplexed and had no answer for the Fennecs in the Cairo International Stadium. That was a traumatising souvenir, but it did not compare to the heartbreak that came during the 2002 AFCON final in Bamako, Mali.

Then, Cisse's dreadlocks were only a few inches in length. With an emerald number 6 ironed onto his sternum and a yellow captain's armband wrapped around his left bicep, he hesitantly advanced to take Senegal's fifth and final penalty of the final. The nerves emanated from Cissé, who never once looked at the Cameroonian goalkeeper Alioum Boukar. On the whistle, he turned on and blasted the ball at the goalkeeper's shin pads. It was a horrific penalty, and while Cameroon celebrated, Cissé collapsed to the floor.

The weight of those successive tactical and mental failures as a player and as a coach at the highest level is the reason why Cissé was under so much pressure ahead of the 2021 AFCON. Yet he managed to right both of those wrongs in Cameroon.

Senegal started the tournament slowly, only defeating Zimbabwe 1-0 in their opening match thanks to a last-minute Mané penalty, before limping to two 0-0 draws against Guinea and Malawi.

Yet Cissé's tactical adjustment of including Watford forward Ismaïla Sarr to bolster the strike force paid dividends as Senegal managed a much more potent attack in the knockout stages. Nonetheless, it was their defensive performances that impressed the most — at no point throughout their seven matches did they trail for even a minute.

In the final they were matched against seven-time winners Egypt who were stellar in the group stages, but turned to an ugly brand of negative football after that.

The 2021 final was uneventful — as many AFCON finals tend to be. Aside from an early penalty miss from Mané, the two sides struggled to create clear scoring opportunities. Senegal, who were on the front foot for most of the match, found themselves in a shootout that Egypt was playing for. The pundits present all insisted this was the ultimate test of mental fortitude and that Senegal were expected to stumble once more. Once again, it came down to Senegal's fifth and final kick.

This time it was Mané who stood 12 yards from the goal. Like his coach also did on that fateful day in 2002, he sprinted during his run-up to the penalty kick and banked on power. This time the ball flew into the net, effectively exorcising the demons that so haunted Senegal since 1965. Cissé again collapsed to the floor in tears, but this time, he was elated. All of the pent-up anxiety from decades of disappointment flew out of the coach and every one of his players. Senegal were finally champions.

'It (the AFCON trophy) was an obsession, revenge, a personal affair,' he would declare, months later. 'It was the fight of my life.'

The post-match celebrations after the final were a sight to behold. The young Senegalese squad danced to Youssou N'Dour's Senegal Rekk (Only Senegal), the de facto team anthem, as did several of Cissé's former team-mates from the 2002 generation who were present as team ambassadors.

Storied former goalkeeper Tony Sylva arrived as goalkeeping coach in 2015 alongside Cissé, Lamine Diatta had team manager duties, while Pape Thiaw, Khalilou Fadiga and Alassane N'Dour also work for the Confederation of African Football in Cameroon. Even El Hadji Diouf made his overbearing presence felt — he can be too much at times, but his immense popularity in Senegal cannot be denied.

Cissé was not obliged to allow such personalities around his squad — not least Diouf and Fadiga, who were among two of his most damning critics in the past. 'This team has the ability to win an Africa Cup of Nations, but that cannot be achieved if Aliou Cissé remains at the helm of the national team,' Diouf said three years ago.

Yet Cissé's ability to forgive and lead is his greatest attribute as both a player and coach. His modus operandi allowed the two generations to intermesh, symbolising a poignant moment where Senegal liberated itself from the shackles of the past and instead came into harmony with its history. For the native of the rebellious Casamance region, leading is innate. Cissé is a descendent of a long line of nobility on both sides of the family. Whether they were judges or imams, his ancestors occupied dignified roles in his community back home.

It must have been a rude awakening being ripped from that status at the age of 9, when his family moved to Champigny-sur-Marne, a greyscale, rough suburb of Paris. For kids of Cissé's generation, the easiest way out of the banlieue was football. As an all-action midfielder that could also deputise in defence, Cissé was an integral player during stints at mid-table clubs in France and England. Even then, Cissé knew that coaching interested him and he noticed that his curiosity wasn't commonplace.

'I wanted to know why I was asked to run so much,' he would recall. 'I was curious to know what the exercises we were offered in training were for. In fact, I was unable to seriously tackle the task until I knew the why and the how. I talked a lot with my coaches because they asked me to put in a lot of effort. I wanted to run well, but I needed to understand. This curiosity has never left me.

'It's interesting to observe what other coaches are doing, but I think you have to forge your own identity and find your own methods. My goal was to draw on all my experiences as a player at the technical and tactical level to become a unique coach.'

Immediately after putting an end to his playing career, Cissé completed his coaching badges in the lower levels of the French footballing pyramid. Prior to the 2012 Olympic Games in London, Cissé was called on by the Senegalese Football Federation to help out as an assistant coach.

It would be there he would first establish relationships with the leaders who later become the cornerstones of the senior men's national team. Left-back Saliou Ciss, central midfielder Cheikhou Kouyaté, Idrissa Gueye and, of course, Sadio Mané were all members of that team who would lose to the eventual champions, Mexico, in the quarter-finals.

Over the 10 years of his coaching career, there has been clear, noted progression for both the coach and his players. Cissé instils discipline, to the point where some of his players jokingly called him 'Jammeh', after the now deposed former Gambian dictator. The discipline, however, is offset by a closeness Cissé enjoys with his players, who he qualifies as having 'much greater knowledge of football than my generation did at their age.'

'I prefer to exchange ideas with my players,' he explained. 'Nothing is unilateral, otherwise we don't progress . . . I'm up against boys who are very connected, but who work in a more personal way than before. To build a collective, I empower them. I also have to explain a lot to them: the reasons for positioning them the way I do, or why we use certain tactics . . .'

For Salim Masoud Said, an African football expert, Cissé's extraordinary man-management skills can perhaps be his x-factor.

'I don't think Cissé is the next coming of Guardiola,' Said said, 'but there's an art to his man-management, his calmness, which has finally transmitted to the team. They are brimming with quality, and you don't need to be a super tactician when you have that.

'So it becomes about: is the team motivated, is morale high, is there a good spirit amongst the group? Do they believe the coach can get them to win? How does the coach make them feel? The Senegal players have always been happy to be led by him.'

What remains to be seen is if those intangibles can translate into obtaining results against some of the very top national teams in the world. Even if Cissé doesn't realise Pelé's irritating prediction that an African nation would win the World Cup before the year 2000, his true legacy will be a trailblazing one. While it is true that the footballing talent around the continent has advanced by leaps and bounds, the results of the continent at the world's premier competition have regressed and many point the finger at the lack of quality on the touchline.

Both Belmadi and Cissé have been the principal architects of a paradigm shift for African coaches. Both are former captains of their national teams. They command ample respect from their players, who see them as big brothers. Hiring former players is usually a win-win — the candidates get a great gig for their first coaching jobs of their careers and, paradoxically, federations pay a lot less for more respected personalities. Cissé only makes around 25,000 euros per month — nowhere near the top earners on the continent.

Coaches such as Radhi Jaïdi at Espérance de Tunis in Tunisia, Walid Regragui at Wydad in Morocco, Benni McCarthy at AmaZulu FC in South Africa are all following in Belmadi's and Cissé's path and may seriously envisage coaching their national teams in the near future.

Cissé can sleep easy knowing that his legacy as a pioneer will forever hold true.

With Patrick Vieira, the Premier League feels more complete

by Dom Fifield

The basic facts of Patrick Vieira's first season in charge of Crystal Palace were not stunningly impressive. But look a little deeper and you will see a club revived . . .

It is a sun-drenched summer evening in south London and Patrick Vieira is taking the mic. His intention is to offer one last thanks to his Crystal Palace players, gathered with their families in front of the dugouts ahead of the post-match lap of appreciation, as well as the thousands of home fans still crammed into the stands, all basking in a last day victory over Manchester United and a season that has exceeded expectations.

'The message is really clear and really simple . . .' opens the Frenchman before the chant whips up to cut him off in his prime.

'He kicks who he wants. He kicks who he wants! Patrick Vieira, he kicks who he wants . . .'

Memories of that pitch invasion at Goodison Park, when Everton fans jubilant at avoiding relegation threatened Vieira to the point that he aimed a kick at a couple, are raw and the potential ramifications of his reaction to a home supporter's goading are still unclear. Vieira has endured three days of regret, castigating himself unnecessarily at having snapped at the Everton fan's pathetically misguided taunts. But, as the home fans launch into a second rendition with more and more taking up the refrain, even he has to muster a sheepish chuckle.

It has been reassuring to see the Frenchman restored to the Premier League. A figure who once set the tone at Arsène Wenger's Arsenal, striding forcefully through midfield and stamping his authority on all-comers, is now inspiring a young, emerging team across the capital. Vieira the manager contrasts markedly with Vieira the player. He offers quiet, thoughtful comment in press conferences as the public face of Palace. He seeks council from Osian Roberts and Shaun Derry, figures of lesser standing, on the touchline during games. A man once considered an on-field firebrand seems to delight in calmly guiding the likes of Wilfried Zaha, Marc Guéhi and Michael Olise towards self-improvement.

There has been the odd impassioned goal celebration, and the occasional wild-eyed difference of opinion with an official, but the fireworks have been relatively rare. The flashpoint on Merseyside had been sparked by one fan's idiocy and provoked a response completely out of keeping with the dignity the 45-year-old displayed since returning to England. But it was an extreme situation. The FA saw sense and, acutely aware of the provocation, didn't levy charges.

Regardless, his reaction was actually a welcome reminder of the quick-tempered player of old — Vieira serving notice that he is still not someone to countenance being pushed around. In that flash of incensed passion, he was recognisable from his playing days. This is the head coach fighting Palace's corner and, beneath that cool exterior, he remains as ferocious as ever. 'Vieira leading from the front,' read the banner unfurled in the Holmesdale Road end prior to kick-off. 'Selhurst stands with you.'

The post-match mood on that final day was celebratory. Palace's first home win over United since 1991 had been a fitting way to sign off a season that had served to revitalise this club. The locals had rejoiced as a young, vibrant team made waves where so many had anticipated toil and trouble. The chorus of delight that greeted the manager on that final afternoon in May reflected the impact he had made.

The raw numbers at season's end did not necessarily scream progression. Palace finished 12th on 48 points, scoring 50 goals in the process, which effectively represented a return to pre-pandemic levels of consistency. There was frustration that they had actually only managed to win 11 games, their joint-worst return since promotion in 2013.

Yet delve only a little deeper into that apparently nondescript mid-table finish and the picture is more revealing. They were beaten only 12 times — just once in their history have they lost fewer times in a season at this level — and, for the second time ever, recorded a positive goal difference. That was testament to a solid defensive set-up and, more significantly, clear improvements in possession.

They built up from the back with ball-playing centre-halves comfortable receiving from their goalkeeper, and midfielders eager to accept in tight areas. For the first time in the elite, they enjoyed the majority of the ball, their 50.9 per cent possession figure up from a meagre 40.1 per cent the previous year. A side who had played on the counter-attack for years was suddenly more at ease dictating the rhythm of contests.

'It's a bit surreal when a legendary player becomes your manager, but there are so many things you can take from him,' said Zaha, who enjoyed his most prolific season at the age of 28. 'He has a lot of ideas and, if you buy into them like everyone has, you can see that it makes a huge difference. Everyone was ready to change and understood what he was telling us would improve our game. We are not just this counter-attacking team anymore.

We keep possession. Now, when we move up the pitch, it is not only with one or two players on the counter-attack against four defenders. We commit as a team.'

As the chairman Steve Parish has jokingly acknowledged, that has made watching the team a considerably less fraught experience. 'All the managers we've had over recent years have done brilliant jobs for us with the resources they have had and we've played in a way we needed to play to do what we needed to do,' he said. 'So there is no criticism at all about anyone who has managed the club. But to watch us out-pass quality teams, keep the ball . . .

'As a chairman when your team don't have much of the ball and the possession stats are down to 30 per cent, you spend most of the games on the edge of your seat. This is different. Possession doesn't always mean you end up with different outcomes in matches, but it is much more enjoyable to watch.

'When we go behind in games, we don't feel like we are down and out. We always feel we can come back. Similarly, when we go ahead now you know it will be really difficult for the opposition to come back at us.'

There had been a rare opportunity to instigate a revolution. The summer of 2021 had seen eight first-team players depart, along with Roy Hodgson and his coaching staff after four seasons of impressive stability. The club, saddled by a hefty wage bill, embraced the bloodletting. It was their chance to instigate a rejuvenation. Those on the outside suggested their approach was an invitation to relegation.

Vieira, sacked by Nice in December 2020, was convinced he was the man to implement the rejig. The board had been looking for the team to be more proactive on the ball and were enthused by his vision, shared in a meeting with Parish on his yacht moored off the Côte d'Azur and in a subsequent Zoom call with other members of Palace's staff.

There was risk on both sides. Vieira, still considered a relative rookie, knew he would have to make an immediate impact to prove he could flourish back in the Premier League. Palace, meanwhile, had looked most seriously at Nuno Espírito Santo — whose approach would have been very different — and the experienced Lucien Favre before turning to Vieira.

There were safer bets out there. But, for all parties, this was the time to be bold and gamble.

As it was, from very early on, the fit seemed right. Where he had been the favourite to be the first Premier League manager to be sacked, he ended up outliving figures far more experienced at clubs who should have been far better placed. The team bought into his ideas and, relatively speaking, flourished. The expected points tally actually had Palace sixth in the final table, over 10 points better off, suggesting their performances merited better. Even so, he conducted this transformation as seamlessly as was conceivable.

Yet what has surprised on-lookers most of all is that Vieira's first outing in the dugout in England, in a corner of the capital with which he had no real previous affinity, has actually felt like a homecoming.

Those behind the scenes at Palace have witnessed the manager's reluctance to summon stories from his playing days when speaking both to his players and the club's staff — he tends to bat away references in that self-deprecating manner of his — but he could not disguise his own delight at being inducted into the Premier League's hall of fame.

Vieira may have been born in Senegal and, having moved to France in his youth, went on to win the World Cup and European Championships with Les Bleus, but he spent the best years of his career at Arsenal. The English game courses through his veins.

For all that, though, he was an iconic figure in *north* London — never south of the river. He was an Arsenal captain, synonymous with The Invincibles and those brutal battles with Roy Keane and Sir Alex Ferguson's Manchester United. He is still cherished by those across the capital, as was clear when he was afforded a rapturous reception when he took Palace to the Emirates in the autumn of 2021. His former club's fans cursed but will have forgiven him soon enough for claiming four points from the sides' two meetings last term.

Yet Vieira has never rammed all those Arsenal connections down the throats of Palace's support. From the outset, he has made clear that was then, this is now, and sought to forge new connections with the club he now oversees. And, if his regular admissions over his first year in charge that it feels 'like I'm at home' are to be believed, he has succeeded.

Maybe he realised that his predecessor, Hodgson, had benefited from a long-standing relationship with the club and the area and saw value in cultivating something similar. More likely he recognised aspects of life in south London from his own upbringing in France. Perhaps from his time in Trappes, an outer-city Parisian banlieue known for its considerable north African immigrant population. Vieira moved there in 1984 at the age of eight with his older brother and an uncle. He would play football out on the street. It was there that he was spotted and first thrust into a local club's youth system.

So perhaps it should not be a surprise that he identifies so readily with those youngsters plucked from south London's melting pot, all eager to make a mark in the game.

At the opening of Palace's category one academy in October 2021, Vieira suggested London, to him, 'always meant "diversity", and diversity is stronger here in south London. This football club is part of the community. It is at the heart of it all. It is one of the reasons we want to develop young players, bringing them through the academy and into the first-team'. He appears to share that outlook.

He has been perfect for this particular project. He takes an active, daily interest in the academy. When it comes to the first-team it was the sporting director, Dougie Freedman, who oversaw 2021's remarkable recruitment drive with guidance from Iain

Moody and the backing of Parish. But Vieira's considerable presence helped secure Palace some of their prime targets in the face of stiff competition. When one last push was required, the hierarchy called in Vieira.

Olise, now a France under-21 international, thrilled at the prospect of working under his compatriot. Guéhi and Conor Gallagher were eager to learn from him. 'When Patrick Vieira tells you he can get the best out of you, you listen,' said Gallagher, whose loan spell from Chelsea yielded his first full England caps. Odsonne Édouard and Joachim Andersen were equally swayed in their decisions to join.

He will know that life is precarious at this level, particularly at clubs of this size who are only ever five or six defeats from a full-scale crisis. But listen to his assessment of his first year in charge and there is a hunger to make this work. 'We will see you all next season with a higher ambition,' he concluded, much to the delight of the crowd, on that Sunday evening at Selhurst Park.

Palace have been grateful to have him. For those of us who admired his impact as a player at Arsenal, enthralled by his regular confrontations with United and the mystique he always carried, the Premier League feels more complete now that he is back.

The Newcastle fans against the Saudi takeover

by Nick Miller

In October 2021 Newcastle were taken over by a group with close links to the Saudi state. 97 per cent of their fans welcomed the takeover, but what of the three per cent that didn't?

'I've never been divorced, but this feels like how a divorce must feel.'

As chief correspondent for the UK's Channel 4 News, Alex Thomson has seen plenty of things that would dumbfound most of us. But the sight of his fellow Newcastle United fans dancing outside St James' Park in Mohammad bin Salman (MBS) masks, celebrating the arrival of the club's new owners, was one step too far.

While not all of them added Saudi flags to their social media profiles, the overwhelming majority of Newcastle fans welcomed the Saudi Public Investment Fund's takeover of the club, which was finally completed in October 2021 after over a year of wrangling.

In an infamous survey by the Newcastle United Supporters

Trust in 2020, 97 per cent of respondents welcomed the then-prospective new owners. A similar poll by fanzine *The Mag* from around the same time suggested that while a little under 40 per cent did have concerns about the human rights record of the Saudi state, it wasn't enough for them to oppose the new regime, with 97.7 per cent favouring them over then-owner Mike Ashley.

A poll by *The Athletic* shortly after the takeover went through also found that, while Saudi's human rights record concerned 83 per cent of respondents, only 29 per cent of those who took part said their misgivings were enough to stop them going to a game or spending money in the club shop.

Fans like Thomson then, are emphatically in the minority. They are there, though: their voices may be drowned out by the sound of opening #cans (a social media trend to celebrate the takeover) and lost among the euphoria, but there are a dissenting few whose moral objections to their club being owned – and used – by MBS and Saudi Arabia must be heard.

At best, these fans have significant internal conflict, unsure as to how they can justify celebrating the money that will now flow through their club when they know the provenance of that cash. At worst, the relationship between some fans and the team they have supported all of their lives is broken; irreparably damaged.

'We've waited a long time to finally be rid of Mike Ashley,' said John-Paul Quinn, 30, a lifelong supporter from County Durham. 'It should be a glorious day, but I've dreaded this takeover since it was first mooted. The club is well shot of Ashley, but it's now in the hands of some of the worst people possible.'

It doesn't need to be repeated here how unpopular Ashley was – and is – on Tyneside. But is his departure worthy of celebration on its own, regardless of who replaces him?

'I had a brief moment of elation knowing that Ashley had gone,' said Alex Howson, a supporter for 25 years, from London. 'But it was soon met with the instant caveats. We're owned by a state, and an atrocious one. All future success will have a caveat. Every signing. Every goal – a reminder where the money came from.'

The denial of a chance to celebrate Ashley's departure properly is just one of the things that generated anger among this sliver of the Newcastle support. That anger is aimed in many different directions: at the Saudi consortium, at their celebrating fellow fans, but most of all at the people who so easily waved the takeover through.

'I'm angry with the Premier League that I've been put in a position where I have to make a moral judgment in order to support the club I've always supported,' says Alex Rowley. 'The main questions have to be laid at the Premier League's door for allowing this.'

Thomson adds: 'My anger isn't directed at Saudi Arabia. Saudi Arabia is an appalling regime. There is torture, murders, women are repressed: we don't have to argue why Saudi Arabia is an appalling regime.

'If it weren't so tragic, it would be comic that the thing that held up the deal from the Premier League was that they were worried so much about – guess what? – money over the piracy deal.'

That was the thing that held the takeover up, rather than moral concerns. Qatari broadcaster BeIn Sports holds the TV rights for the Premier League in the Middle East, but to get around that in Saudi Arabia, the feed is simply pirated and broadcast under the name BeoutQ: so they were both stealing their coverage, and trolling their neighbours. Eventually the issue was resolved and the takeover allowed to go through.

'I think for many Newcastle fans, the issue of human rights abuses by Saudi Arabia has probably largely always been filed under "Horrible stuff that happens far away",' says one Newcastle fan, who blogs under the name Bob Helpful.

'Now, within 48 hours of the takeover being thrust upon them, they are being expected to make judgements and decisions about how matters they've never had to think about before impact their support for the club.'

For others, the decision is a little less agonising. Ben Etterley, 47, has supported Newcastle since he was 10 years old. He grew up in nearby Ashington and used to save up his school dinner money to go to games when he was a youngster. But he is also a member of Amnesty International and a campaigner against the death penalty. For him, this wasn't much of a moral quandary.

'It's not a choice for me. For me, it's not difficult because it's just a game. A *fucking brilliant* game, but just a game,' he says. 'We're the customers — if we stop making the market for the product, the market would change. If football fans en masse said, "I'm not supporting the World Cup in Qatar", would the World Cup have gone to Qatar? Maybe I'm naive. But I'd rather be naive than feel guilty.

'I remember reading a tweet from someone when the takeover was first mooted, when they said, "I'll care when someone is beheaded in Eldon Square (in Newcastle city centre)". It was one of those moments when you thought, "I just can't believe I'm reading this".'

The takeover hasn't just been welcomed by everyday fans. The Newcastle United Supporters Trust released a statement after the takeover was approved that began, 'Dear His Excellency Yasir Al-Rumayyan . . .' and only got more sycophantic from there.

In some respects, they are in a tricky position. If their purpose is to reflect the views of Newcastle fans, they can't really ignore that potentially around 97 per cent are in favour of this new ownership. But there are ways of representing those views that don't ignore the bigger issues at play.

'I won't renew (my membership of the Trust) when it comes to next year, following that statement,' says Rowley. 'It was just uncautiously welcoming, with no acknowledgement of the very complicated issues. It was abundantly clear that I'm not repre-sented by the Trust at all.'

One argument has been that, because they have no say in who actually owns the club, there's little point in challenging that ownership now they are in place. However, while the takeover had been in limbo, they encouraged fans to write to their MP to campaign in its favour. The 'Nothing to do with us, guv!' excuse doesn't really wash.

'The Trust state that they "will act responsibly as a guardian of the future of Newcastle United" but are these really the people we want to trust with the future of our club?' says Quinn. 'Does the club now become a vehicle for the promotion of the Saudi state and their enterprises? They don't appear to have considered the wider implications for our game of this deal but instead have welcomed it with open arms. In truth, I feel let down by that.'

Rowley adds: 'The Trust has actively campaigned to insert themselves into that conversation, so they can't then absolve themselves of the responsibility of considering all the aspects that are at play. I just felt they bottled it.'

There was also a statement from United With Pride, the 'official Newcastle United LGBT+ inclusive supporters' group'.

They acknowledged that Saudi Arabia 'as a country is one of the least tolerant for LGBTQ+ and gender rights anywhere in the world', but offered no condemnation and speculated that Newcastle being owned by the state could help change that.

What of those fans who are delighted? What would the dissenters say to them?

'I wouldn't say anything to them,' says Channel 4's Thomson, 'because these are people who passionately want their club to succeed, as I passionately want my club to succeed. I just happen to be in a different place. I happen to think that things like human rights and things like murder actually do matter. And that they're ultimately more important than whether my football club is doing well.'

Howson adds: 'I've read and listened to the views of fellow fans I have huge respect for — some quite literally laughing off the Saudi issue, stating that it's nothing to do with them. I've never felt so disconnected to the club.'

Those who greeted the takeover with such unquestioning glee made the conflicted feelings of many even worse.

'The fan reaction to this announcement made it much more upsetting,' said Rowley. 'The fanbase needs to grow up and just understand that this is happening. And yes, you can't stop it, but go into it with an adult head on. These questions would be asked if it was any club.'

The latter point is an important one to make, to emphasise that this is not just some vendetta against Newcastle; some unspecified agenda against that club in particular. These questions would be levelled at the supporters of any club in this position.

So what now? There was little talk of or even appetite for a 'phoenix' club, a version of FC United of Manchester set up by Newcastle fans opposed to how the current entity are being run.

Which leaves fans who don't feel they can support this new version of Newcastle in a curious position. Some had already disassociated themselves from the club during the crushing nothingness of the Ashley years. But what about a season-ticket holder like Bob Helpful now?

'I think I probably will stop going to home games and at the very least and pack in my season ticket,' he says. 'It's a gesture, probably an empty one, and not one I expect will be echoed by many. Of course, I'll still *support* Newcastle, I'd rather never watch football again than support another team.'

'You can't switch off your love for a club and a place,' says Thomson. 'You can't. But at the same time, football is or should be about the head as well as the heart a wee bit. I cannot go near or condone or take any joy from any success that now happens.'

Quinn concurs: 'I find it hard to see how I will ever go to the ground again, under owners who I cannot accept. In all honesty, I have never felt more disconnected from my club than I do right now.'

Etterley has plans to start following Berwick Rangers of the Scottish fifth tier, broadly because they don't play in the English leagues so there's absolutely no chance of any direct conflict. Rowley said he might start watching sixth-tier Darlington, but his feelings towards Newcastle will remain . . . complicated.

'I'm not sure how I'll feel until I start watching them,' he says. 'Will I forget about these feelings I have now? Will I start to dis-associate them in my mind? I'm a little bit worried if that does happen, because then it's basically a justification for the sportswashing.'

But, ultimately, something has changed for him and will never be the same again:

'It's just two distinct Newcastle Uniteds now: it's the one that I grew up with being besotted by in the '90s with Kevin Keegan and then later Bobby Robson. And this one.'

'I was speaking to my friend who's an avid Spurs fan,' said Thomson, before the first game under the new regime, against Tottenham. 'I told him I hope they win 3-0.'

For a small section of the Newcastle support, that seems to sum it all up.

A version of this article first appeared on The Athletic.

In search of the Premier League's most average player

by Duncan Alexander

In a world where we are encouraged to have the most extreme opinions imaginable, there's comfort in the average. So who is the Premier League's most comforting player?

In these polarised times it's too easy to be drawn into those footballing debates that never end. Who is better: Messi or Ronaldo? Who is history's greatest icon: Pelé or Maradona? Do you say Nou Camp or Camp Nou? Why does James Milner's career follow the same timeline as *Grand Designs*? Sometimes it feels like it will never end, the arguments, the debates, the circular discussions . . . the *banter.*

Well maybe it's time to take a stand against football's extremities and celebrate the middle — the ponderous meat in the sporting sandwich we all love so much. Because, let's be honest, unless you support Manchester City or Liverpool, or Fulham and/ or Norwich, most seasons will be pretty much the same year on year. Does it really look like fun being a Rotherham fan in 2022?

In 2017 they got relegated from the Championship, in 2018 they got promoted from League One, in 2019 they got relegated from the Championship, in 2020 they got promoted from League One, in 2021 they got relegated from the Championship and in 2022 they got . . . promoted from League One. I simply don't care how many incidents there were with pigeons, Rotherham United, simply pick a division and enjoy it.

Of course, there are clubs and players who respect the art of keeping it pretty average. Rochdale famously lounged about in the fourth tier from 1974 to 2010, doing little else but nurturing beetroot canning expert and future England World Cup star Rickie Lambert. And if we look at the history of the famed English league, jab our finger in the air and loudly proclaim that finishing somewhere between 10th and 12th is 'pure mid-table vibes' then I am pleased to announce that the most average team in Our League System's history are Stoke City, who have finished in one of those positions on 30 occasions, an incredible figure that puts them eight clear of the next club, Sheffield United on 22.

Some median ultras were delighted with Manchester United's performance in the Premier League in 2021-22. Yes, the troubled superclub may have exchanged many millions in wage packets for a record low Premier League points tally, but they also contrived to finish the season with a goal difference of zero. A club like Manchester United finishing with a zero GD is like staring at a Piet Mondrian painting. It looks simple, almost childlike, but you try and recreate it if you can. Neoplasticism, they call it. The painting style I mean. Meanwhile, students of the Own Goals and Gaffs (sic) video series may be pleased to learn that Millwall FC, the club invented by Danny Baker in the 1980s, have ended seasons with a zero goal difference on five occasions, more than any other English league side.

And let's not forget the truly seismic footballing events of 1966. I refer, of course, not to the overhyped World Cup tournament in England (aka Get Pelé, Don't Get Hawkeye), but rather to the breathtakingly balanced 1965-66 Moroccan domestic league championship, won by — and you may well be ahead of me here — Wydad Athletic Club with 57 points from 26 games, just a point ahead of Raja Club Athletic on 56.

I say 'just ahead' of their Casablanca rivals, but they were just ahead of the entire division. Third placed Renaissance Sportive de Settat finished on 54 points, as did fourth place. Fifth place had 53, sixth and seventh ended on 52, eighth and ninth on 51 and 10th to 12th on 50 points. That left the two relegation spots, filled by Club Omnisport de Meknès and Moghreb Atlético Tetouan on 49 points. Both ended the season a couple of wins from third place and three wins from winning the title. That's what we want from our football. Balance and poise. Grace and beauty.

A word of warning: extreme polarisation fans, drunk on joy from seeing Manchester City hit 100 points in 2018 and witnessing Liverpool regularly smash through the 90-point mark and not win the title, are right now signalling aggressively at the 1996-97 Premier League campaign, statistically the most even season the reformed league has ever churned out. Only 35 points separated champions Manchester United from 18th place Sunderland, which theoretically was good, but the reality was no one really remembers much at all about that season and Stig Inge Bjørnebye got into the PFA Team of the Year. Look, sometimes things can be too average, and I say that as an average fan.

Nevertheless, if we accept the correct notion that the true magic and joy of football is contained within the amorphous middle, then is it not right to try and find and celebrate the Premier League's most middling players from the 2021-22 season? Because it's all too easy to stand at barbecues and say stuff like 'yeah I really can't see anyone closing the gap on City and Liverpool' or 'Norwich need to regroup in the Championship and come back and give it a proper go.'

Everyone thinks it, sadly too many people say it out loud. How much better would it be to lean in conspiratorially and quietly say,

'Hey, do you want to know the most average player in the Premier League in 2021-22? And this isn't opinion, by the way, this is worked out with . . . data.' Yes ok, a few people will recoil in fear and walk away but true thinkers, true dreamers, will stare at you open-mouthed and rapt as you reveal what you are about to discover for yourself.

So in the words of TFI Friday house band Texas, let's work it out.

Essentially this is going to be a gigantic process of elimination until we are left with the one true hero of averageness, so let's start at a macro level and get rid of some teams. For starters we can lose anyone in the top four or the relegation zone. Some of your players might have indeed been a bit average but your side's good/bad (delete as applicable) season means they just have to deal with that themselves.

Similarly those sides who qualified for Europe or who only just survived can go as well. I'm also not going to consider Newcastle United because we all know they experienced a ridiculously polarised season. Godawful in the first half, mysteriously improved in the second.

That leaves us then with a solid rump of teams: Aston Villa, Brentford, Brighton & Hove Albion, Crystal Palace, Leicester City, Southampton and Wolverhampton Wanderers. The slightly-less-than-magnificent seven. Let the process commence.

Appearances

Right, so we cannot be having anyone who has played every game during the season. That simply isn't average behaviour, so that immediately rules out Conor Coady and Matty Cash. Coady in particular did not have an average season as the famously goal-shy defender went Goal Mad in 2021-22 with four of them — one more than Jack Grealish provided at Manchester City. We also cannot consider players with just a handful of games, which sadly rules out such magnificent names as Jaden

Philogene-Bidace. No, we must choose from a select band of players who played somewhere between 15 and 28 games. A middle band; a land of hope.

Goals

Look, even the median lads can pop up with a goal now and again so we're not going to consider anyone who ended the season on a big fat zero. That's not an average season, that's just a rubbish one. As always, outliers have to be eliminated, so Jamie Vardy is knocked out straight away as the numbers say that he scored 15 goals in only 25 appearances – despite world-renowned experts on topical football podcasts justifiably saying he would struggle to reach 10. So no, Jamie Vardy does not get in. None of the other players in this already thinned-down list of 33 even reached double figures, so all of them can still be considered.

Assists

Assists are never as high as goals. Even Kevin De Bruyne has switched to scoring himself these days, so we have to be careful here. It's tempting to eliminate any remaining player who didn't get credited with one this season but we also need to be aware of the aggressive uncle at a wedding scene, the sort of man who will loudly announce that 'assists aren't even a thing. They're nonsense.' You can't lose the crowd that early, so all the no-assist men are still in. We can, though, eliminate three players with a frankly continental total of five Premier League assists in 2021-22, namely Nathan Redmond, Kelechi Iheanacho and Michael Olise.

Results

Now all the players in line to land this incredible honour played for mid-table teams in 2021-22 so we are not expecting huge discrepancies between games won and games lost, but interestingly* none of the remaining 30 players won exactly the same number of games as they lost. Once again our job here is to bin off outliers, so goodbye Adam Armstrong (W4 L11), Adam Webster (W10 L4) and a host of other players not called Adam. Things are getting real: like a badly planned international squad, we're down to 21 players.

Age

The ageing process harrows us all and footballers are no different. When we're handing out awards like 'Most Average Player of 2021-22' we have to avoid both youngsters and old timers. The former are just starting out and knowledge of how median their season was could be construed as . . . mean. Meanwhile the latter are old, and might take it badly and hunt me down. So no one born before the Premier League started in 1992 (farewell Marc Albrighton, Danny Welbeck, Christian Benteke, Stuart Armstrong, Big Phil Coutinho, Jonny Evans and Shane Duffy), and no one born in the era I have owned a mobile phone, so au revoir to Trincão, Valentino Livramento, Rayan Aït-Nouri and Mads Roerslev.

Advanced Metrics

That's right, even an award as primal as this one cannot escape the looming hand of the modern game, with its xG and its xA and all the other ones, specifically designed by fun-hating scientists to ruin the sport forever and/or help you work out what's going on. We are down to 10 players here and, I'll be honest, there's quite a lot of Leicester City players. Which passes the eye test, because they were pretty average in the 2021-22 Premier League, weren't they?

Other options remaining include Adama Traoré, but he is immediately disqualified because he left halfway through the season to JOIN FC BARCELONA, which is very much not the action of an

---

* is it? Not sure.

average man. 'How are we going to use your science stuff?' you ask. Well, we're going to look at expected goals and actual goals, and expected assists and actual assists and look at players who have very similar values in each. Because that's what the Average Man does, isn't it? He does exactly what you expect.

And when we do this a name surfaces. Perhaps not the name you were thinking of (alternatively: perhaps it was) but, on reflection, a name — and indeed a player — that is surely worthy of this most median of honours. Here are the raw facts:

- He played 28 times
- He scored one goal from an xG of 1.63
- He assisted twice from an xA of 2.57
- He won 11 games and lost nine
- He was born in September 1998, on the day before Belle & Sebastian released 'The Boy with the Arab Strap' as prophesied
- He had a duel success rate of 47% (yeah, pretty average)
- His name? Kiernan Dewsbury-Hall

And, let's be honest, his surname, which yes, does sound a bit like a stately home, gave rise to some of the most average tweets we saw in the entirety of 2021-22. So congratulations to Kiernan Dewsbury-Hall and remember: this doesn't mean you played badly and it doesn't obscure the fact that you played very well on occasion, but it does mean that in the midst of millions of data points collected during the 30th Premier League season, you were in the middle of many players who also played for mid-table sides. And do you know what? That's just fine.

Football under the Taliban: what it means for Afghan women

by Nancy Frostick

When the Taliban returned to Afghanistan in 2021, the women's national football team feared they would be among the first to be targeted. Many of them escaped to new lives . . .

'For the girls based in Kabul, in a split second everything they had worked for for 20 years was lost. And my heart just broke for them.'

Shabnam Mobarez pauses and exhales with a breath that carries the weight of her despair down the phone line from the United States to the UK.

The former Afghanistan women's national team captain has done everything in her power to get her team-mates and friends evacuated from the country after it fell back under Taliban rule in August 2021, but she knows that will not be enough. The futures of millions of women and girls will look very different now and there is little she can do except continue to keep their story alive.

'For now, I see no hope for girls playing in Afghanistan. This regime will not support it and it's going to be super dangerous. Even if they establish anything and try to play in private, it's still something that, if it's discovered, means they could lose their lives because they want to play sport so much. I see no hope inside Afghanistan, but I hope we can come together from outside to represent the country that we knew and still be able to compete. I wish and hope that's possible.'

Afghanistan fell quickly to Taliban forces last summer following the withdrawal of Western troops in August, starting with territory in rural areas before the capital Kabul was taken within 10 days. TV channels across the world were flooded with images of citizens rushing to airports in the hope of obtaining visas to leave the country as panic and fear gripped a population that had lived outside the restrictions of the regime for two decades.

In the midst of the chaos and among those most fearing for their lives were Mobarez's Afghanistan-based team-mates who knew that a terrifying fate awaited them if they failed to make it out in time. Under the last Taliban regime, life as a woman in the country was brutal — denied education, requiring a male family member to accompany them any time they left the house and threatened with public beatings for disobedience.

Upon their return to power last year, the country's youngest female mayor said that she was waiting for the Taliban to come and kill her. The minister of education, Rangina Hamidi, told the BBC that she might 'pay the price for joining a government position' and did not know if she would live to see the morning.

There was no football for men either during the first regime, with most sports banned between 1984 and 2002. This time around the Taliban are trying a more media-aware approach and have allowed the men's national team to continue even if their draconian measures relating to women have once again become the norm.

Even once US forces had overthrown the regime in 2001, life was not easy for women and girls wanting to play football. Societal attitudes changed slowly until, in 2007, a women's national team was formed by the Afghanistan National Olympic Committee.

'Our team has been one that has literally defined the word resilient,' said Mobarez. 'We have fought through everything. Before the Taliban we fought through so many obstacles, especially the players in Kabul. They had to go through hell to get to practice — there were people who would throw stones at them and spit at them. Even taxi drivers didn't want to take them to practice because they believe it's a game for boys and girls should not be a part of it.

'Most of the players coming from inside Afghanistan were not physically prepared because they did not do the same training as the foreign players. It breaks my heart because they weren't given that opportunity — they weren't given the proper gear, proper balls.'

Mobarez is 26 years old and started playing football in her youth growing up in Denmark, having left Afghanistan with her family towards the end of the last Taliban regime in 2001. Playing for Denmark was originally her career goal, but hearing of the Afghanistan women's national team and then visiting the country for the first time since her family left changed her life.

'Seeing how the women were treated in the country as a whole, that's when I decided that I was not going to pursue anything else but to try to develop football in Afghanistan,' she says. 'That's what I knew would bring joy to the women of Afghanistan and would give them hope to allow them to dream to become a football player. My first trip there in 2014 was a life-changing trip because it showed me that that was where I needed to be — and that was my mission from then on, because it's where I was needed the most.

'On the streets people were just not accepting of a woman playing any kind of sport, especially not soccer. But I did see some positive change. When I went in 2014 it was very messed up, how the girls were treated. In 2018 there was a bit of development and we were supported a bit more. Even men would come and watch us play. That felt like a baby step in the right direction and was reason for hope then.'

To even reach a point where the national team was able to play its first major tournament in 2010 gave the women a bond that runs deeper than just being team-mates. Mobarez considers them her sisters, bound together in adversity that extends further back than their escape from the Taliban in 2021.

In 2018, *The Guardian* revealed that FIFA was investigating allegations of physical and sexual abuse suffered by team members at the hands of men from the country's football federation, including its president, Keramuddin Keram. Kit maker Hummel tore up their sponsorship deal with the federation as a result while Keram was handed a lifetime ban and a fine of 1 million Swiss Francs by FIFA.

The team also had vastly inferior training conditions to their male counterparts as Mobarez recalls sessions held days before a friendly against Jordan in 2018 on a 7-a-side pitch — no full size pitches had previously been made available to women despite them being expected to play matches on them.

And then came the events of last summer when Mobarez and fellow former national team captain Khalida Popal, along with the help of a small team at FIFPRO, football's global players' union, were called into action to evacuate players. Popal, living in Denmark, and Mobarez, based in New Jersey, were in contact with their team-mates throughout the evacuation operation. Not all were able to leave with their family members, while Popal and former national team coach Haley Carter told them to shut down their social media accounts and asked people to stop sharing photos of female athletes in order to protect their identities.

'I was in contact with some of the players and it took them about three days (to get out)', says Mobarez. 'The girls were super strong throughout the whole process. They had to go through checkpoints and at every checkpoint one of the girls was explaining to me that she could breathe between the checkpoints but when she was at one, she literally could not breathe. She knew if she did something wrong or said something wrong, anything at all, they could pull her from the car and shoot her there and then.

'I tried to stay in touch with them as much as I could really to bring them some positivity but there was nothing I could tell them. I couldn't tell them that everything was going to be okay because I knew that the situation was life and death and I didn't want to give them false hope for the future. I was trying to be optimistic and trying to tell the players there that they should spend some time with their families, because if they got evacuated they might miss them.

'The future was so unsure and I had to be careful with the words that I chose because I didn't want to give them hope and then in a week the Taliban might have found them. It's heartbreaking.'

Part of the difficulty in getting the players out was finding a country willing to grant the necessary visas so that they could pass through the checkpoints to the airport, which was overrun with people desperate to escape. Harrowing footage showed people clinging onto the wings and landing gear of planes as they took off from Kabul, including 19-year-old national youth team player Zaki Anwari. He is one of many to have fallen to their deaths.

After much struggle and applications to five different govern-ments, the team at FIFPRO realised that the visa process was moving quickest with the Australian authorities. Through a mammoth effort, they managed to relocate over 100 people to Australia to start a new life.

'Part of the first job of explaining this to governments was to make them understand that the very act of these women playing football was an act of defiance,' says Jonas Baer-Hoffmann, FIFPRO general secretary. 'It was effectively a human-rights protest in itself. Then many of them also became more actively involved in the protests and the process of change in the country, so a few of them were very high profile.

'We initially started with a list of four players with the worst risk situations, but from there the list grew as we worked through the process and ultimately it became more than 100 people. We were certain that if we were not able to get them out during those days then we were pretty certain that their lives and their safety were at risk. There were reports in the aftermath of people who did get killed with similar backgrounds who were also athletes, so it was probably a correct risk assessment that they would not have survived.'

It was not just the women's team that needed help to leave the country — eventually players and their families who were part of the youth and development teams were also evacuated and made their way to the UK. They were at the airport on the day that a suicide bomber detonated explosives at the perimeter gate in an attack that killed 170 Afghans and 13 United States service members. The senior women's team players had passed through the area and managed to get out just 48 hours before the airport shut down.

The 31 players and 101 family members of the youth and development team's struggle did not end up leaving Afghanistan as they first had to wait for two months in a hotel and were unable to leave until the UK granted visa papers for the entire group. They reached England in November 2021 and have since been invited to train at Leeds United and Dulwich Hamlet as well as meeting UK government officials.

Men's football in Afghanistan has continued for now, with their first match since the Taliban's return taking place in November 2021 against Indonesia in Turkey.

Very few players are actually based in Afghanistan; the squad for the friendly included players from 14 different countries, including two based in the UK. Noor Husin and Maziar Kouhyar played for Dartford and Hereford respectively in the sixth tier at the time. Both left Afghanistan in an attempt to escape the war and the Taliban when they were children.

'My dad is seen (by the Taliban) as a collaborator and every one of my family, including me, is under threat of being executed,' Kouhyar told *The Sun*. 'We have relatives that are now in hiding.'

As for the women's team, who played their last competitive matches in the 2018 CAFA Women's Football Championship and had three fixtures in Women's Asian Cup qualifying cancelled in September 2021 after the team's evacuation, the future is less certain. Many are starting again in a new country, learning a new language and in a new culture. Dreaming of a chance to represent their country again is not impossible but is, at this stage, improbable.

'It's very hard to put into words what I feel because it's too many things,' says Mobarez. 'Sometimes I feel guilty because I think to myself, how was I so lucky to get out of there back in 2001? Why was it me and my family who got out? There are other girls just like me and they are not going to know anything. They are not going to know that our country had amazing football players and our country has female football players.

'They are going to have a very dark childhood. The girls who are super young right now, we don't know what the future holds for them but they are not going to be able to dream or do anything. They knew a Kabul that was free where they were allowed to go out and do so many things.

'My heart really hurts for them.'

Son Heung-min, the underrated global superstar

by Charlie Eccleshare

Son Heung-min has been one of the best players in the Premier League since joining Tottenham in 2015. But he barely gets the recognition such a status deserves: why?

At what point does an 'underrated' player become so talked about in those terms that the description no longer applies?

Back in the day, hugely decorated internationals like Claude Makélélé, Gilberto Silva and Darren Fletcher were so often described in this way that the moniker started to lose all meaning. The thought also occurred: underrated by whom? These were all players who were hoovering up trophies and were rated extremely highly by their elite managers who picked them every week and gave them a huge amount of responsibility.

Perhaps in those instances the 'underrated' element came more from the fact that they played in one of the least glamorous positions, and it could be used almost interchangeably with 'unsung hero'. Again, as with players like James Milner who have also been given that epithet, there must come a point when a player is described as 'unsung' so frequently they are in fact a 'sung (if such a thing exists) hero'.

What then to make of Tottenham Hotspur striker Son Heung-min who, fresh from jointly winning the 2021-22 Golden Boot with 23 Premier League goals, does appear to be that rare thing of someone who is genuinely underrated?

First, a recap of how good Son is. He averaged just over 20 goals per season across all competitions in six straight seasons since his second year at Spurs in 2016, often massively outscoring his tallies for expected goals (xG), which evaluates the quality of chances falling his way. In 2021-22 for instance, Son scored 23 Premier League goals from an xG of 15.9. That essentially means he's scored 7.1 goals more than would have been anticipated based on how good his chances were (only Kevin De Bruyne had a higher differential with 8.7). In 2020-21 he also outscored his Premier League xG by 7.1 goals, while in 2016-17 he did so by 7.3. In other words he is a truly world-class finisher, which is obvious to anyone who has ever seen him play.

And so on the idea of him being underrated, there are a few ways we can try and quantify this. The lack of recognition when it comes to individual awards is one avenue. Son was bizarrely not even on the shortlist for the six-man Professional Footballers' Association Premier League Player of the Year. The shortlist was compiled by members of the PFA, so it was an oversight from Son's fellow professionals, who deemed Conor Gallagher — admittedly impressive on loan at Crystal Palace — more deserving of a place than the man who ended up being the league's leading goalscorer (none of which were penalties, and alongside seven assists).

Son was also overlooked by those paid to watch the Premier League, finishing 14th in the Football Writers' Association (FWA) player of the year award. The voting took place between late March and 27 April, which could partly explain why Son, who finished the season so strongly, was overlooked. But it's still striking to see that Son picked up 0.5 per cent of the vote, just above Joel Matip and just below Diogo Jota.

Journalists in strange judgement call shock etc etc.

As for his peers, he has never even been among the six nominated for the PFA Player of the Year awards, let alone won it, has only been in their Premier League team of the year twice and didn't make it in 2021-22 despite sharing the Golden Boot.

But it's not just fellow players and media who have tended to overlook Son. Despite his phenomenal consistency over the last six seasons — only Harry Kane, Mohamed Salah and Sadio Mané (just) have scored more non-penalty goals in the top flight since the start of 2016-17 — he has barely been linked with a move to one of Europe's heavyweights, either inside or outside the Premier League.

Speaking to those who know Son, they think part of the reason for this is his relative lack of ego. He is not someone who wants or needs to be touted around to the biggest clubs. He is also exceptionally loyal to Spurs, and signing a four-year deal in 2021 was the equivalent of saying to any potential suitors: please don't bother. That Son did so at a time when Harry Kane was trying to leave and Spurs were on the back of a pretty wretched season in which they finished seventh shows his level of dedication. The deal had been agreed in principle the previous November, but even then Spurs were not in the Champions League and overall some way behind the biggest clubs in England.

Son also signed a five-year contract in 2018, effectively shutting the door on Manchester City, who had signed Kyle Walker from Spurs the previous summer and were interested in bringing the South Korean to the Etihad. That was probably the closest he ever came to even being the subject of transfer speculation, and it was a story that was over before it had even begun.

'Maybe it's to do with his humility,' says a source who knows Son well, trying to explain the player's relative lack of recognition. 'Albeit he's a huge global star, but there isn't a circus that surrounds him. That's probably a contributing factor.

'It's great for Spurs — the more under the radar the better for them — but I struggle to think of someone having as good a season as him and not being in contention for the main awards.'

'I think the underrated thing is partly because he's so loyal to Spurs,' adds another. 'For example if he was seriously linked to United or Real or showed any kind of impression he would like a new challenge there could be more interest from fans outside of Tottenham, from those clubs. But he always says he wants to stay at Spurs so is loved by their fans and other clubs know he is not attainable.'

Son's loyalty to Spurs then goes some way to explaining why no bigger club has ever seriously attempted to try and prise him away from north London. But what about the wider football community's tendency not to fully appreciate him?

The view in South Korea is that the perception of Son would be very different if the striker had a different nationality. 'A lot of Korean fans say that if Son was an English player he would be valued a lot more highly,' explains Lee Sung-mo, a South Korean football journalist who covered Son for five years in England. 'That's what they're saying in the biggest fan communities. If he were English, Brazilian or German he'd be competing for the Ballon d'Or.'

'From a UK point of view we feel he is underrated,' adds Rachel Hur, a London-based British-Korean European football correspondent for *Sports Dong-a*. 'We feel he could be hyped up more, but maybe because he's an Asian player he's less so.

'We've accepted over the years that it's just how it is. Maybe if he was a British player, England would go mad about him.

'We have no idea why . . . I don't think it's a negative thing as such, and I'm not sure if the perception has changed this season. He's still not seen as being in the same bracket as world-class players that people rave about.'

The point about perceptions around Son being partly based on his nationality is an interesting one. There does seem to be little doubt that he would be viewed differently if he came from a traditional footballing superpower. As it is, Son is often compared to his compatriot Park Ji-sung, who had so much success with Manchester United. But other than their nationality the two have little in common as players. Where Park's game was based more on his energy and versatility in midfield, Son is a lightning-quick attacker whose pace and power makes him more akin to Mané and Salah — or fellow Spurs legend Gareth Bale.

Son may also be the victim, a little like Kane, of being so clinical that he can almost appear mechanical. Typically in this country the preference has been for more mercurial talents who are a bit more unpredictable in what they produce. Son, by contrast, is lethally effective and extremely consistent — off either foot you know he will almost always hit the target (no elite Premier League goalscorer has scored a higher proportion of their non-headed goals with their weaker foot than Son's 43 per cent). He's unlikely to do anything flashy unless he absolutely has to or thinks that doing so will give him the best chance of scoring.

Son, after all, was coached as a youngster by his father, who did not let his children join a competitive team until they were teenagers, instead forcing them to partake in repetitive drills that would improve their technique. You can see the benefits of those repetitions in Son's perfectly honed shooting ability.

In any case, even if Son is underrated in England, he is absolutely adored by the two most important groups to him: his fans back home and the Tottenham supporters. There is now quite a lot of overlap between those two groups given how many Koreans support Spurs because of Son's success there. Tottenham are well aware of this and the commercial opportunities therein, and toured South Korea in 2022. The Korean women's captain Cho So-hyun also plays for Tottenham.

'He is completely hero-worshipped in South Korea' says Lee. 'He's the biggest national star at the moment among the fans.'

Another Korean source adds that he is even bigger back home than K-pop group BTS, asking for anonymity for fear of upsetting the band's legions of fans.

'Koreans go absolutely mad for Son,' says Hur. 'He's definitely not underrated there and is very much hyped-up, getting all the praise and media attention.

'Everyone in South Korea follows Spurs now because of him, whereas at first it was about Son and wanting him to move to a bigger club. But Spurs is such a big club there now that it's one of the best-supported teams. That's changed a lot over the last few years.'

Whether it will remain the case after Son leaves is an interesting one, with industry experts pointing to the fact that a lot of younger fans support players rather than teams. But for the moment Tottenham have a hugely dedicated fanbase in Korea, as evidenced by the fans who travel over for every game and, while in London, make the pilgrimage to the Spurs training ground to try and catch a glimpse of their hero.

Son's huge marketability was reflected by him signing with the sports division of Hollywood talent agency CAA Base towards the end of 2020. Huge stars like Cristiano Ronaldo and José Mourinho are among the company's clients, underlining the potential that many brands see in Son. It's impressive that he remains as grounded as he is given his huge profile back home.

And as well as being hero-worshipped in Korea, Son is loved by Tottenham staff and supporters.

'We know Spurs fans adore him, speaking to them over the last few years, and he does feel that love,' says Hur.

This mutual affection between Son and the Tottenham supporters is part of the reason why those close to him say he is not especially bothered by the lack of wider recognition. And with a World Cup coming up where Korean fans are hopeful Son can fire them into the knockout rounds, he has a chance to become even more popular in his home country. There's also a view among regular Son watchers that even as he ages, he is only going to get better. That's certainly the direction of travel so far for Son, who has just enjoyed his most prolific ever season at Spurs.

Surely he can't remain underrated much longer?

Qatar splits Bayern and their fans

by Raphael Honigstein

The relationship between German clubs and their fans has always been a tricky one: particularly when they get into bed with a regime like Qatar . . .

A sold-out Allianz Arena match against Freiburg in November 2021 saw the post-lockdown return of the human 'T', the logo of shirt sponsors Telekom, formed in the stands by 58 company interns who receive free tickets in return for dressing up like sperm from Woody Allen movie *Everything You Always Wanted to Know About Sex* for 90 minutes.

Whereas said marketing stunt has been going on for so long that nobody takes much notice anymore, let alone offence, another of Bayern Munich's commercial tie-ups involving white outfits continues to attract criticism and satirical derision among sections of the fanbase.

During the 2-1 win, supporters in the Südkurve, the stadium's die-hard section, raised a banner depicting Bayern's CEO Oliver Kahn and chairman Herbert Hainer as willing operators of a sports-washing laundromat, turning blood-stained shirts into clean, Qatar-branded robes.

'For money, we clean anything,' it read. Cue a camera cut to Kahn and Hainer in the stands, looking glum.

A sub-group of Bayern ultras called Munich's Red Pride have sporadically protested their club's shirt-sleeve sponsorship deal with Doha Airport/Qatar Airways ever since the arrangement started in January 2016.

They held up placards lambasting former CEO Karl-Heinz Rummenigge's 2017 insistence that Bayern were again going to Qatar for their winter training camp because of 'superstition' (as previous visits had been followed by them winning the Bundesliga). They ridiculed Rummenigge and former chairman Uli Hoeness saying that Bayern would find 'ideal conditions' in Doha as money-motivated and blinkered, and wondered aloud whether cash was simply 'more important than human rights' for the perennial German champions.

The intervention from the terraces seemed to strike a bigger nerve than usual, however.

It was the first to target the club's new leadership duo of Kahn and Hainer, after the latter had emphasised Bayern's mission of spreading 'social values' at the turn of the year, and felt topical in an international context, too: the subject of reputation-laundering through football having gained renewed attention in the wake of the Newcastle United takeover by Saudi Arabia's public investment fund (PIF).

In addition, the banner coincided with a members' proposition designed to take the debate from the Südkurve into the mainstream.

Michael Ott and handful of co-authors who are not part of organised supporter groups also wanted the members' assembly on 25 November to vote on the club 'doing anything within the necessary legal and actual possibilities of influence' on Bayern Munich plc that's running the professional football operation 'to let contracts with Qatar Airways or other companies majority-owned by the Emirate of Qatar lapse at the next possible opportunity, and to not extend them or to re-sign them'.

The current contract with Qatar Airways runs until 2023.

Bayern Munich plc is 75 per cent owned by Bayern club members. It's doubtful whether the proposition can technically bind the supervisory board that controls Kahn and the other members of the plc into taking such a specific decision, even if it does make it to a vote and wins a majority.

Ott, a Mainz-based lawyer, estimates its chances of passing as '50-50'. But in a sense he's more interested in 'a public debate about the club's moral responsibilities' than a specific outcome.

'In January 2020, a fan club organised a podium discussion and flew in immigrant workers from Qatar, they invited a human rights expert and a club representative — but no one from Bayern came', Ott told *The Athletic*. 'I felt ashamed of being a fan that day. And I told myself: this cannot stand'.

Bayern did not comment on the proposition before the AGM. There was no comment on the banner, either. The club would be within their rights to confiscate such fan signs that haven't been cleared for sentiment and compliance with technical restrictions in advance but there's no appetite to send in the stewards and escalate the situation. As long as the protest doesn't involve hate speech or personal insults, the bosses at the Bayern's Säbener Strasse HQ decided to bear having their morals questioned publicly.

The Bundesliga club's democratic set-up — they are majority-owned by the members, who vote in the leaders — encourages fans to voice their concerns, sometimes loudly, sometimes pointedly, sometimes in a fashion that's downright embarrassing for those in charge.

Attempts to speak to Munich's Red Pride were unsuccessful. They only number about 30 people but their protest can't be fobbed off as a minority view within the organised fanbase. A Südkurve insider says 'their opposition, or at least their unease, about the Qatar deal is widely shared'.

Bayern have particularly political ultras who have repeatedly stood up against racism, antisemitism, homophobia and against what they perceive as the ills of modern football, such as the spring's mooted Super League and high ticket prices. Whether less committed members of the club's estimated nine-million-strong fanbase in Germany alone care quite as much about the human rights record of a sleeve sponsor is harder to ascertain.

For Bayern, there are about 20 million reasons to continue with Qatar as a sponsor. That's a fairly significant €100 million since January 2016, roughly the combined cost of five seasons of Robert Lewandowski's services.

Ironically, the very Bundesliga '50 plus 1' regulations that prevent its clubs being taken over by outside investors force them to pursue a strategy of commercial tie-ups that will throw up deals with some of the same non-Western countries that invest in football in a more direct manner elsewhere.

That dynamic is especially relevant for Bayern, a club who have outgrown their own saturated domestic market — local car-maker BMW will not pay €20 million to have 58 workers form their logo in the ground — and now compete with top sides across Europe who are able to call upon non-organic revenues.

They weren't naive about facing a backlash when they weighed up doing the deal five years ago. They talked to NGOs, who told them they could do it, provided they spoke out about human rights publicly. The club thought that both impossible and counter-productive, embarking on a policy of soft, behind-the-scenes discussions and symbolic gestures — such as having their women's team travel to Doha and visit local schools — instead.

'Our view is that change doesn't happen through rejection, only through dialogue,' Rummenigge told *The Athletic* in April 2021. A cop-out? Perhaps. But even Qatar expert Regina Spöttl, of Amnesty International Germany, has spoken out against football turning its back on the country.

'Going there is better than a boycott,' Spöttl told German newspaper *Tagesspiegel* in April.

The government ministers Bayern consulted encouraged them to sign the contract in any case, in line with then-chancellor Angela Merkel's drive to attract investment from the Emirate into the German economy at the time. There's 'nothing wrong from a foreign policy point of view', then-foreign minister Frank-Walter Steinmeier declared in 2016, once the cooperation was announced.

The question at the heart of the matter is this: should football clubs be more discerning about doing commercial deals than governments and corporations would be?

'We're a football club but also an economic entity that cannot survive without economic partnerships', Rummenigge told newspaper *Die Welt* in March. 'We're no different to Volkswagen, Daimler, Deutsche Bank or others who cooperate with Qatari partners economically.' Qatar has a significant stake in those and other German blue-chip companies.

Freelance journalist and Bayern supporter Justin Kraft, one of Ott's co-signees, is not convinced by that line of argument.

'Bayern aren't simply a corporation', Kraft says. 'They don't simply have customers but fans, who look at these things from a much more emotional angle. They (the supporters) care about the moral implications, not just finances.'

Ott agrees: 'Whether you buy from a specific company is a personal choice but you don't have much influence beyond that. As a fan, you do. You can try and get your club to behave in a moral way. And if you have this opportunity, it's your moral duty to use it. It's worth fighting for, because it's your club. You only have that one.'

These idealistic concerns are the polar opposite of the blind faith of the 'Right or wrong, it's my club' brigade who dominate much of the discourse on anglophone social media.

Supporters such as Kraft, Ott and Munich's Red Pride love their club so much they focus on the wrong, not the right, out of a sense of disappointment that Bayern fall short of a high moral benchmark.

The club's long history of corporate social responsibility, from saving rival clubs by playing in lucrative testimonials to providing help for refugees, material support for the local Jewish football club — former chairman Kurt Landauer was persecuted by the Nazis in the 1930s — and sizeable donations for the victims of flooding, might have made things worse, in a strange way: it's created an expectation that they'll always be on the easily-identifiable right side of the debate on social matters.

Human Rights Watch and the UN's International Labour Organization (ILO) have recently said the situation of immigrant workers has improved in Qatar, though LGBT individuals still face discrimination. But at what point would it be enough for Bayern's internal critics? Or, assuming for a moment that Ott's proposal succeeds, who'd then be left that's deemed acceptable in a world of globalised sponsorships? Are arrangements with Chinese or Turkish companies OK, in principle?

'I can't really answer that, I don't know where exactly the red line is either,' Ott admits. 'But I don't think it's my job to define the red line. In fact, I think it's nearly impossible to do this in a general way. It probably will have to be evaluated from case to case.

'For now, however, it is sufficient to say that Qatar has, in any case, crossed the red line, in my opinion. It would be good if Bayern could sit down with experts and fans and figure out where their red line is, and become more sensitive, generally speaking.'

Regardless of the outcome, the club will have to continue to figure out what kind of principles they can still afford to have.

But maybe it's unrealistic to believe they'll somehow be better at finding coherent answers than anyone else trying to succeed in this deeply compromised world of ours.

A version of this article first appeared on The Athletic

2021-22 in the EFL: the year of the young manager

by Adrian Clarke

The grizzled old gaffer in camel coat and shiny shoes is dead . . . well, sort of, but it's clear that more clubs are favouring new, fresh ideas over old-school nous and experience.

Modern head coach > old-fashioned gaffer. That was the vibe at dugout level right across a 2021-22 EFL campaign that fully embraced the winds of change.

Old school wheeler-dealer types, long-ball merchants, those who list 'I know the division' as a key skill set, and tactics-averse motivators were not quite outlawed, but many were quietly shuffled to one side.

For this was the year of the developer.

Young coaches with newly harvested ideas and a background in improving footballers (a remarkable new concept!) were given a greater opportunity to shine, and the results were staggeringly positive.

In League Two, so often a graveyard of the past-it boss getting one last crack on reputation alone, a steady stream of owners gave enterprising newcomers a platform to show their skills.

For starters, the champions Forest Green Rovers were led by 39-year-old rookie Rob Edwards. Owner Dale Vince had persuaded the former Wolves defender to quit his role as head coach of England under-16s to take his first post at senior level, and it was a gamble that paid off handsomely.

Edwards' intelligent coaching and innovative tactical approach quickly improved the players at his disposal, and during an incredible 19-match spell that saw Halloween, Guy Fawkes Night, Christmas, New Year and even Valentine's Day pass without a defeat. They were simply untouchable.

Watford liked what they saw. They cheekily swooped in for Edwards before he'd even had time to dry clean his champagne-soaked clobber.

Eighty-seven miles down the road from the sleepy Gloucestershire town of Nailsworth, Exeter City's Matt Taylor was another first timer that will look back on 2021-22 with great fondness. Stepping up from his duties as the Grecian's under-23 head coach to replace Paul Tisdale in 2018, the former Exeter defender steadily built a side capable of achieving automatic promotion.

On a shoestring budget the self-sustainable, fan-owned club relied heavily on Taylor's coaching potential to make them competitive. And it was a challenge the 40-year-old rose to, guiding a young side filled with academy graduates to the runners-up spot.

Another next-gen manager, Joey Barton, claimed the third automatic promotion place courtesy of a frankly outrageous 7-0 final day victory at home to Scunthorpe United. The Bristol Rovers boss will always have his critics, but having already steered previous employers Fleetwood Town into the League One play-offs, his coaching credentials are indisputably sound.

In the League Two play-off picture this pattern of coach-led influence continued. Northampton Town's Jon Brady was promoted from head coach of the under-18s and made the transition look easy in his first full season in charge at Sixfields. But for a scarcely believable goal difference swing on the last day of the season he'd have earned an impressive top-three finish.

Like the Cobblers, Swindon Town were also vanquished in the play-offs, but the way they were stylishly reinvented by 41-year-old Ben Garner shouldn't be ignored. He'd built his reputation as a bright footballing mind as an academy coach at Crystal Palace, climbing the ladder to take on assistant roles at Selhurst Park and the Hawthorns.

In his first senior job at Bristol Rovers, Garner's possession-based philosophy didn't translate into winning football, but Swindon has been a better fit. Building a brand-new team that were still learning one another's names at the start of the campaign, he cultivated one of the most watchable footballing sides seen at this level for many years.

Swindon had 51 more shots in open play and produced 132 more sequences of 10-plus passes than anyone else in League Two. They may not have been promoted, but Garner's coaching beliefs shone brightly and earned him a move to Charlton.

Sutton United's Matt Gray and Newport County's James Rowberry are two more first-time managers worthy of praise. Neither man had been a number one before taking their respective roles, but both impressed.

Gray's Sutton missed out on the play-offs by one place in their debut EFL season, and were unfortunate to lose the Papa Johns' Trophy Final in extra time to Rotherham United.

At 29 Rowberry became one of the youngest coaches in the world to earn UEFA Pro Licence status, and eight years on he is busy creating an exciting new identity for the Exiles.

Keen followers of fashion, Salford City and Barrow took the plunge too. Neil Wood, the 39-year-old Manchester United under-23s coach replaced Gary Bowyer at Salford, while Barrow turned to 37-year-old Pete Wild, who excelled in the National League with Halifax Town.

Appointing thirty-somethings in their managerial nappies also held a strong appeal for a growing number of League One's powerbrokers. In fact, between August 2021 and May 2022, seven of the 11 managers appointed in the third tier were under the age of 40. The eldest was returning Morecambe boss Derek Adams, at the grand old age of 46.

Ambitious Ipswich Town snapped up former Manchester United coach Kieran McKenna in December, and the 35-year-old galvanised an unhappy fanbase with an attractive style of play that had them flooding back through the Portman Road turnstiles.

Plymouth Argyle's Steven Schumacher, 38, and MK Dons head coach Liam Manning, 36, were two other young 'uns excelling in first-time roles at the helm of EFL clubs. The Pilgrims may have suffered a late season dip in form, but the former Bury midfielder impressed when asked to fill the void left by Ryan Lowe's sudden move to Preston.

When the relatively unknown Manning arrived at Stadium MK in August 2021, he was two years younger than captain Dean Lewington, but he immediately built on the excellent work of predecessor Russell Martin.

Manning started out as an academy coach (yep, another one!) at Ipswich Town. Later he went on to work with West Ham United's Under-23s before going overseas to become New York City's academy director, and later head coach of Belgian side Lommel.

Retaining MK Dons' adventurous possession-based style, while pairing it with a more secure defensive platform, his team made big improvements to claim 24 additional points compared to the previous campaign. Finishing third on 89 points, MK eventually lost to Wycombe Wanderers in the play-offs, but their precocious head coach is now managerial hot property.

It is easy to forget that Wigan Athletic's Leam Richardson is another head-coach-newbie-done-good. Having served his appren-ticeship as number two to Paul Cook at Accrington, Chesterfield, Portsmouth, and Wigan — interspersed with the odd caretaker role — the 42-year-old grabbed an opportunity to fly solo with the Latics during the COVID-19 pandemic.

Backed in the transfer market by new owners, he built a new team from scratch, dispelling the notion that too many summer transfers can be disruptive. Blending physicality with tactical nous, Richardson's Latics were crowned champions, two points ahead of long-time leaders Rotherham United.

The Wigan head coach also happened to save the life of star striker Charlie Wyke, who suffered a cardiac arrest in training. Calmly administering CPR moments after the front man had collapsed, he crucially initiated the resuscitation process before a doctor arrived on the scene.

For all the bluster around how the Championship season is always such an exhausting slog, a survival of the fittest, the 2021-22 success stories indicate tactical savviness is very much the trump card.

Eddie Howe, Sean Dyche, Rafa Benítez, Nuno Espírito Santo, Chris Wilder, Dean Smith, Daniel Farke, Thomas Frank and Marcelo Bielsa all inspired promotions in recent seasons. Bright footballing minds, one and all; they share an ability to improve individual players, while also implementing distinct and effective playing styles.

In short, they know their way around a chalkboard and this was a running theme again at the top end of English football's second tier. Scott Parker, who spent a year coaching Tottenham Hotspur's under-18s side prior to returning to senior level, stood out as one of the shrewdest operators.

Yes, he was backed heavily by the Bournemouth board en route to a second-placed finish, but his acute focus on every tactical detail helped get the Cherries over the line — his second Premier League promotion by the age of 41.

He didn't go up with Huddersfield Town in the end, but Carlos Corberan is arguably the poster boy for this wave of fledgling head coaches. He was young at 39 (✓), stepped up from a developmental role with Leeds United's under 23s (✓), spent time cutting his teeth as a number two (✓), his coaching improved the team and individuals without spending money (✓), and he was also an absolute whizz when it came to devising super-clever strategies (✓).

It's the full set in this fashion-conscious time.

Ditching the Bielsa-style tactics he tried (and flopped with) before, Corberan flipped things around to earn a reputation as a tactical tinkerer supreme. Switching shapes on a game-by-game, half-by-half, quarter-by-quarter basis to react to issues, or proactively seek out weaknesses in the opposition, Huddersfield Town were extraordinarily awkward opponents.

One minute they'd be sat deep ready to pounce on the counter, the next they would have four up front playing keep-ball inside the final third. Keeping up with their game plan was a complicated process.

Manic inside his technical area, obsessing about every minor detail, there's definitely a bit of Pep Guardiola in Corberan's make-up. To complete that comparison, he might just have over-thought his play-off final approach beneath the Wembley arch.

With a heavy focus on stifling their opponents that day, a ploy that worked well, his pre-occupied Terriers didn't manage a shot on target of their own in a 1-0 loss to Nottingham Forest.

The two defeated play-off semi-final gaffers, Nathan Jones and Paul Heckingbottom, are also far more track suit than trench coat.

Heckingbottom worked in the academies at Barnsley and Sheffield United, stepping up from a role with the club's under-23s to almost steer the Blades to promotion. A natural training ground coach with bright ideas and an affinity with the club's supporters, he elevated his reputation in 2021-22.

The same can be said of Luton Town's Jones (a former assistant to Chris Hughton) who enjoyed a wonderful campaign of over-achievement at Kenilworth Road. The intense, effervescent Welshman was long regarded as one of the best coaches around, and by shifting to a more power-based style of play he extracted every ounce of potential from his small squad of players.

Bedecked in tight black training gear on a match day, wearing moulded boots and his heart on his sleeve, Jones was very much Luton Town's 12th man on the side lines. Without his energy and coaching prowess, Hatters fans would not have been able to dream of top-flight football.

The EFL's final act of another absorbing season was to send Nottingham Forest on their way to the promised land and it was fitting that one of the country's best developers was the mastermind of it.

After obtaining his UEFA Pro Licence at the age of just 29, Steve Cooper went on to run the Wrexham and Liverpool academies, before steering England's under 17s to World Cup glory in 2017.

Brilliant with young players, astute in his creation of the team's identity, a natural tactical analyst, but also somebody who 'kills Forest's players with kindness', according to defender Joe Worrall, Cooper's positive style of inclusive management was a roaring success.

He took the two-time European champions on an unimaginable journey from the Championship relegation zone to promotion in eight magical months. Cooper's Forest were the story of the season in the EFL.

This isn't the death knell for grey-haired gaffers in suits and shiny shoes. Far from it. The wisdom and knowledge they boast should never be discounted, and Carlo Ancelotti is proof personified that you don't need to be a modern, or genius tactical coach to scale footballing mountains.

But there can be no denying the breeze is blowing in another direction. Right across the EFL in 2021-22 there was a bold willingness to try something, or somebody different. And it was largely successful too. Fresh ideas are being valued as a higher currency than proven experience.

THE TOTALLY FOOTBALL BOOK

The Inter Totally Quiz

Think you know more about football than the
Totally pundits? Well . . . it's quite possible you're
right – but this is your chance to prove it . . .

THE QUESTIONS

Champions League finals

1) Who won the first Champions League final, after it had been rebranded from the European Cup in 1993?

2) John Terry famously missed a penalty in the 2008 Champions League final shootout, but who was the other Chelsea player to miss?

3) Who scored Bayern Munich's goal in the 1999 final against Manchester United?

4) Which player, who later moved to England, scored twice for Borussia Dortmund in the 1997 final?

5) Who scored the winning penalty for Milan in the 2003 final?

6) What do the 2000, 2003, 2008, 2013, 2014, 2016, 2019 and 2021 finals have in common?

7) What do the finals in 2005 and 2007, 2009 and 2011, 2014 and 2016, and 2019 and 2022 have in common?

8) Four members of the Porto team that started the 2004 Champions League final under José Mourinho went on to play for Chelsea: name them.

9) Who was the first English player to score in a Champions League final for a non-English club?

10) Which team has appeared in six Champions League finals but lost five of them?

Answers on page 299

Missing clubs

1) Which name is missing from this list of Robbie Keane's permanent clubs? Wolves, Coventry, Inter, XXXXX, Tottenham, Liverpool, Tottenham, LA Galaxy, ATK

2) Which name is missing from this list of Ronaldo's permanent clubs? Cruzeiro, PSV, Barcelona, Inter, Real Madrid, XXXXX, Corinthians

3) Which name is missing from this list of Gary Lineker's permanent clubs? Leicester City, Everton, Barcelona, Tottenham, XXXXX

4) Which name is missing from this list of James Milner's permanent clubs? Leeds United, Newcastle, XXXXX, Manchester City, Liverpool

5) Which name is missing from this list of Emile Heskey's permanent clubs? Leicester, Liverpool, Birmingham, XXXXX, Aston Villa, Newcastle Jets, Bolton Wanderers

6) Which name is missing from this list of Ándrea Pirlo's permanent clubs? Brescia, XXXXX, AC Milan, Juventus, New York City FC

7) Which name is missing from this list of Ángel Di Maria's permanent clubs? Rosario Central, XXXXX, Real Madrid, Manchester United, PSG

8) Which name is missing from this list of David James's permanent clubs? Watford, Liverpool, Aston Villa, West Ham, XXXXX, Portsmouth, Bristol City, Bournemouth, IBV, Kerala Blasters

9) Which name is missing from this list of Jermain Defoe's permanent clubs? West Ham, Tottenham, Portsmouth, Tottenham, Toronto FC, Sunderland, XXXXX, Rangers, Sunderland

10) Which name is missing from this list of Dimitar Berbatov's permanent clubs? CSKA Sofia, Bayer Leverkusen, Tottenham, Manchester United, XXXXX, Monaco, PAOK, Kerala Blasters

Answers on page 300

Golden Boots

1) Which player has won the most Premier League Golden Boots, with four?

2) Three English players shared the Premier League Golden Boot in 1997-98: which three?

3) Three African players shared the Premier League Golden Boot in 2018-19: which three?

4) Name the two English players to have won the World Cup Golden Boot.

5) Who won the first Premier League Golden Boot? He's also the only player to win it by scoring goals for different teams in the season.

6) Which player, while at Benfica, won the first ever European Golden Boot in 1968?

7) Two Brazilians won the European Golden Boot in the 1990s: one was Ronaldo, playing for Barcelona, and the other played for Porto — who?

8) Just Fontaine holds the record for the most goals scored by a World Cup Golden Boot winner at a single tournament, in 1958 — how many did he score?

9) Three Germans have won the World Cup Golden Boot — which three?

10) What did the winner of every World Cup Golden Boot from 1978 to 1998 have in common?

Answers on page 301

Managers

1) Didier Deschamps became the third man to win the World Cup as a player and a coach in 2018 — who were the first two?

2) For how many years did Sir Alex Ferguson manage Manchester United?

3) At which club did José Mourinho start his managerial career?

4) Which two clubs have Thomas Tuchel and Jürgen Klopp both managed?

5) What do these managers have in common: Stefano Pioli, Giovanni Trapattoni, Alberto Zaccheroni, Leonardo?

6) Which club has been managed by Tony Pulis, Sam Allardyce, Alan Pardew, Roy Hodgson and Neil Warnock?

7) Name any of the national teams, other than England, that Sven-Göran Eriksson has managed.

8) What have Miguel Muñoz, Giovanni Trapattoni, Johan Cruyff, Carlo Ancelotti, Frank Rijkaard, Pep Guardiola and Zinedine Zidane all done that nobody else has?

9) Dave Mackay did it in 1975, Howard Kendall did it in 1985 and 1987, Kenny Dalglish did it in 1986, 1988, 1990 and 1995, George Graham did it in 1989 and 1991: specifically, what is 'it'?

10) Who was the first manager from outside the UK and Ireland to win the English title?

Answers on page 302

Euro '96

1) Ireland didn't qualify for Euro '96 – who beat them in the play-off?

2) Who did England draw 1-1 with in the opening game?

3) Why was the consolation goal the Netherlands scored in their 4-1 defeat to England significant?

4) Against which team did Karel Poborský score his famous 'scoop' goal?

5) Which of the following grounds DID NOT host a game at the tournament: City Ground, Villa Park, Highbury, Hillsborough, Elland Road.

6) Who did the Czech Republic beat on penalties in the semi-final?

7) Which of the following England players DID NOT take a penalty against Germany in the semi-final: Paul Gascoigne, David Platt, Paul Ince, Teddy Sheringham?

8) Who scored both of Germany's goals in the final?

9) Who finished as the tournament's top scorer?

10) And which defender was named as the player of the tournament?

Answers on page 303

English clubs in Europe

1) Who were the first English club to win a major European trophy?

2) Who were the first English club to compete in the European Cup?

3) Which English team won the first ever UEFA Cup in 1972, after it had been rebranded from the Inter-Cities Fairs Cup?

4) Who were the teams that Nottingham Forest beat in the finals when they won the 1979 and 1980 European Cups?

5) Who were the first English club to beat Bayern Munich at the Olympiastadion in European competition?

6) Who beat Arsenal on penalties in the 2000 UEFA Cup final?

7) Who competed in the 2013-14 Europa League despite playing their domestic football in the Championship?

8) Who played in the only ever European Super Cup to be contested between two English teams in 2019?

9) Who were the first English club to win a European trophy after they were readmitted to UEFA competition, when the ban following the Heysel disaster expired?

10) What is the next stadium in this sequence: the Camp Nou, the Atatürk Stadium in Istanbul, the Luzhniki Stadium, the Allianz Arena Munich, the Wanda Metropolitano in Madrid, and . . .

Answers on page 304

Italia '90

1) What is the name of Cameroon's match-winner when they shocked Argentina in the opening game?

2) Who scored the winning penalty in Ireland's second round victory over Romania?

3) Against which team did Roger Milla score twice in extra time, taking advantage of a goalkeeping error, in the second round?

4) Against which team did David Platt score a 120th-minute volley to put England into the quarter-finals?

5) Where was England's semi-final defeat to West Germany held?

6) Who was fouled for the penalty that decided the final in West Germany's favour?

7) What was Pedro Monzón the first player to ever do?

8) Which Yugoslavian was named as young player of the tournament?

9) Toto Schillaci was the surprise top-scorer in the tournament: which club was he playing for at the time?

10) Which two future Premier League-winning managers were in Italy's squad at the tournament?

Answers on page 305

Who am I?

1) I started my career at the biggest club in my country before moving to Germany. I joined an exceptionally wealthy club shortly before they became exceptionally wealthy. I left that club in 2019 to manage the club at which I started my career.

2) I played in Germany, Italy and the USA. I managed the Hungary and Bulgaria national teams. I won the World Cup and a Ballon d'Or. I lost two European Cup/Champions League finals in dramatic circumstances.

3) I won the Spanish title twice with a big team but it's not the club I am most associated with. I scored a lot of goals for a big English team but only won one league title with them. I had to delay signing for that team for a year after a serious injury.

4) I have played for both Milan teams, but I am most associated with another Serie A giant. I have appeared in two Champions League finals but won neither. I have both scored and missed a high profile penalty for my country.

5) I played the majority of my career in Italy but I am not Italian. I scored in a Champions League final while on loan at an Italian club. I once held the world transfer record when moving between two Italian clubs.

6) I won the Champions League with my first club, then followed the manager I won it with to his new club in England. I also won the league title in Spain. I won one European Championship and lost in the final of another.

7) I moved to England in 1997, signed by the manager who gave me my debut in my home country. I spent one season in Spain before returning to England for the final three seasons of my career. I have scored in a World Cup final.

8) I spent 13 years at my first club where I won eight national titles and the Champions League. From there I moved to England where I spent two seasons. I finished my career in America. I have won the World Cup.

9) I moved to England from Real Sociedad and won the Champions League the season after that. I went on to win the Champions League again with a club from my home country. I finished my playing career at a German club.

10) I won the Premier League with my boyhood club but moved to another club in the same city in controversial circumstances, but I won the Champions League with that second club. I later played in Italy and the USA.

Answers on page 306

Missing managers

1) Which name is missing from this run of permanent Aston Villa managers? Paul Lambert, Tim Sherwood, Rémi Garde, XXXXX, Steve Bruce

2) Which name is missing from this run of permanent Tottenham managers? Juande Ramos, Harry Redknapp, XXXXX, Tim Sherwood, Mauricio Pochettino

3) Which name is missing from this run of permanent Real Madrid managers? José Mourinho, Carlo Ancelotti, XXXXX, Zinedine Zidane, Julen Lopetegui

4) Which name is missing from this run of permanent Nottingham Forest managers? Aitor Karanka, XXXXX, Sabri Lamouchi, Chris Hughton, Steve Cooper

5) Which name is missing from this run of permanent West Ham United managers? Sam Allardyce, Slaven Bilić, David Moyes, XXXXX, David Moyes

6) Which name is missing from this run of permanent Celtic managers? Neil Lennon, Ronny Delia, Brendan Rodgers, XXXXX, Ange Postecoglou

7) Which name is missing from this run of permanent Crystal Palace managers? Alan Pardew, Sam Allardyce, XXXXX, Roy Hodgson, Patrick Vieira

8) Which name is missing from this run of permanent Newcastle United managers? Graeme Souness, Glenn Roeder, XXXXX, Kevin Keegan, Joe Kinnear

9) Which name is missing from this run of permanent Ireland managers? Steve Staunton, XXXXX, Martin O'Neill, Mick McCarthy, Stephen Kenny

10) Which name is missing from this run of permanent Everton managers? Walter Smith, David Moyes, Roberto Martínez, XXXXX, Sam Allardyce

Answers on page 307

Stadia

1) Which Football League ground has hosted a cricket Test match?

2) Which of these venues has never hosted an FA Cup final: the Oval, Stamford Bridge, Anfield, Old Trafford, Goodison Park?

3) What do the following stadia have in common, in relation to World Cup finals: Estadio Centenario in Montevideo, Stadio Nazionale in Rome, Wembley in London, Olympiastadion in Munich, Estadio Monumental in Buenos Aires, Stade de France in Paris?

4) Which team used Wembley as their home ground for Champions League games in the 1990s?

5) Which stadium hosted the game with the highest attendance in World Cup history?

6) Which clubs share the Stadio Luigi Ferraris as their home?

7) In which stadium was the 2022 Champions League final scheduled to be held before it was switched to Paris?

8) Who calls the Estadio de la Cerámica their home?

9) In which year did the rebuilt Wembley open?

10) Dundee and Dundee United's grounds are just over 300 metres apart: what are those grounds called?

Answers on page 308

Goalkeepers

1) What is the award given to the best goalkeeper in Spain every season?

2) As of 2022, who is the only goalkeeper to win the Ballon d'Or?

3) How did Manchester United goalkeeper Alex Stepney dislocate his jaw during a game in 1975?

4) What do Gianpiero Combi, Dino Zoff, Iker Casillas and Hugo Lloris have in common?

5) How much (in £) did Juventus pay Parma for Gigi Buffon in 2001?

6) From which team did Bayern Munich sign Manuel Neuer in 2011?

7) José Luis Chilavert, maverick goalscoring goalkeeper, played for which national team?

8) Which of these goalkeepers did not score a Premier League goal in their career: Peter Schmeichel, Tim Howard, Paul Robinson, Rob Green

9) Which goalie saved the crucial penalty against England at Euro 2004, after removing his keeping gloves?

10) Which two goalkeepers were involved when Louis van Gaal substituted one for the other for a penalty shootout at the 2014 World Cup?

Answers on page 309

Missing letters

1) S____ A____ scored the title-winning goal for M____ C____ in 2012

2) R____ M____ won the first E____ C____

3) J____ K____ has won league titles in E____ and G____

4) B____ C____ managed N____ F____ for 18 years

5) L____ M____ won the B____ d'____ in 2018

6) W____ H____ signed C____ T____ and J____ M____ in 2006

7) F____ T____ played 786 times for R____

8) O____ H____ managed B____ M____ and B____ D____

9) P____ J____-____ played 100 times for S____ K____

10) E____ t____ H____ was S____ M____'s assistant at FC T____

Answers on page 310

THE TOTALLY FOOTBALL BOOK

World Cup finals

1) Who did Uruguay beat in the final of the first World Cup in 1930?

2) Why was the final match of the 1950 World Cup between Uruguay and Brazil not technically 'the final'?

3) Which player, who would later go on to lead Brazil to two finals as a manager, scored for them in the 1958 final?

4) Geoff Hurst scored a hat-trick in the 1966 final, but who got England's other goal?

5) In which stadium was the 1982 final held?

6) Which three players missed penalties for Italy in the 1994 final shootout?

7) Who was originally named on the team sheet to play up front for Brazil in the 1998 final, until Ronaldo was deemed fit to start?

8) In 2014, Mario Götze was the first player since Rudi Völler in the 1986 final to do what?

9) What did Mario Mandžukić become the first to do in the 2018 final?

10) What do the 1934, 1966, 1978, 2010 and 2014 finals have in common?

Answers on page 311

Career paths

Which players do these career paths belong to – permanent clubs only, all players made their debuts after 1990 but have all retired.

1) Piacenza, Parma, Atalanta, Juventus, Milan

2) Crewe Alexandra, Liverpool, Charlton, Tottenham, Fulham, Blackburn

3) Metz, Marseille, Arsenal, Villarreal, Aston Villa, FC Goa

4) Chemnitzer FC, Kaiserslautern, Bayer Leverkusen, Bayern Munich, Chelsea, Bayer Leverkusen

5) Grêmio, PSG, Barcelona, Milan, Flamengo, Atlético Mineiro, Querétaro, Fluminense

6) Blackburn, Newcastle, Manchester City, Aston Villa, Stoke City

7) Norwich, Blackburn, Chelsea, Celtic, Birmingham, Aston Villa

8) Marsonia, NK Zagreb, Dinamo Zagreb, Wolfsburg, Bayern Munich, Atlético Madrid, Juventus, Al-Duhail, Milan

9) Marseille, Arsenal, Manchester City, Antalyaspor, West Ham, Anderlecht

10) Ajax, Real Madrid, Inter, Galatasaray, Nice, Al-Gharafa

Answers on page 312

European Championships

1) Who won the first ever European Championships, in 1960?

2) Which two countries have won the Euros the most times, with three each?

3) Which was the first tournament to feature a classic 'finals' format of group stages followed by knockouts all held at the same time?

4) What was notable about the winning penalty in the Euro '76 final shootout?

5) Who finished top scorer in Euro '88?

6) England were famously knocked out in the first round of Euro '92, but which other 'big' team, a former European champion, was also knocked out in that group?

7) Who scored France's 94th minute equaliser in the final of Euro 2000?

8) Who was the Spain manager when they won Euro 2008?

9) Eder scored the winning goal for Portugal in the Euro 2016 final: which Premier League team was he contracted to in the previous season?

10) Which English players scored their penalties in the Euro 2020 final shootout?

Answers on page 313

Squad numbers

1) Which number did Paul Gascoigne wear at the 1990 World Cup?

2) Which number is traditionally worn by left-backs in Brazil?

3) Thierry Henry famously wore 14 for Arsenal and Barcelona, but which number did he typically wear with France?

4) Which number did goalkeeper Rui Patrício wear while at Wolves?

5) Who wore No. 5 for Liverpool when they won the 2005 Champions League?

6) To which Premier League great does this sequence of squad numbers belong: 24, 22, 18, 22?

7) Gigi Buffon chose to wear 88 on his shirt while at Parma but had to change it: why?

8) How were the squad numbers for Argentina's 1978 World Cup winning squad chosen, leaving midfielder Ossie Ardiles wearing No.2, defender Luis Galván with 7 and Ricky Villa wearing 22?

9) When Cristiano Ronaldo joined Real Madrid he couldn't wear his favoured No.7 because Raúl had it: what number did he wear in his first season in Spain?

10) Which squad number links the following players: Michael Ballack, Park Ji-sung, Alessandro Nesta, Thomas Müller

Answers on page 314

2021-22 in the Premier League

1) Who were the only team to do the double over Manchester City?

2) Who did Cristiano Ronaldo make his second debut for Manchester United against?

3) What was the score in both league games between Manchester City and Liverpool?

4) A consortium led by Serbian media mogul Dragan Šolak completed their takeover of which club in January?

5) Against which team did Steven Bergwijn score in the 95th and 97th minutes to earn Spurs a comeback 3-2 win in January?

6) Who mocked Arsenal for celebrating 'like they won the league' after their 1-0 victory over Aston Villa in March?

7) Manchester United finished the season with goal difference of zero: when was the last time they didn't have a positive goal difference?

8) Which two players shared the Premier League Golden Boot?

9) How many points separated Manchester City and Liverpool from the start of the 2018-19 season to the end of the 2021-22 season?

10) Ten managers lost their jobs this season: name as many as you can.

Answers on page 315

2021-22 in the EFL

1) Who was sacked as Nottingham Forest manager in September, after they won just one point from seven games?

2) Which Bournemouth player was diagnosed with Hodgkin's lymphoma early in the season? He later announced that he was in remission after treatment.

3) Fulham beat three teams 7-0 this season: name any of them.

4) Which Championship club signed Andy Carroll in January?

5) What is the name of the Nottingham Forest goalkeeper that saved three Sheffield United penalties to beat them in their play-off semi-final?

6) Henri Lansbury, Cameron Jerome and Robert Snodgrass all played for which Championship club, who reached playoffs?

7) Which former Celtic hero was appointed as Fleetwood Town manager in May?

8) Who were the two losing semi-finalists in the Championship play-offs?

9) Which Wycombe player made the final appearance of his professional career, aged 40, in the League One play-off final?

10) Nottingham Forest won the Championship play-off final — when was the last time they played in the Premier League?

Answers on page 316

2021-22 in Women's football

1) Which US international did Arsenal sign, only for her to leave the club before the end of the season?

2) Who became England's record goalscorer when she scored a hat-trick against Latvia in January?

3) Who won the Ballon d'Or in November?

4) Who retired in August after a career in which she won 316 caps, scored 134 goals for her country, won two World Cups and two Olympic gold medals?

5) Why was PSG midfielder Kheira Hamraoui in the news in November?

6) Why was the FA Cup final played between Arsenal and Chelsea in December unusual?

7) What did Ada Hegerberg do for the first time in five years, in March?

8) What was the score in the Champions League Clasico, as Barcelona faced Real Madrid in front of a record 91,553 crowd in March?

9) How many Champions League titles had Lyon won when they defeated Barcelona in the final in Turin?

10) Georgia Stanway left Manchester City at the end of the season to join which European side?

Answers on page 317

2021-22 in European football

1) Barcelona condemned 'violent and disdainful acts' against their manager Ronald Koeman following their 2-1 defeat to Real Madrid in October: who did they condemn?

2) What happened two days after that?

3) Why was Lyon's game against Marseille abandoned in November?

4) Why was Christian Eriksen forced to cancel his Inter contract in December?

5) From which club did Juventus sign Dušan Vlahović in January?

6) Which club won the Turkish Süper Lig, their first title in 38 years?

7) Union Saint-Gilloise finished top of the Belgian league in the regular season: which English club are they associated with?

8) Borussia Dortmund sacked their manager immediately after the end of the season: name that manager.

9) Milan won Serie A with a Frenchman in goal for most of the season: name him.

10) Which former Premier League player was Ajax's top-scorer as they won the Eredivisie?

Answers on page 318

2021-22 in European trophies

1) Who beat Roma 6-1 in the early stages of the Europa Conference league, but were later knocked out of the competition by José Mourinho's side?

2) Which German giant did Rangers beat in the first knockout round of their Europa League campaign in February?

3) What was the name of the Moldovan minnows that beat Real Madrid in the Champions League group stage?

4) Who missed the crucial penalty when Rangers lost to Eintracht Frankfurt in the final?

5) Who scored a hat-trick for Real Madrid as they dramatically turned their Champions League tie against PSG around?

6) Which team knocked Manchester United out of the Champions League?

7) Which side knocked Juventus and Bayern Munich out of the Champions League?

8) Kevin Trapp was in goal for Eintracht Frankfurt when they knocked Barcelona out of the Europa League in April. What was notable about his previous appearance at the Camp Nou?

9) Where was the Europa Conference League final held, between Roma and Feyenoord?

10) Real Madrid's Champions League victory was their fifth since 2014: which three players started all five finals?

Answers on page 319

2021-22 in international football

1) Who beat Italy in their World Cup qualifying play-off?

2) Who did Portugal beat in their play-off?

3) Why was the Brazil v Argentina World Cup qualifier interrupted in September?

4) Cristiano Ronaldo became the highest scorer in men's international football history in September 2021 when he scored his 111th goal for Portugal: whose record did he break?

5) Which Premier League goalkeeper was the hero for Argentina as they won the 2021 Copa America?

6) Why was England's World Cup qualifier against Andorra in October briefly in doubt?

7) Who scored the winner for France as they beat Spain in the Nations League final in October?

8) Who finished top scorer in the Africa Cup of Nations?

9) Who scored the decisive penalty for Senegal as they beat Egypt in the Afcon final?

10) Which country sealed a spot at their first World Cup since 1986 when they beat Jamaica 4-0 in March?

Answers on page 320

2021-22 in trivia

1) What was unusual about the goalkeeper who started Comoros's Africa Cup of Nations quarter-final against Cameroon?

2) Name the two Hollywood actors who bought National League side Wrexham in October.

3) Manchester City suspended a partnership with cryptocurrency firm 3Key in November: was this because a) the firm was owned by Sheikh Mansour and it was deemed a conflict of interest, b) the firm went out of business or c) doubts emerged over whether the firm actually existed?

4) Which League One side knocked Newcastle out of the FA Cup in January?

5) What did referee Janny Sikazwe do to provoke baffled reactions at the end of the Mali v Tunisia match in the Africa Cup of Nations?

6) Why did Virgil van Dijk give Kepa Arrizabalaga a good hard stare after scoring a penalty past him in the Carabao Cup final shootout?

7) Who missed the decisive penalty to give Liverpool the win in that final?

8) Why were the Egypt players distracted during the penalty shootout in their World Cup qualifying play-off against Senegal?

9) Which Premier League team named a starting XI with 1-11 squad numbers, against Liverpool in August?

10) Which very expensive striker had just seven touches in 90 minutes during a game against Crystal Palace in February?

Answers on page 321

2021-22 in transfers

1) Which player, who shortly afterwards moved to Serie A on loan, tweeted in August: 'All I want to do is go where I'm wanted and where I'm going to play @Arsenal.'

2) For which Qatari team did James Rodríguez sign in September?

3) From which Italian team did Arsenal sign Takehiro Tomiyasu in August?

4) Chelsea sold Tammy Abraham to Roma after they bought Romelu Lukaku, but who did Inter sign from Roma to replace Lukaku?

5) Who did Manchester City sell to Barcelona in January?

6) Who was Newcastle's first purchase after they were taken over by the Saudi Arabian Investment Fund?

7) Which Spanish club did Anthony Martial join on loan in January?

8) In January Aston Villa signed Lucas Digne from Everton, but who did Everton sign from Aston Villa?

9) Philippe Coutinho joined Aston Villa on loan from Barcelona. Where else had Coutinho played on loan since moving to Barca from Liverpool in 2018?

10) Name the young forward that Manchester City signed from River Plate in January, immediately loaning him back to the Argentinean club.

Answers on page 322

2021-22 in managers

1) Name the three men who managed Watford this season, in the correct order.

2) Xavi took over as Barcelona manager in November: which Qatari team did he move from?

3) A 4-1 defeat to which side was the final straw for Manchester United before they sacked Ole Gunnar Solskjær?

4) Who took charge of United after Solskjær was sacked but before Ralf Rangnick was appointed until the end of the season?

5) And at which club was Rangnick director of football before joining United?

6) Which manager, upon his appointment, described his new club as calling like 'a siren song', presenting the image of them as a mermaid tempting him to be dashed on the rocks?

7) Who was sacked by West Brom in February, replaced by Steve Bruce?

8) Who was the manager that led Senegal to the Africa Cup of Nations title?

9) What links Erik ten Hag and the man who Ajax chose to replace him, Alfred Schreuder (apart from the fact they're both bald)?

10) Neil Warnock announced his retirement in April. He famously won eight promotions during his managerial career, but with which club was his most recent promotion?

Answers on page 323

2021-22 in memoriam

1) Jimmy Greaves passed away in September — which of these London clubs did he NOT play for: Chelsea, West Ham, Fulham, Tottenham?

2) Roger Hunt also died in September. He held the Liverpool all-time scoring record until 1993 — who broke it?

3) Ron Flowers passed away in November. He was a member of England's 1966 World Cup winning squad, but for which club did he play the majority of his career?

4) Real Madrid legend Paco Gento died in January. How many times did he win the European Cup with them?

5) Freddy Rincón passed away in April. Which Spanish club did he play for in the 1990s?

6) Agent Mino Raiola died in April. His first ever deal was reportedly to take a Dutch player from Serie A to Nottingham Forest — which player?

7) German great Gerd Müller passed away in August. He held the record for most goals at World Cups (14) for 32 years — who broke it in 2006?

8) Frank O'Farrell passed away in March. He's most widely known for succeeding Matt Busby at Manchester United, but which Second Division team did he take to the FA Cup final in 1969?

9) Walter Smith died in October. How many league titles did he win over two stints as Rangers manager?

10) The manager who signed Henrik Larsson for Celtic passed away in January. Who was that manager?

Answers on page 324

THE ANSWERS

Champions League Finals

1) Marseille

2) Nicolas Anelka

3) Mario Basler

4) Karl-Heinz Riedle

5) Andriy Shevchenko

6) They were contested by clubs from the same country

7) They were contested between the same teams

8) Paulo Ferreira, Ricardo Carvalho, Maniche, Deco. Half a point for José Bosingwa, who was an unused substitute

9) Steve McManaman — for Real Madrid in 2000

10) Juventus

Missing clubs

1) Leeds United

2) AC Milan

3) Nagoya Grampus Eight

4) Aston Villa

5) Wigan Athletic

6) Inter

7) Benfica

8) Manchester City

9) Bournemouth

10) Fulham

Golden Boots

1) Thierry Henry

2) Chris Sutton, Dion Dublin and Michael Owen

3) Mo Salah, Sadio Mané and Pierre-Emerick Aubameyang

4) Gary Lineker (1986) and Harry Kane (2018)

5) Teddy Sheringham

6) Eusébio

7) Mário Jardel

8) 13

9) Gerd Müller (1970), Miroslav Klose (2006) and Thomas Müller (2010)

10) They all won it with the same amount of goals — six

Managers

1) Franz Beckenbauer and Mário Zagallo

2) 27

3) Benfica

4) Mainz and Borussia Dortmund

5) They have all managed both Inter and AC Milan

6) Crystal Palace

7) Mexico, Ivory Coast or the Philippines

8) Won the European Cup/Champions League as a player and a manager

9) Won the English league title as a manager having previously won it as a player

10) Arsène Wenger

Euro '96

1) The Netherlands

2) Switzerland

3) It meant they qualified for the knockout phase on goals scored, ahead of Scotland

4) Portugal

5) Highbury

6) France

7) Paul Ince

8) Oliver Bierhoff

9) Alan Shearer

10) Matthias Sammer

English clubs in Europe

1) Tottenham — the 1963 Cup Winners' Cup

2) Manchester United in 1956-57

3) Tottenham

4) Malmö and Hamburg

5) Norwich City in 1993

6) Galatasaray

7) Wigan Athletic

8) Liverpool and Chelsea

9) Manchester United — the 1991 Cup Winners' Cup

10) The Estádio do Dragão in Porto — they're the stadia where English teams have won the Champions League.

Italia '90

1) François Oman-Biyik

2) David O'Leary

3) Colombia

4) Belgium

5) The Stadio delle Alpi in Turin

6) Rudi Völler

7) Get sent off in a World Cup final

8) Robert Prosinečki

9) Juventus

10) Carlo Ancelotti and Roberto Mancini

Who am I?

1) Vincent Kompany

2) Lothar Matthäus

3) Ruud van Nistelrooy

4) Leonardo Bonucci

5) Hernán Crespo

6) Ricardo Carvalho

7) Emmanuel Petit

8) Bastian Schweinsteiger

9) Xabi Alonso

10) Ashley Cole

Missing managers

1) Roberto Di Matteo

2) André Villas-Boas

3) Rafa Benítez

4) Martin O'Neill

5) Manuel Pellegrini

6) Neil Lennon

7) Frank de Boer

8) Sam Allardyce

9) Giovanni Trapattoni

10) Ronald Koeman

Stadia

1) Bramall Lane

2) Anfield

3) They are the stadia where the hosts have won the World Cup

4) Arsenal

5) The Maracana in Rio De Janeiro — the final match of the 1950 World Cup

6) Sampdoria and Genoa

7) The Gazprom Arena in St Petersburg

8) Villarreal

9) 2007

10) Dens Park and Tannadice Park

Goalkeepers

1) The Ricardo Zamora Trophy

2) Lev Yashin, in 1963

3) Shouting at his defenders

4) They all captained their countries to win the World Cup

5) £32 million

6) Schalke 04

7) Paraguay

8) Rob Green

9) Ricardo

10) Jasper Cillessen and Tim Krul

Missing letters

1) Sergio Agüero scored the title-winning goal for Manchester City in 2012

2) Real Madrid won the first European Cup

3) Jürgen Klopp has won league titles in England and Germany

4) Brian Clough managed Nottingham Forest for 18 years

5) Luka Modrić won the Ballon d'Or in 2018

6) West Ham signed Carlos Tevez and Javier Mascherano in 2006

7) Francesco Totti played 786 times for Roma

8) Ottmar Hitzfeld managed Bayern Munich and Borussia Dortmund

9) Park Ji-sung played 100 times for South Korea

10) Erik ten Hag was Steve McClaren's assistant at FC Twente

World Cup finals

1) Argentina

2) The winner that year was decided by a four-team group: it just happened that the last match was between the two teams that could win it

3) Mário Zagallo

4) Martin Peters

5) The Santiago Bernabéu, Madrid

6) Franco Baresi, Daniele Massaro, Roberto Baggio

7) Edmundo

8) Score after coming on as a substitute

9) Score a goal and an own goal

10) They were all decided in extra time

Career paths

1) Filippo Inzaghi

2) Danny Murphy

3) Robert Pires

4) Michael Ballack

5) Ronaldinho

6) Shay Given

7) Chris Sutton

8) Mario Mandžukić

9) Samir Nasri

10) Wesley Sneijder

European Championships

1) USSR

2) Germany and Spain

3) 1980 in Italy

4) Antonín Panenka scored his famous chip and thus invented a style of penalty

5) Marco van Basten

6) France

7) Sylvain Wiltord

8) Luis Aragonés

9) Swansea City

10) Harry Kane and Harry Maguire

Squad numbers

1) 19

2) 6

3) 12

4) 11

5) Milan Baroš

6) Paul Scholes

7) It's a number associated with Nazis and the far right

8) They were allocated by alphabetical order

9) 9

10) 13

2021-22 in the Premier League

1) Tottenham

2) Newcastle

3) 2-2

4) Southampton

5) Leicester

6) Ashley Young

7) 1989-90

8) Son Heung-min and Mo Salah

9) One

10) Xisco Muñoz, Steve Bruce, Nuno Espírito Santo, Daniel Farke, Dean Smith, Ole Gunnar Solskjær, Rafa Benítez, Claudio Ranieri, Marcelo Bielsa, Sean Dyche

2021-22 in the EFL

1) Chris Hughton

2) David Brooks

3) Blackburn Rovers, Reading and Luton Town

4) West Brom

5) Brice Samba

6) Luton Town

7) Scott Brown

8) Luton Town and Sheffield United

9) Adebayo Akinfenwa

10) 1999

2021-22 in Women's football

1) Tobin Heath

2) Ellen White

3) Alexia Putellas

4) Carli Lloyd

5) She was dragged out of her car and attacked by two masked men after a team meal.

6) It was the 2020-21 final, delayed due to COVID-19

7) Play for Norway

8) 5-2 to Barca

9) Eight

10) Bayern Munich

2021-22 in European football

1) A group of Barcelona fans who blocked Koeman's car from leaving the Camp Nou

2) Barcelona sacked Koeman after a 1-0 loss to Rayo Vallecano

3) Crowd trouble saw L'OM's Dimitri Payet struck by a bottle

4) Italian regulations prevent sportspeople playing with defibrillators fitted, as Eriksen did after his cardiac arrest during Euro 2020

5) Fiorentina

6) Trabzonspor

7) Brighton & Hove Albion

8) Marco Rose

9) Mike Maignan

10) Sébastien Haller

2021-22 in European trophies

1) Bodø/Glimt

2) Borussia Dortmund

3) FC Sheriff Tiraspol

4) Aaron Ramsey

5) Karim Benzema

6) Atlético Madrid

7) Villarreal

8) He was in goal for PSG in the infamous 'remontada' game when Barca scored three times after the 88th minute to win in 2017

9) Tirana, Albania

10) Luka Modrić, Karim Benzema and Dani Carvajal

2021-22 in international football

1) North Macedonia

2) Turkey

3) Officials from the Brazilian health authority arrived at the stadium during the game, accusing four Argentinean players of breaking COVID-19 regulations

4) Ali Daei of Iran

5) Emi Martínez

6) There was a fire at the stadium on the day before the game

7) Kylian Mbappé

8) Vincent Aboubakar

9) Sadio Mané

10) Canada

2021-22 in trivia

1) He was an outfield player forced to play there after their three specialist keepers were ruled out

2) Ryan Reynolds and Rob McElhenney

3) c) Doubts emerged over whether the firm actually existed

4) Cambridge United

5) He blew for full-time after 86, then 89 minutes

6) Kepa had moved to his right in an attempt at mind games — Van Dijk put his penalty to that side anyway

7) Kepa Arrizabalaga

8) Fans in the crowd were shining laser pens in their faces

9) Burnley

10) Romelu Lukaku

2021-22 in transfers

1) Ainsley Maitland-Niles

2) Al-Rayyan

3) Bologna

4) Edin Džeko

5) Ferran Torres

6) Kieran Trippier

7) Sevilla

8) Anwar El Ghazi

9) Bayern Munich

10) Julián Álvarez

2021-22 in managers

1) Xisco Muñoz, Claudio Ranieri, Roy Hodgson

2) Al-Sadd

3) Watford

4) Michael Carrick

5) Lokomotiv Moscow

6) Roy Hodgson at Watford

7) Valérien Ismaël

8) Aliou Cissé

9) They were both assistant to Steve McClaren at FC Twente

10) Cardiff, in 2018

2021-22 in memoriam

1) Fulham

2) Ian Rush

3) Wolverhampton Wanderers

4) Six

5) Real Madrid

6) Bryan Roy

7) Ronaldo

8) Leicester City

9) 10

10) Wim Jansen

THE TOTALLY
FOOTBALL
BOOK

On This Day

**Every day is an anniversary of something in football:
from the biggest events in the history of the game, the
most extraordinary feats, great victories and calamitous
defeats, through to the time a referee kicked a player
and the time a manager head-butted a player . . .**

January 1

Stanley Matthews became the first footballer to be knighted, in 1965: Alf Ramsey would be given the same award two years later. In 1997, Bryan Robson appeared in his last game as a player, for Middlesbrough, where he had been player-manager since 1994.

January 2

1971 saw tragedy at Ibrox, when 66 people died in a crush during an Old Firm game, the number of spectators trying to exit the ground via Staircase 13 causing barriers to collapse. In 2015, Steve Gerrard announced he would leave Liverpool at the end of the season, for LA Galaxy.

January 3

BBC Radio's Sports Report, complete with the iconic theme tune and James Alexander Gordon reading the classified football results, was broadcast for the first time in 1948. In 2010, Manchester United were knocked out of the FA Cup by rivals and League One side Leeds United.

January 4

A nadir of the pre-VAR/goal-line technology days in 2005, as a Pedro Mendes shot for Portsmouth was fumbled over the line by Manchester United's Roy Carroll, but the goal wasn't given. 1994 saw a Premier League classic, when Liverpool came from three down to draw 3-3 with United.

January 5

Roy Hodgson took charge of the last game of his disastrous spell in charge of Liverpool in 2011, a dispiriting 3-1 defeat to Blackburn leaving them only four points off the relegation zone. In

1995, Leeds United agreed a deal to sign Tony Yeboah from Eintracht Frankfurt for £3.4 million.

January 6
Manchester United's ill-conceived trip to the Club World Championship in 2000, which had seen them pull out of the FA Cup, reached something of a low as David Beckham was sent off against Mexican side Necaxa. In 2012, Thierry Henry rejoined Arsenal, on loan from New York Red Bulls.

January 7
One of the great FA Cup giant-killings occurred in 1989, as Coventry City were beaten 2-1 by non-League side Sutton United, only two years after winning the tournament. Mark Bosnich was sacked by Chelsea in 2003, after he tested positive for cocaine.

January 8
Kevin Keegan announced his resignation as Newcastle United manager in 1997, just days after they had beaten Tottenham 7-1. Three of the Togo national team were killed after they were attacked by terrorists as they travelled to the 2010 Africa Cup of Nations in Angola.

January 9
Sven-Göran Eriksson resigned as Lazio manager in 2001, in order to take the England job. He was due to make the move in the summer, but Lazio's form collapsed so he left early. 2009 saw one of Alex Ferguson's 'mind games' pay off as Rafa Benítez delivered his 'facts' press conference.

January 10
Manchester United broke the British transfer record in 1995, when they signed Andy Cole from Newcastle for £7 million. It was a good date for United transfers: in 2006 they signed Patrice

Evra from Monaco. In 1996, Terry Venables announced he would step down as England manager after Euro 96.

January 11

David Beckham announced he would be leaving Real Madrid for LA Galaxy in 2007. Chelsea caused some consternation in 2004 when they faced Charlton on a pitch that appeared to be almost entirely sand. In 2008, they signed Nicolas Anelka from Bolton for £15 million.

January 12

Cristiano Ronaldo became the first Premier League player to be voted FIFA World Player of the Year in 2009. Chelsea signed one of the previous players to hold that title, as George Weah joined them from Milan in 2000: he celebrated by scoring on his debut that night against Spurs.

January 13

David Seaman announced his retirement in 2004, only a few months after signing for Manchester City, because of a persistent shoulder injury. In 1994, Arsène Wenger gave a young Thierry Henry his first senior contract, at Monaco. Aston Villa signed Juan Pablo Ángel in 2001.

January 14

In 1969 Matt Busby announced he would retire as Manchester United manager at the end of the season. There was an extraordinary incident in 2018 in France, as referee Tony Chapron kicked Diego Carlos of Nantes, then sent him off, after an accidental collision in a game against PSG.

January 15

In 2000, Ipswich defender Gary Croft played against Swindon Town while wearing an electronic ankle tag — he had been released from prison for driving while disqualified. In 2006, Sven-Göran Eriksson was stung by the 'Fake Sheikh' – also known as *News of the World* journalist Mazher Mahmood.

January 16
Kevin Keegan made a dramatic return as Newcastle manager in 2008, 11 years after resigning. In 2001, Alex Ferguson announced that he would be retiring when his contract ended at the conclusion of the following season, but ultimately changed his mind.

January 17
1998 saw one of the Premier League's more memorable celebrations, as Temuri Ketsbaia marked his goal for Newcastle against Bolton by removing his shirt, kicking the advertising boards and attempting to remove his boots.

January 18
In 1961, the maximum wage of £20 a week (£17 in the summer) was abolished: Johnny Haynes would later become the first £100-a-week footballer. David Sullivan and David Gold took over West Ham in 2010. Southampton appointed Mauricio Pochettino as manager in 2013.

January 19
Kaká turned down the opportunity to sign for Manchester City in 2009, with chief executive Garry Cook famously later saying the Brazilian's club Milan had 'bottled' the transfer. Chelsea pulled off a more successful deal in 2004, agreeing a fee with Rennes for goalkeeper Petr Čech.

January 20
Paolo Maldini made his Milan debut in 1985, aged just 16. He would go on to play for the club for another 24 years, winning

seven Serie A titles and five European Cups. In 2006 another 16-year-old, Theo Walcott, signed for Arsenal from Southampton for an initial £5 million, rising to £12 million.

January 21

In 2005 Ken Bates, using some of the proceeds from selling Chelsea to Roman Abramovich took over Leeds United. Peter Shilton played the 1,005th and final match of his Football League career in 1997, for Leyton Orient against Wigan. Emiliano Sala tragically died in a plane crash in 2019.

January 22

A First Division match between Arsenal and Sheffield United became the first English football fixture to be broadcast on the radio in 1927. In 2002, Manchester United signed Diego Forlán. 2018 saw the inauguration of former Milan great George Weah as the new president of Liberia.

January 23

West Ham's Jermain Defoe set what was then a post-war goalscoring record in 2001 when he found the net in 10 consecutive games while on loan at Bournemouth. In 2006, Sven-Göran Eriksson announced that he would step down as England manager after that year's World Cup.

January 24

In 1999, Ole Gunnar Solskjær scored his second-most dramatic late goal for Manchester United, as he netted an injury-time winner against Liverpool in the FA Cup third round. In 1996, Newcastle agreed the transfer that some believed scuppered their title bid: Faustino Asprilla, from Parma.

January 25

Eric Cantona 'scissor kung-fu kicked' Crystal Palace fan Matthew Simmons – who claimed he had merely shouted 'it's an early bath for you Mr Cantona!' – after being sent off at Selhurst Park in 1995. In 1997, Trevor Sinclair scored his famous bicycle kick for QPR against Barnsley.

January 26

In a Setubal hospital in 1963, José Mourinho came kicking and screaming – presumably literally – into the world. It was also the birthday of Tottenham's great manager Bill Nicholson, in 1919. 1993 saw the lowest-attended Premier League game, just 3,039 watching Wimbledon v Everton.

January 27

A spicy 2002 FA Cup tie between Arsenal and Liverpool saw three players sent off, including Jamie Carragher who was hit by a coin but threw it back into the crowd. In 2006, Robbie Fowler re-signed for Liverpool, from Manchester City. West Ham signed Paolo Di Canio in 1999.

January 28

In 1961, Denis Law scored six goals for Manchester City against Luton, but still lost the tie: the game was abandoned due to a waterlogged pitch, and Luton won the re-staged game. In 1994 Graeme Souness resigned as Liverpool manager, and Terry Venables was given the England job.

January 29

Steve McManaman became the first high-profile English player to take advantage of the Bosman ruling, as he agreed a deal to leave Liverpool for Real Madrid in 1999. Chelsea signed Scott Parker for £10 million in 2004. In 2014, Yohan Cabaye left Newcastle for PSG.

January 30

England manager Glenn Hoddle gave an interview to *The Times* in 1999 in which he suggested disabled people were paying for sins in a previous life. He was eventually sacked. In 2008 Cristiano Ronaldo scored a famous free kick against Portsmouth, leaving David James rooted.

January 31

In 2011, one of the more dramatic transfer deadline days saw Chelsea pay £50 million for Fernando Torres, with Liverpool replacing him by signing Andy Carroll from Newcastle for £35 million. In 1994, Roy Evans was appointed Liverpool manager, replacing Graeme Souness.

February 1

Roy Keane and Patrick Vieira squared up in the tunnel before Manchester United's 4-2 win at Arsenal in 2005. Sunderland scored three own goals in a 3-1 loss to Charlton in 2003. In 2006 Sol Campbell left Highbury in the middle of an error-strewn performance for Arsenal against West Ham.

February 2

In 1991 Arsenal lost to Chelsea, their only league defeat on their way to the title. In 2009 Robbie Keane returned to Tottenham from Liverpool, having only moved to Anfield six months earlier. Graeme Souness was sacked as Newcastle manager in 2006, replaced by Glenn Roeder.

February 3

The weather in England was so bad in 1940 that only two of 56 matches were able to go ahead, one of which ended Plymouth 10 Bristol City 3. In 1992, Kevin Keegan was appointed Newcastle manager for the first time. Arsenal signed Andrey Arshavin in 2009, from Zenit St Petersburg.

February 4

Alan Shearer became Newcastle's leading goalscorer in 2006: his strike against Portsmouth was his 201st, overtaking Jackie Milburn. In 2004 10-man Manchester City came back from 3-0 down to beat Spurs in the FA Cup. Mick McCarthy was appointed Ireland manager in 1996.

February 5

John Terry was stripped of the England captaincy in 2010, after reports he had an affair with Wayne Bridge's ex-partner, Vanessa Perroncel. Newcastle came back from 4-0 down to draw 4-4 with Arsenal, in 2011. Hereford beat Newcastle to pull off one of the great FA Cup upsets in 1972.

February 6

In 1958, 23 people, including eight members of the Manchester United side, died as their plane crashed at Munich airport. Ole Gunnar Solskjær scored four goals as a substitute in United's 8-1 win over Nottingham Forest in 1999. George Gillett and Tom Hicks bought Liverpool in 2007.

February 7

A UEFA summit in 1996 decided that two teams would be able to qualify for the Champions League from each country. George Best scored six for Manchester United against Northampton Town in 1970. The 39th game, a Premier League idea to introduce an extra fixture, was proposed in 2008.

February 8

Fabio Capello resigned as England manager in 2012, after the FA took the captaincy away from John Terry following allegations he had racially abused Anton Ferdinand. Inverness Caledonian Thistle beat Celtic in 2000, prompting the headline: 'Super Caley go ballistic Celtic are atrocious.'

February 9

Trevor Francis became Britain's first £1 million footballer when he signed for Nottingham Forest from Birmingham City in 1979. Chelsea sacked Luiz Felipe Scolari in 2009. In 1985, an unexploded World War Two bomb caused Sheffield United v Oldham to be postponed.

February 10

In 1996, Grimsby manager Brian Laws threw a plate of chicken wings at his player Ivano Bonetti's face, breaking his cheekbone. The first Primera Liga game in Spain took place in 1929: Real Madrid beat CD Europa 5-0. West Ham were awarded the Olympic Stadium in 2011.

February 11

Michael Owen made his debut for England in 1998 against Chile, but Marcelo Salas grabbed the headlines, scoring a sensational volley in a 2-0 win. Luis Suárez refused to shake Patrice Evra's hand in 2012, the first time the two had met since Suárez was banned for racially abusing Evra.

February 12

England were beaten in a Wembley World Cup qualifier for the first time in 1997, Italy winning 1-0. Wayne Rooney's England debut was in 2003, against Australia. In 2011, he scored a sensational overhead kick against Manchester City. World Cup winner Gordon Banks died, aged 81, in 2019.

February 13

Arsène Wenger offered to replay Arsenal's FA Cup win over Sheffield United in 1999, after Kanu had intercepted a throw intended to return the ball to the Blades following an injury, setting up Marc Overmars for the winner. In 2002, Youri Djorkaeff signed for Bolton from Kaiserslautern.

February 14

Bob Paisley, the legendary Liverpool manager, died at the age of 77 in 1996. Fulham appointed Felix Magath as their manager in 2014. In 2015, Aston Villa hired Tim Sherwood. Kevin Keegan announced he would leave Newcastle in 1984: he departed his final game, against Liverpool, via helicopter from the centre circle.

February 15

It was the beginning of the end for David Beckham at Manchester United in 2003, after Alex Ferguson cut him over the eyebrows by kicking a boot which hit Beckham in the head. The Premier League's first ever sacking occurred in 1993, when Chelsea dismissed Ian Porterfield.

February 16

Leicester City players were ejected from a resort in La Manga in 2000, after high jinks resulted in Stan Collymore spraying team-mates and other guests with a fire extinguisher. In 1957 Egypt became the first ever Africa Cup of Nations winners after beating Ethiopia 4-0 in the final.

February 17

David Platt scored four as England beat San Marino 6-0 in 1993, in their ultimately doomed World Cup qualifying campaign. Kevin Keegan was appointed England manager, initially for just four games, in 1999. Mike Ashley rebranded St James' Park as the Sports Direct Arena in 2012.

February 18

Edwin van der Sar finally conceded a goal in 2009, as Peter Løvenkrands's strike for Newcastle against Manchester United made it 1,311 minutes without letting one in, a Premier League record at the time. Gary Lineker scored all four as England beat Spain 4-2 in a 1987 friendly.

February 19

Old Trafford staged its first match in 1910, when Manchester United played Liverpool. In 2011 Chelsea were knocked out of the FA Cup by Everton, their first defeat in the competition since March 2008. Alan Shearer made his England debut in 1992, scoring in a 2-0 win over France.

February 20

One of the great FA Cup ties saw Liverpool and Everton draw 4-4 in 1991. In 1995, George Graham was found guilty of accepting improper payments from agent Rune Hauge and was sacked by Arsenal. In 1992, the FA approved the formation of the Premier League.

February 21

In 2004 goalkeeper Brad Friedel scored a 90th minute equaliser for Blackburn versus Charlton, only to concede moments later. In 2007 Liverpool became the first English club to beat Barcelona at the Camp Nou in a Champions League tie. Arsenal and Thierry Henry beat Real Madrid 1-0 in 2006.

February 22

Kenny Dalglish shocked the world by resigning as Liverpool manager in 1991, still deeply affected by the aftermath of the Hillsborough disaster. Arsenal signed Nicolas Anelka from PSG in 1997. In 1956, the first floodlit league game in England took place between Portsmouth and Newcastle.

February 23

In 2017, Claudio Ranieri was sacked by Leicester City, just nine months after leading them to the most unlikely league title win of all time. Stanley Matthews died in 2000 at the age of 85. In 2008, Arsenal's Eduardo suffered a horrific leg break after a late tackle by Birmingham City's Martin Taylor.

February 24

Swansea won their only major trophy, beating Bradford 5-0 in the League Cup final in 2013. Spurs won the same competition, their first trophy in nine years, in 2008. James Hayter scored the quickest hat-trick in Football League history in 2004, bagging three in two minutes 20 seconds.

February 25

Liverpool completed the first leg of their 2001 treble by beating Birmingham City in the League Cup final. A spicy 2007 edition saw three sent off as Chelsea beat Arsenal 2-1. Marcus Rashford made his Manchester United debut in 2016, scoring two past FC Midtjylland in the Europa League.

February 26

Portsmouth became the first Premier League club to enter administration, when they dropped into the financial blackhole in 2010, immediately being docked nine points. Liverpool beat Cardiff on penalties in the 2012 League Cup final. Pat Jennings made his 1,000th appearance in 1983.

February 27

José Mourinho won his first trophy in English football, as Chelsea beat Liverpool to lift the 2005 League Cup. Birmingham City shocked Arsenal to win that same trophy in 2011. In 2010, a Ryan Shawcross challenge seriously broke Aaron Ramsey's leg. Bayern Munich were formed in 1900.

February 28

In 2005 Delia Smith took the microphone at Norwich's game against Manchester City to ask the home fans, 'Where are you? Let's be 'avin' you!' They lost 3-2 and were ultimately relegated. Sven-Göran Eriksson's first game in charge of England in 2001 ended in a 3-0 win over Spain.

February 29

Middlesbrough won the only major trophy in their history as they defeated Bolton in the 2004 League Cup final. Stuart Pearce took charge of his only game as England caretaker manager, after Fabio Capello's resignation in 2012: it ended in a 3-2 defeat to the Netherlands at Wembley.

March 1

Newcastle manager Alan Pardew was sent off for headbutting Hull midfielder David Meyler during their game in 2014. In 2015, Chelsea beat Tottenham in the final of the League Cup, the first trophy of José Mourinho's second spell. Arjen Robben agreed to join Chelsea from PSV in 2004.

March 2

Liverpool beat Manchester United in the final of the 2003 League Cup, with Steven Gerrard and Michael Owen scoring the goals. Dennis Bergkamp scored THAT goal against Newcastle in 2002, when he turned and spun Nikos Dabizas perfectly/flukily, depending on your point of view.

March 3

Chris Armstrong became the first Premier League player to fail a drugs test in 1995 – he tested positive for cannabis. In 1983, Bristol Rovers boss Bobby Gould fined himself £200 for comments to a referee. In 2017 Raymond Kopa, the great France and Real Madrid attacker, died aged 85.

March 4

Manchester United hammered Ipswich Town 9-0 in 1995, with Andy Cole helping himself to five. In 1967, the first League Cup final to be played at Wembley saw Third Division QPR beat holders West Brom 3-2. Chelsea sacked André Villas-Boas in 2012, Roberto Di Matteo his replacement.

March 5

Nani was sent off as Bayern Munich beat Manchester United in 2013, in what would turn out to be Alex Ferguson's last ever Champions League game. In 1993, David Sullivan bought Birmingham City. Kosovo played its first ever official international friendly in 2014, drawing 0-0 with Haiti.

March 6

Dirk Kuyt scored a hat-trick from a cumulative distance of about six yards as Liverpool beat Manchester United 3-1 in 2011. Real Madrid were officially established in 1902. In 2006 Sunderland sacked Mick McCarthy in a season which eventually saw them win just 15 points.

March 7

The 'forgotten five' members of England's 1966 World Cup winning squad – Nobby Stiles, Roger Hunt, Ray Wilson, George Cohen and Alan Ball – were honoured with MBEs. Bobby Moore was transfer-listed by West Ham in 1974.

March 8

The first international game played in England and the second international ever took place in 1873: England beat Scotland 4-2. Ronaldinho scored one of the Champions League's most iconic goals, his toe-punt against Chelsea, in 2005.

March 9

If the world didn't know about José Mourinho before, they did in 2004 when his Porto knocked Manchester United out of the Champions League and he ran down the touchline in celebration. His future club Inter were founded in 1908. Jock Stein was appointed Celtic manager in 1965.

March 10

Third tier Wycombe Wanderers knocked Leicester City out of the FA Cup in 2001, the winner scored by Roy Essandoh, a last-minute replacement striker they had found via Ceefax. David Beckham returned to Manchester United in 2010, playing for Milan in a Champions League tie.

March 11

Large sections of Old Trafford were destroyed by World War II bombs in 1941: the damage was such that Manchester United couldn't play there until 1949. In 2017 Lincoln City became the first non-League team to play in an FA Cup quarter-final since 1914. They lost 5-0 to Arsenal.

March 12

Frank Lampard became the first midfielder to score four in a Premier League game when Chelsea beat Derby 6-1 in 2008. Pelé played in London for the only time in his career, when Santos played a friendly against Fulham in 1973. Mick McCarthy was appointed Sunderland manager in 2003.

March 13

El-Hadji Diouf was banned for two games by UEFA and fined £5,000 by a Glasgow court after he spat at some Celtic fans during their game against Liverpool in the 2003 UEFA Cup. The Premier League and the EFL were suspended in England due to the spread of COVID-19 in 2020.

March 14

Fernando Torres tore Manchester United asunder as title-chasing Liverpool won 4-1 at Old Trafford in 2009. In 1998 another United home defeat saw Marc Overmars give Arsenal a 1-0 win and set them on course to win the league. David Moyes was appointed Everton manager in 2002.

March 15

Liverpool were founded in 1892 when Everton, the original tenants of Anfield, had a disagreement with landlord John Houlding and left for their own stadium across Stanley Park. Third Division Swindon Town caused a huge upset by beating Arsenal in the 1969 League Cup final.

March 16

The Battle of Bramall Lane in 2002 saw three Sheffield United players sent off and two more injured in a hugely bad-tempered game against West Brom: the Baggies were 3-0 up when the final player went off, and the result stood. Tottenham sacked George Graham in 2001.

March 17

Fabrice Muamba suffered a cardiac arrest on the pitch during Bolton's game against Spurs: his heart stopped for 78 minutes before doctors revived him. Don Revie was appointed Leeds manager in 1961. Diego Maradona's time at Napoli ended in 1991 after he tested positive for cocaine.

March 18

Perhaps the finest day in Fulham's history came in 2010, when they came back from 4-1 down on aggregate to beat Juventus 5-4 in the Europa League last 16. Clint Dempsey scored the clinching goal with the most perfect, floating chip imaginable. Ajax was formed in Amsterdam in 1900.

March 19

Five months after undergoing heart surgery, Gérard Houllier returned to the Liverpool dugout for their 2-0 Champions League win over Roma in 2002. Middlesbrough signed Paul Gascoigne from Rangers in 1998. Barnet appointed Martin Allen for the fifth time in 2018.

March 20

The Jules Rimet trophy was stolen from Westminster Central Hall in London in 1966: it was found under a hedge by Pickles the dog seven days later. Lev Yashin, legendary Russian goalkeeper, died in 1990 aged 60. Liverpool's bid to go unbeaten in 1987-88 ended with defeat to Everton after 29 games.

March 21

Vinnie Jones was booked after just three seconds of a game between Chelsea and Sheffield United in 1992. In 1999 Tottenham won the League Cup, beating Leicester 1-0 in the final. Leeds sacked manager Terry Venables in 2003: Peter Reid replaced him and saved them from relegation.

March 22

Steven Gerrard was sent off 38 seconds after coming on in his final ever Liverpool v Manchester United game in 2015. In 1994 United hero Eric Cantona was sent off against Arsenal, his second red card in four days. Wayne Rooney scored for United from the halfway line against West Ham in 2014.

March 23

Newcastle owners Freddie Shepherd and Douglas Hall were caught calling Geordie women 'dogs' and bragging about ripping fans off for replica shirts in 1998. The first official women's football match in England took place in 1895, when a northern XI beat their southern counterparts 7-1.

March 24

Robbie Fowler unsuccessfully tried to persuade referee Gerald Ashby not to award him a penalty for Liverpool against Arsenal in 1997: he missed the spot kick, but Jason McAteer scored the rebound. In the first game played at the rebuilt Wembley in 2007, Italy U21s drew with England 3-3.

March 25

Ian Botham, better known as one of England's greatest cricketers, made his debut in the Football League when he came on for Scunthorpe United against Bournemouth in 1980. Wimbledon won 1-0 at Norwich in 2003: the game was notable because there were just 10 away fans present.

March 26

Paolo Di Canio scored his magnificent volley for West Ham against Wimbledon in 2000: it was voted Premier League goal of the season. David Beckham won his 100th England cap when he played a friendly against France, becoming – at the time – the country's fifth centurion.

March 27

Robbie Fowler was fined by UEFA for showing a message supporting striking Liverpool dockers during a Cup Winners' Cup game against Brann Bergen in 1997. Harry Kane scored 79 seconds into his England debut in 2015. Kevin Keegan managed his first England game in 1999, a 3-1 win over Poland.

March 28

Glenn Hoddle left Southampton in 2001 in order to take over his boyhood club Tottenham. Also in 2001, seven Manchester United players started for England in their World Cup qualifier against Albania: it equalled the record of seven Arsenal players, set in 1934 against Italy.

March 29

Derby County's relegation was confirmed in 2008 with a 2-2 draw against Fulham: it was the earliest a team had ever suffered a Premier League relegation. Sergio Agüero announced he was leaving Manchester City at the end of the season in 2021, after a decade at the club.

March 30

Peter Ridsdale resigned as chairman of Leeds in 2003, with the club in serious financial trouble after his excessive spending on players allowed them to 'live the dream'. Stiliyan Petrov announced he had been diagnosed with leukaemia in 2012 – he later made a full recovery.

March 31

Two months after kung-fu kicking Crystal Palace fan Matthew Simmons, Eric Cantona declared in 1995: 'When the seagulls follow the trawler, it's because they think sardines will be thrown into the sea.' In 2001, David Rocastle died at 33 from non-Hodgkin's lymphoma.

April 1

Alan Shearer took over as Newcastle United manager as they tried to avoid relegation in 2009. Wendy Toms became the first female official to be added to the Football League list in 1995. Also that day, Nottingham Forest beat Sheffield Wednesday 7-1, then the Premier League's record away win.

April 2

Newcastle's Lee Bowyer and Kieron Dyer were sent off for fighting in a game against Aston Villa in 2005. Ken Bates bought Chelsea for £1 in 1982. José Mourinho's 150-game unbeaten home run – stretching back to 2002 at Porto – ended in 2011 when Real Madrid lost to Sporting Gijon.

April 3

Arguably the greatest Premier League game ever took place, when Liverpool beat title-chasing Newcastle 4-3 in 1996. In 1999, Robbie Fowler was in trouble after celebrating a goal by pretending to snort the six-yard line. Sheffield moved to Wembley in 1993: Wednesday beat United in the FA Cup semi-final.

April 4

Duncan Edwards made his debut for Manchester United in 1953. In 1892 West Brom beat Darwen 12-0: with Nottingham Forest's win over Leicester Fosse by the same score in 1909, it's still the biggest English top-flight win ever. Ray Wilkins passed away at the age of 61 in 2018.

April 5

Leeds United fans Kevin Speight and Christopher Loftus were killed in Istanbul before their UEFA Cup semi-final against Galatasaray in 2000. In 2009 Federico Macheda burst onto the scene by scoring a late winner for Manchester United against Aston Villa to keep them in the title race.

April 6

José Mourinho dodged a UEFA ban for Chelsea's 2005 Champions League quarter-final tie against Bayern Munich: he was smuggled into the dressing room in a laundry bin. In 1994 the FA cancelled an England v Germany friendly when they belatedly realised it was scheduled for Hitler's birthday.

April 7

Bayern Munich beat Manchester United on away goals in the 2010 Champions League quarter-final. Ryan Giggs scored what would turn out to be a crucial equaliser in the first leg of United's 1999 Champions League semi-final against Juventus. Paul Gascoigne broke his leg in Lazio training in 1994.

April 8

Coventry City defender David Busst suffered a horrific broken leg against Manchester United in 1996: after 26 operations, the injury ended his career. Manchester City looked to have thrown away the 2012 Premier League title after Mario Balotelli was sent off in their 1-0 defeat at Arsenal.

April 9

Alan Shearer made his full debut for Southampton in 1988, and scored a hat-trick: he remains the youngest to achieve that feat in the top flight. Daniel Amokachi scored twice in Everton's 4-1 win over Spurs in the 1995 FA Cup semi-final, after bringing himself on as substitute.

April 10

Steve Bruce scored a 97th-minute winner as Manchester United beat Sheffield Wednesday to keep them on track for the title in 1993. David Beckham's 2002 World Cup was in doubt after he broke a metatarsal. Mohamed Al-Fayed welcomed Michael Jackson to a Fulham game in 1999.

April 11

Billy Wright became the first ever England player to earn 100 caps after appearing against Scotland in 1959. The 2017 Champions League quarter-final between Borussia Dortmund and Monaco was postponed after the BVB coach was attacked by a bomb en route to the game.

April 12

The first international match at Wembley saw England and Scotland draw 1-1 in 1924. In 1999 Michael Owen suffered the injury that would change his career: he tore one of his right hamstring muscles, which never reattached itself, meaning he was hampered for the rest of his career.

April 13

Chesterfield were denied a place in the 1997 FA Cup final, after officials failed to spot a shot had gone over the line – they drew 3-3 with Middlesbrough, who won the replay. In 2014 Liverpool looked on course for their first title since 1990 after they beat Manchester City 3-2 at Anfield.

April 14

Ryan Giggs scored one of the most iconic goals in FA Cup semi-final history when he danced through the Arsenal defence in 1999. Chelsea and Liverpool shared a madcap 4-4 draw in their Champions League quarter-final second leg in 2009: Chelsea went through, 7-5 on aggregate.

April 15

The lives of 97 Liverpool fans were lost in 1989 after over-crowding and policing errors caused a crush in the Leppings Lane end during their FA Cup semi-final against Nottingham Forest. A 2016 coroner's inquest eventually ruled that the 97 had been unlawfully killed.

April 16

Graeme Souness left Rangers to become Liverpool manager in 1991. Leicester won their first major trophy in 33 years when they beat Middlesbrough in a League Cup final replay in 1997. In 1983 Oxford United owner Robert Maxwell announced plans to merge the club with Reading.

April 17

Alan Shearer played what turned out to be the final match of his career in 2006, scoring in a 4-1 win over Sunderland. In 2011 Arsenal took the lead over Liverpool in the 97th minute, but still ended up not winning, as the visitors equalised with a 111th minute penalty from Dirk Kuyt.

April 18

Steve Morrow scored Arsenal's winner in the 1993 League Cup final against Sheffield Wednesday, but in the post-match celebrations Tony Adams picked him up and dropped him, breaking his arm. In 2021 Europe's biggest clubs announced their intention to form the Super League.

April 19

Bobby Charlton made his England debut in 1958, just two months after the Munich air disaster: he scored the first of his 49 international goals. Liverpool reached the 2001 UEFA Cup final by beating Barcelona in the semi-final at Anfield. José Mourinho was sacked by Tottenham in 2021.

April 20

Arsenal announced that Arsène Wenger would be stepping down as manager in 2018, after 22 years in charge. Oxford United won the only major trophy in their history in 1986, beating QPR to lift the League Cup. Two days after it was announced, the Super League collapsed in 2021.

April 21

A big date for Roy Keane: in 1999 he produced an extraordinary performance to lead Manchester United to the Champions League final, as they beat Juventus in Turin. Two years later, he was sent off for his assault on Alf-Inge Haaland. In 2013, Luis Suárez bit Chelsea's Branislav Ivanović.

April 22

Robin van Persie scored a hat-trick as Manchester United clinched the Premier League title in 2013 by beating Aston Villa. A year earlier they effectively blew their title chances after drawing 4-4 with Everton. In 2004 Ron Atkinson was caught making racist comments about Marcel Desailly.

April 23

Ronaldo scored a sensational hat-trick at Old Trafford as Real Madrid beat Manchester United 6-5 on aggregate in their 2003 Champions League quarter-final. In 2001 Ruud van Nistelrooy, having recovered from a cruciate knee injury a year earlier, finally signed for Manchester United.

April 24

2012 saw Chelsea's extraordinary Champions League semi-final win against Barcelona, Fernando Torres's goal capping a game they'd played over half of with 10 men. In 1996, Graeme Souness enraged half of Istanbul by planting a Galatasaray flag in the centre circle of Fenerbahce's pitch.

April 25

Arsenal were confirmed as Premier League champions in 2004, as they drew 2-2 at Tottenham on their way to completing a season unbeaten. Two years later they reached the Champions League final by beating Villarreal. In 2007, England 1966 World Cup winner Alan Ball died at the age of 61.

April 26

Nottingham Forest announced that Brian Clough would retire at the end of the season in 1993, with the club's relegation imminent. Manchester United came into being when Newton Heath rebranded themselves in 1902. Michael Owen scored his 100th Liverpool goal in 2003.

April 27

Steven Gerrard slipped as Liverpool lost 2-0 to Chelsea in 2014, effectively ending their title hopes. Massimo Maccarone scored an injury-time winner as Middlesbrough came back from 3-0 down on aggregate to beat Steaua Bucharest to reach the 2006 UEFA Cup final.

April 28

2013 saw the saddest game ever, as Reading and QPR drew 0-0, a result that saw both of them relegated. In 1973, Jackie and Bobby Charlton played their final league games for Leeds and Manchester United respectively. Luiz Felipe Scolari turned down the England job in 2006.

April 29

Kevin Keegan declared he would 'love it' if Newcastle beat Manchester United to the title in 1996, responding to Alex Ferguson's suggestion that other teams tried harder against his team than Keegan's. Gary Lineker scored his 48th and final England goal against Russia in Moscow in 1992.

April 30

Chelsea won the first Premier League title under Roman Abramovich in 2005, after they beat Bolton 2-0. Liverpool played their last game in front of the Kop terrace in 1994. Ligue 1 scrapped their season in 2020, in the wake of the COVID-19 pandemic: PSG were named champions.

May 1

Alf Ramsey was sacked as England manager in 1974 after failing to qualify for the World Cup. 38 years later, Roy Hodgson was confirmed as England manager after Fabio Capello's departure. In 2007 Liverpool reached the Champions League final by beating Chelsea in a penalty shootout.

May 2

Leicester City were confirmed as 5,000-1 Premier League champions in 2016 after Tottenham could only draw with Chelsea. Manchester United won their first title in 26 years in 1993. The 'Matthews final', when Stan Matthews inspired Blackpool to beat Bolton in the FA Cup final, took place in 1953.

May 3

Liverpool beat Chelsea in the 2005 Champions League semi-final thanks to Luis Garcia's 'ghost goal', about which José Mourinho is still annoyed. Arsenal won the Premier League in 1998 by beating Everton 4-0, making Arsène Wenger the first manager from outside the UK and Ireland to win the title.

May 4

Arsenal beat Parma in Copenhagen to win the 1994 Cup Winners' Cup. The FA announced the appointment of Steve McClaren as England manager in 2006. In 1949, 18 members of the 'Grande Torino' team that had dominated Italian football died in a plane crash outside Turin.

May 5

Bert Trautmann broke his neck in the 1956 FA Cup final, but played on. Manchester City were relegated in 1996 when they drew with Liverpool: they wrongly thought a point would keep them up. Liverpool threw away a 3-0 lead at Crystal Palace to effectively hand City the title in 2014.

May 6

Tottenham won the 1961 FA Cup final, becoming the first team since 1897 to win the double. Michael Owen scored on his debut in 1997, although Liverpool's 2-1 defeat to Wimbledon saw Manchester United crowned champions. Ryan Giggs played his last ever game in 2014.

May 7

'Lasagnegate': Spurs lost 2-1 at West Ham in 2006 with several players suffering from suspected food poisoning, so Arsenal's win in their last game at Highbury saw them finish fourth. Liverpool produced an astonishing comeback to beat Barcelona in the 2019 Champions League semi-final.

May 8

Sir Alex Ferguson announced his retirement in 2013, after 26 years at Manchester United. In 1999, Jimmy Glass, an on-loan keeper, scored a last-minute goal to keep Carlisle in the Football League. Tottenham came from 3-0 down to beat Ajax in the 2019 Champions League semi-final.

May 9

England played their first ever international at Wembley against non-British or Irish opposition in 1951, beating Argentina 2-1. Chelsea won the league in 2010 by emphatically beating Wigan 8-0. In 1936 Bernard Joy, the last ever amateur to represent England, made his international debut.

May 10

Liverpool beat Everton in the 1986 FA Cup final to seal the double, a week after beating them to the First Division title. Real Zaragoza beat Arsenal in the 1995 Cup Winners' Cup final after Nayim lobbed David Seaman from 50 yards. Chelsea appointed Ruud Gullit as their manager in 1996.

May 11

56 people died after a fire engulfed a stand at Valley Parade during a Bradford City game in 1985. Manchester United beat Liverpool in the 1996 FA Cup final. Chelsea beat Liverpool in 2003 to qualify for the Champions League, without which Roman Abramovich may not have bought them.

May 12

Alan Sunderland scored the winner for Arsenal against Manchester United in one of the most dramatic FA Cup finals in 1979. Blackburn were relegated in 1999, four years after they won the title. Michael Owen scored twice to give Liverpool a 2-1 win over Arsenal in the 2001 FA Cup final.

May 13

Sergio Agüero scored the most dramatic Premier League goal ever as Manchester City won the 2012 Premier League title. Carlos Tevez scored against Manchester United to help West Ham stay up in 2007. Chelsea won the 1998 Cup Winners' Cup, a Gianfranco Zola goal beating Stuttgart.

May 14

Blackburn Rovers won the Premier League title in 1995, despite losing on the final day to Liverpool. Wimbledon won the 1988 FA Cup by beating Liverpool, just 11 years after becoming a Football League club. Tottenham played their final ever game at the old White Hart Lane in 2017.

May 15

Arsenal completed their 'invincible' season in 2004. In 2005 West Brom became the first team who were bottom at Christmas to survive in the Premier League. Spurs became the first English team to win a major European trophy, beating Atlético Madrid 5-1 in the 1963 Cup Winners' Cup final.

May 16

Manchester United won the Premier League in 1999, the first part of the treble. Liverpool completed their own treble in 2001 when they beat Alaves 5-4 in the UEFA Cup final. Sadio Mané scored the quickest ever Premier League hat-trick in 2015, for Southampton against Aston Villa.

May 17

Middlesbrough lost the 1997 FA Cup final to Chelsea, their second cup final loss to add to relegation that season. Arsenal won their first trophy in nine years when they beat Hull in the 2014 FA Cup final. Portsmouth won the 2008 FA Cup final – their first since 1939 – beating Cardiff 1-0.

May 18

Arguably the greatest European Cup final of them all saw Real Madrid beat Eintracht Frankfurt 7-3 in 1960. Eric Cantona announced his retirement, aged just 30, in 1997. Tottenham won the 1991 FA Cup final against Nottingham Forest, but Paul Gascoigne shattered his knee.

May 19

Chelsea beat Bayern Munich on penalties in their own stadium to win the 2012 Champions League. Alex Ferguson took charge of his final ever Manchester United game in 2013, a 5-5 draw with West Brom. Lazio beat Real Mallorca to win the last ever Cup Winners' Cup, in 1999.

May 20

Liverpool beat Everton 3-2 in the 1989 FA Cup final, just five weeks after the Hillsborough disaster. Everton won it in 1995, beating Manchester United 1-0 thanks to a Paul Rideout goal. Bobby Moore made his England debut in 1962: Jimmy Greaves scored a hat-trick in a 4-0 win over Peru.

May 21

Manchester United beat Chelsea in the first ever all-English Champions League final in 2008, Edwin van der Sar the hero in the penalty shootout. Another shootout saw Arsenal win the 2005 FA Cup, Patrick Vieira scoring the winner against Manchester United. FIFA was founded in 1904.

May 22

Manchester United won the second leg of their treble, beating Newcastle 2-0 in the 1999 FA Cup final. They also won in 2004, beating Millwall 3-0. Wembley hosted its first European Cup final as Milan beat Benfica 2-1 in 1963. Chelsea sacked Carlo Ancelotti after a game at Everton in 2011.

May 23

A training-ground row with Mick McCarthy saw Roy Keane banished from the Ireland 2002 World Cup squad. Pippo Inzaghi scored both for Milan as they beat Liverpool in the 2007 Champions League final. England suffered their worst ever defeat in 1954, losing 7-1 to Hungary in Budapest.

May 24

Steve McManaman scored as Real Madrid beat Valencia 3-0 in the 2000 Champions League final. Newcastle were relegated from the Premier League after defeat to Aston Villa in 2009. Steven Gerrard played his last ever game for Liverpool in 2015: he scored as they lost 6-1 to Stoke.

May 25

Liverpool came back from 3-0 down to win the 2005 Champions League final on penalties against Milan. Celtic became the first British team to win the European Cup, when they beat Inter 2-1 in 1967. Stan Mortensen and Tommy Lawton got four each as England beat Portugal 10-0 in 1947.

May 26

Manchester United scored twice in the last few minutes to beat Bayern Munich in the 1999 Champions League final, completing English football's first treble. Aston Villa won the European Cup in 1982, also beating Bayern 1-0 in the final. Gary Lineker made his England debut in 1984.

May 27

Michael Owen scored against Morocco in 1998, making him England's youngest ever scorer. All First Division teams resigned from the Football League in 1992, leading to the formation of the Premier League. Barcelona beat Manchester United in the 2009 Champions League final.

May 28

Nottingham Forest retained the European Cup in 1980, beating Hamburg in the final with John Robertson scoring the only goal. The 'dentist's chair' emerged into the public consciousness, as several England players were pictured on a boozy night out in 1996.

May 29

There was tragedy in Brussels, as 39 Juventus fans were crushed to death in the Heysel Stadium before the 1985 European Cup final against Liverpool. Manchester United became the first ever English team to win the European Cup, beating Benfica 4-1 in the final at Wembley in 1968.

May 30

Nottingham Forest won the European Cup in 1979, beating Malmö 1-0 in Munich. Liverpool won the 1984 edition, beating Roma in their own stadium on penalties. Theo Walcott became England's youngest ever player after making his debut against Hungary in 2006.

May 31

Glenn Hoddle omitted Paul Gascoigne from the 1998 World Cup, a hugely controversial decision at the time. Chelsea signed Andriy Shevchenko for £30 million from Milan in 2006. Alex Ferguson was sacked for the only time in his career, dismissed by St Mirren in 1978.

June 1

England played their first ever game at the newly rebuilt Wembley Stadium in 2007, a 1-1 draw with Brazil that also saw the return to the national team of David Beckham. Martin O'Neill left Leicester to take over at Celtic in 2000. Chelsea appointed Carlo Ancelotti in 2009.

June 2

José Mourinho arrived at Chelsea in 2004. Just four days after being elected for a fifth term in 2015, Sepp Blatter announced he would step down as FIFA president amid corruption allegations. UEFA banned English clubs from European competition after the Heysel disaster in 1985.

June 3

José Mourinho arrived for his second spell as Chelsea manager in 2013, declaring himself to be 'the happy one'. England thrashed Jamaica 6-0 in a pre-2006 World Cup friendly, Peter Crouch scoring a hat-trick and missing a penalty. Rafa Benítez left Liverpool in 2010.

June 4

Chelsea signed Eden Hazard from Lille in 2012, for £32 million. Mark Hughes resigned from Blackburn Rovers in order to take over at Manchester City in 2008. In 1977, Scotland beat England 2-1, after which the Wembley goalposts were broken and the pitch dug up by jubilant fans.

June 5

Alan Mullery became the first ever England player to be sent off, during their 1-0 defeat to Yugoslavia in the 1968 European Championship semi-final. The other semi-final, between Italy and the USSR, was decided by a coin toss. Roberto Martínez took over at Everton in 2013.

June 6

Another England sending off: this time Ray Wilkins against Morocco in 1986, the first man to be sent off for England at a World Cup. Jacques Santini took over as Tottenham manager in 2004: he lasted 13 games. Gareth Southgate took over from Steve McClaren at Middlesbrough in 2006.

June 7

Gordon Banks made THAT save from Pelé during England v Brazil at the 1970 World Cup. David Beckham scored a penalty against Argentina at the 2002 World Cup. Robbie Keane broke the Ireland caps record in 2013, scoring a hat-trick against the Faroe Islands in his 126th game.

June 8

One of the biggest World Cup shocks ever saw Cameroon beat defending champions Argentina in the opening game of the 1990 World Cup. Euro 96 kicked off, as England drew 1-1 with Switzerland. Sepp Blatter was elected as FIFA president for the first time in 1998.

June 9

Paul Ince became the first black player to captain England in 1993: unfortunately it was in a 2-0 defeat to the USA, leading to the headline 'Yanks 2 Planks 0'. Chelsea signed Marcel Desailly from Milan in 1998. Liverpool signed future captain Jordan Henderson from Sunderland in 2011.

June 10

The second ever World Cup was won by Italy in 1934, beating Czechoslovakia 2-1 in Rome. England won the prestigious 'Le Tournoi' in 1997. A winger called Ryan Wilson captained England schoolboys against Germany in 1989 – he would later become known as Ryan Giggs.

June 11

Cristiano Ronaldo signed for Real Madrid from Manchester United in 2009, for a then-world record fee of £80 million. Archie Gemmill scored his famous goal for Scotland vs the Netherlands at the 1978 World Cup as they won 3-2. Herbert Chapman became Arsenal manager in 1925.

June 12

England drew 1-1 with the USA at the 2010 World Cup, after Rob Green's error gave the Americans an equaliser. Chelsea signed Cesc Fàbregas from Barcelona in 2014. Pat Jennings made his 119th and final appearance for Northern Ireland, against Brazil at the 1986 World Cup.

June 13

The first European Cup final in 1956 saw Real Madrid beat French side Stade Reims 4-3. Malcolm Glazer completed his take-over of Manchester United in 2005. Julen Lopetegui was sacked as Spain coach days before the 2018 World Cup, after agreeing to take the Real Madrid job.

June 14

England were knocked out of the 1970 World Cup, beaten 3-2 by West Germany. Chelsea signed Frank Lampard from West Ham in 2001. Manuel Pellegrini was appointed Manchester City manager in 2013. Liverpool won the title in 1947 – the latest ever finish to a non-COVID English league season.

June 15

Paul Gascoigne scored a spectacular goal and David Seaman saved a penalty as England beat Scotland 2-0 at Euro 96. The highest ever score in a World Cup finals match saw Hungary beat El Salvador 10-1 in 1982.

June 16

Bryan Robson scored 27 seconds into England's opener at the 1982 World Cup, as they went on to beat France 3-1. Rafa Benítez was appointed Liverpool manager in 2004. Tottenham became the first English football club to be floated on the London Stock Exchange in 1983.

June 17

David Beckham left Manchester United and signed for Real Madrid in 2003. Wayne Rooney became the youngest ever European Championship goalscorer when he found the net against Switzerland at Euro 2004: Swiss striker Johan Vonlanthen broke that record four days later.

June 18

England beat the Netherlands 4-1 at Euro 96, the goals scored by Alan Shearer and Teddy Sheringham. Co-hosts South Korea produced a huge shock by knocking Italy out of the 2002 World Cup. Bolton made one of the more implausible signings of 2002: Jay-Jay Okocha.

June 19

Benito Mussolini came up with a spicy motivational tactic for Italy in the 1938 World Cup final against Hungary: he sent them a telegram that read 'win or die'. Luckily for all concerned, they won 4-2 to retain the trophy in the Stade Olympique de Colombes in Paris.

June 20

Arsenal signed Dennis Bergkamp from Inter for £7.5 million in 1995. Alan Shearer made his last ever appearance for England as they were knocked out of Euro 2000 after losing to Romania. England drew 2-2 with Sweden at the 2006 World Cup, but Michael Owen ruptured his knee.

June 21

Brazil won the 1970 World Cup, beating Italy 4-1 in the final in Mexico, Pelé scoring his final ever World Cup goal. In 2002 they knocked England out of the World Cup, their 2-1 win sealed by Ronaldinho lobbing David Seaman. Chelsea appointed André Villas-Boas as manager in 2011.

June 22

Diego Maradona scored two memorable goals as Argentina beat England 2-1 in the 1986 World Cup quarter-finals. Graham Poll infamously booked Croatia's Josip Šimunić three times in their 2006 World Cup game against Australia. England beat Spain on penalties at Euro 96.

June 23

In 1968 a tragedy occurred at El Monumental stadium when 74 fans were crushed to death at the end of a game between Boca Juniors and River Plate. Jermain Defoe scored the only goal as England beat Slovenia at the 2010 World Cup to qualify for the second round.

June 24

Luis Suárez bit a player for the third time in his career, this time Giorgio Chiellini at the 2014 World Cup. England lost in the Euro 2004 quarter-finals, to Portugal on penalties. West Germany and the Netherlands met in a spicy affair at the 1990 World Cup, when Frank Rijkaard spat in Rudi Völler's hair.

June 25

Liverpool won their first league title since 1990 in 2020. West Germany beat Austria 1-0 at the 1982 World Cup, which put them both through to the knockouts. Argentina won the 1978 World Cup, beating the Netherlands in the final. The Dutch got their trophy, beating the USSR at Euro 88.

June 26

Denmark beat Germany in one of the all-time great upsets to win the 1992 European Championships. Germany beat England on penalties in the semi-final of Euro 96. Marc-Vivien Foé tragically collapsed and died on the pitch during Cameroon's game against Colombia in 2003.

June 27

Michel Platini scored as France beat Spain 2-0 in the final of Euro 84. England crashed out of Euro 2016, losing 2-1 to Iceland. Leeds sacked David O'Leary in 2002, a year after reaching the Champions League semi-finals. Manchester United signed Teddy Sheringham in 1997.

June 28

Russia's 6-1 win over Cameroon at the 1994 World Cup saw two goalscoring records: Oleg Salenko scored five times, the most in a single game, while Roger Milla became the tournament's oldest scorer at 42. In 2015, England's Women reached the World Cup semi-finals for the first time.

June 29

Spain beat Germany 1-0 in the final of Euro 2008. 17-year-old Pelé scored twice in Brazil's 1958 World Cup final win over Sweden. The USA beat England at the 1950 World Cup: it was such an upset that one newspaper assumed the 1-0 score was an error and reported a 10-0 England win.

June 30

Germany won Euro 96, beating the Czech Republic in the final thanks to Oliver Bierhoff's golden goal. Brazil won the 2002 World Cup by beating Germany 2-0 in the final, Ronaldo scoring both. David Beckham was sent off as England were knocked out of the 1998 World Cup by Argentina.

July 1

English – and arguably European and world – football was changed forever in 2003 when Roman Abramovich bought Chelsea. England Women lost in the semi-final of the 2015 World Cup to Japan. Spain won the 2012 European Championships, thrashing Italy 4-0 in the final.

July 2

In 1994 Colombian defender Andrés Escobar was shot and killed in Medellín, 10 days after he scored an own goal against the USA at the World Cup. France added Euro 2000 to their World Cup win when David Trezeguet scored a golden goal to defeat Italy in the final.

July 3

England finally won a penalty shootout, beating Colombia at the 2018 World Cup. Sol Campbell signed for Arsenal on a free transfer from Tottenham in 2001. André Villas-Boas was appointed as Tottenham manager in 2012. Arsenal signed Robert Pires from Marseille in 2000.

July 4

West Germany beat Hungary 3-2 in the 1954 World Cup final: the Magyars had won their group game 8-3. England lost to West Germany on penalties in the semi-final of the 1990 World Cup. Greece won Euro 2004, beating Portugal in the final. Liverpool signed Fernando Torres in 2007.

July 5

In 1996 Manchester United made what seemed at the time like a minor signing, paying £1.5 million for Ole Gunnar Solskjær. Chelsea signed Chris Sutton for £10 million in 1999. Steven Gerrard looked to be on his way out of Liverpool in 2005, having told them he wanted to join Chelsea.

July 6

Steven Gerrard announced he had changed his mind, rejected Chelsea and signed a new contract at Liverpool in 2005. David Ginola signed for Newcastle from PSG in 1995 for £2.5 million. Former Thai Prime Minister Thaksin Shinawatra completed his takeover of Manchester City in 2007.

July 7

England appointed Bobby Robson as their new manager in 1982. Former England boss Sven-Göran Eriksson became Manchester City manager in 2007. Pelé made his debut for Brazil in 1957 aged 16, scoring against Argentina. Ashley Cole left Chelsea in 2014, signing for Roma.

July 8

Germany dished out one of the great humiliations as they beat Brazil 7-1 in the 2014 World Cup semi-final. West Germany beat Argentina 1-0 in the 1990 World Cup final, thanks to an Andreas Brehme penalty. Toni Schumacher levelled Patrick Battiston in the 1982 World Cup semi-final.

July 9

Italy beat France on penalties to win the 2006 World Cup, after Zinedine Zidane had been sent off for butting Marco Materazzi. Five years earlier, in 2001, Zidane had become the most expensive player of all time when Real Madrid bought him from Juventus for £46 million.

July 10

The USSR beat Yugoslavia in the first ever European Championships final in 1960. Newly promoted Tottenham pulled off a coup in 1978 when they signed World Cup winners Ossie Ardiles and Ricky Villa. Mo Johnston became the first publicly Catholic player to join Rangers in 1989.

July 11

Italy and Marco Tardelli were celebrating after beating West Germany in the 1982 World Cup final. Spain beat the Netherlands 1-0 in the 2010 World Cup final. Italy beat England on penalties in the Euro 2020 final at Wembley. Luis Suárez moved from Liverpool to Barcelona in 2014.

July 12

Zinedine Zidane's two headers and uncertainty around Ronaldo set France on their way to winning the 1998 World Cup final against Brazil. Bill Shankly shocked Liverpool by resigning as manager in 1974. Manchester United signed Juan Sebastián Verón for £28.1 million in 2001.

July 13

The first World Cup games were played in 1930: France beat Mexico 4-1 and the USA beat Belgium 3-0. Carlos Tevez joined Manchester City in 2009. George Graham was barred from football for a year in 1995 for taking illegal payments. Leicester appointed Claudio Ranieri in 2015.

July 14

Patrick Vieira left Arsenal in 2005 to sign for Juventus. Raheem Sterling moved from Liverpool to Manchester City in 2015. The Calciopoli punishments were handed down for corruption in Italian football in 2006, with Juventus stripped of two league titles and relegated to Serie B.

July 15

Didier Deschamps became the third man to win the World Cup as a player and coach when France beat Croatia in 2018. Blackburn broke the British transfer record in 1994 when they paid £5 million for Chris Sutton. In 1989 England winger Laurie Cunningham died in a car crash aged 33.

July 16

The final match of the 1950 World Cup saw Uruguay break Brazilian hearts by winning 2-1 at the Maracanã. Brazil got some revenge 39 years later by beating Uruguay in the final of the 1989 Copa America. Shaun Wright-Phillips moved from Manchester City to Chelsea for £21 million in 2005.

July 17

The first ever World Cup final to be decided by penalties saw Brazil beat Italy in 1994. Liverpool appointed Gérard Houllier to be co-manager with Roy Evans in 1998. In 1991 22 clubs signed the 'Founder Members Agreement' that would eventually lead to the Premier League being formed.

July 18

On a Leicester pre-season tour in 2002, Dennis Wise broke team-mate Callum Davidson's cheekbone after an argument over a game of cards. In 2000 Nicky Barmby became the first player to move from Everton to Liverpool in 41 years. Pelé played his final game for Brazil in 1971.

July 19

One of the great World Cup upsets took place in 1966, with North Korea beating Italy 1-0, and on the same day Portugal beat Brazil 3-1. Roy Keane left relegated Nottingham Forest to sign for Manchester United in 1993. Liverpool signed Peter Crouch from Southampton in 2005.

July 20

In 1871, FA secretary Charles Alcock proposed the establishment of the FA Cup. The FA legalised professional football in 1885, under pressure from leading clubs. Ronaldinho snubbed Manchester United and joined Barcelona in 2003. Chelsea signed Didier Drogba from Marseille in 2004.

July 21

In 1991 David Platt moved from Aston Villa to Bari for a then-record sum of £5.5 million. John White, a key member of Tottenham's 1961 double winners, was killed after being struck by lightning in 1964. Steven Gerrard announced his international retirement in 2014 after winning 114 caps.

July 22

Rio Ferdinand moved from Leeds United to Manchester United in 2002 for £29.1 million, the first big sale made by Leeds as their spending caught up with them. The Emirates Stadium staged its first game in 2006, a testimonial for Dennis Bergkamp. Liverpool signed Didi Hamann in 1999.

July 23

England beat Argentina 1-0 in the 1966 World Cup quarter-final with Geoff Hurst, who had replaced the injured Jimmy Greaves, scoring. Argentina captain Antonio Rattin was sent off and Alf Ramsey stopped his players swapping shirts with their opponents, who he called 'animals'.

July 24

Real Madrid signed Luís Figo from rivals Barcelona for a world record fee of £38 million in 2000, after some shrewd manoeuvres by Florentino Pérez. Bruce Grobbelaar, Hans Segers and John Fashanu were all charged with match fixing in 1995 – all three were cleared two years later.

July 25

Didier Drogba re-signed for Chelsea in 2014, two years after the end of his first spell at the club. Arsenal signed Jens Lehmann from Borussia Dortmund in 2003. In 1993, Brazil lost a World Cup qualifier for the first time as they were defeated 2-0 by Bolivia in La Paz – nearly 12,000 feet above sea level.

July 26

Alan Shearer moved to Blackburn Rovers from Southampton in 1992 for a British record transfer fee of £3.6 million plus David Speedie. Bobby Charlton scored both for England as they beat Portugal 2-1 in the 1966 World Cup semi-final. Bob Paisley became Liverpool manager in 1974.

July 27

Chelsea signed Ricardo Carvalho for £19.8 million in 2004, the second of Porto's Champions League winning side to follow José Mourinho to London that summer. Ruud van Nistelrooy left Manchester United for Real Madrid in 2006. Les Ferdinand signed for Tottenham in 1997.

July 28

Sergio Agüero completed his £36 million move from Atlético Madrid to Manchester City in 2011. Robbie Keane moved from Coventry to Inter for £13 million in 2000. Also that day Barcelona signed Marc Overmars and Emmanuel Petit from Arsenal for a combined fee of £30 million.

July 29

Alan Shearer became the world's most expensive footballer when he moved from Blackburn to Newcastle United for £15 million in 1996. Tottenham signed Jürgen Klinsmann in 1994. Liverpool signed Robbie Keane from Spurs for £19 million in 2018: he would go back six months later.

July 30

England won the 1966 World Cup, beating West Germany 4-2 in the final at Wembley thanks to a hat-trick by Geoff Hurst, the other goal scored by Martin Peters. Uruguay won the first ever World Cup in 1930, defeating Argentina 4-2 in the final. Everton signed Romelu Lukaku for £28 million in 2014.

July 31

Bobby Robson, former England, Ipswich, Barcelona and Newcastle manager, passed away from cancer in 2009, at the age of 76. Fulham pulled off a coup by signing Edwin van der Sar from Juventus in 2001. Michael Carrick moved from Tottenham to Manchester United in 2006.

August 1

The first ever Women's Olympic Football tournament culminated in 1996, as hosts the USA beat China 2-1 in the gold medal match. Steve McClaren began work as England manager in 2006: he would last 16 months and 18 games. Arsenal won the 2020 FA Cup, beating Chelsea 2-1.

August 2

Nicolas Anelka finally got his move from Arsenal to Real Madrid, moving to the Spanish capital for £20 million and Davor Šuker. Bolo Zenden left Barcelona to sign for Chelsea in 2001 for £7.5 million. Manchester United agreed an £80 million deal to sign Harry Maguire in 2019.

August 3

Thierry Henry joined Arsenal from Juventus for £11 million in 1999. John Charles moved for what turned out to arguably be the most successful stint abroad for a British player, when he left Leeds for Juventus in 1957. Real Madrid agreed a deal to sign Xabi Alonso from Liverpool in 2009.

August 4

In 2005 Phil Neville left Manchester United after 15 years at the club, signing for Everton. Aston Villa appointed Martin O'Neill as their manager in 2006. Iker Casillas announced his retirement from football in 2020: he made 725 appearances for Real Madrid but ended his career at Porto.

August 5

Chelsea's post-Roman Abramovich takeover spending continued in 2003 as they signed Joe Cole from West Ham and Juan Sebastián Verón from Manchester United. 1970 saw the first ever penalty shootout in English football, when Manchester United beat Hull 4-3 in the Watney Cup.

August 6

Laurent Koscielny left Arsenal to join Bordeaux in 2019: he had refused to join the Gunners' pre-season tour when they wouldn't release him from his contract. Pat Jennings moved from Tottenham to Arsenal in 1977. 20,000 Newcastle fans turned out to welcome Alan Shearer in 1996.

August 7

Manchester United signed Dion Dublin from Cambridge for £1 million in 1992. Bradford City played their first top flight game in 77 years in 1999, beating Middlesbrough 1-0. Diego Forlán announced his retirement in 2019 after a 21-year career. Arsenal signed Santi Cazorla from Malaga in 2012.

August 8

Eric Cantona scored his first hat-trick in English football, as Leeds United beat Liverpool 4-3 in the 1992 Charity Shield. Norwich lost the first game of the 2009-10 League One season 7-1 to Colchester, then promptly poached their manager, Paul Lambert.

August 9

Willian left Chelsea in 2020, and would go on to sign for Arsenal. Martin O'Neill resigned as Aston Villa manager in 2010. Chelsea won the 2009 Community Shield, a result significant because it was their first ever penalty shootout victory.

August 10

Liverpool made the most significant signing in their history in 1977, when they bought Kenny Dalglish from Celtic for £440,000. Kevin Keegan and Billy Bremner were sent off for fighting in the 1974 Charity Shield. Steve McClaren dropped David Beckham from his first England squad in 2006.

August 11

The unthinkable happened in 2021 when Lionel Messi left Barcelona, after spending his entire career there, to sign for PSG. Frank Lampard's first game in charge of Chelsea didn't go well, as they lost 4-0 to Manchester United in 2019.

August 12

Cristiano Ronaldo completed his move from Sporting to Manchester United for £12.24 million in 2003. Fulham signed George Best and Rodney Marsh in 1976, to add to Bobby Moore. Bruce Rioch was sacked by Arsenal in 1996, paving the way for Arsène Wenger to take over.

August 13

Michael Owen left Liverpool to sign for Real Madrid in 2004, moving for £8 million plus Antonio Núñez. The first ever game at Pride Park was abandoned in 1997 after the floodlights failed during Derby's game against Wimbledon. Manchester City signed Mario Balotelli in 2010.

August 14

Arsenal signed Patrick Vieira and Rémi Garde in 1996. Sarina Wiegman was confirmed as England Women manager in 2020. Barcelona hit rock bottom that day when Bayern Munich beat them 8-2 in the Champions League semi-final, with Philippe Coutinho – on loan from Barca – scoring twice.

August 15

The Premier League began in 1992, with Brian Deane scoring the first goal of the new era for Sheffield United against Manchester United. Cesc Fàbregas left Arsenal to sign for Barcelona in 2011. Dean Ashton broke his ankle in 2006, an injury that ultimately forced him to retire.

August 16

Teddy Sheringham scored the first televised Premier League goal, netting for Nottingham Forest against Liverpool in 1992. Cristiano Ronaldo made his first debut for Manchester United in 2003. Steve McClaren took charge of his first England game, a 4-0 win over Greece in 2006.

August 17

David Beckham scored from the halfway line in Manchester United's season opener against Wimbledon in 1996. Wayne Rooney made his senior debut for Everton, against Tottenham in 2002. Fabrizio Ravanelli scored a hat-trick versus Liverpool on his Middlesbrough debut in 1996.

August 18

James Milner moved from Aston Villa to Manchester City for around £24 million in 2010. Jack Walker, owner of Blackburn Rovers, died aged 71 in 2000. PSG qualified for their first ever Champions League final after beating RB Leipzig in 2020. Ashley Cole retired in 2019.

August 19

Alan Hansen made the most infamous incorrect prediction in football punditry when he declared Manchester United 'would win nothing with kids' in 1995: they went on to win the double. Chelsea signed Michael Essien in 2005. Coventry signed Robbie Keane from Wolves in 1999.

August 20

Jürgen Klinsmann made a dramatic debut for Tottenham in 1994, scoring against Sheffield Wednesday and performing his famous 'dive' celebration. Manchester United signed Dwight Yorke from Aston Villa in 1998. Real Madrid signed Jonathan Woodgate from Newcastle in 2004.

August 21

The first ever substitute in an English league match came in 1965, when Keith Peacock replaced Mike Rose for Charlton in their 4-2 defeat to Bolton. Liverpool agreed to sign Mario Balotelli in 2014. Tony Yeboah scored his sensational volley for Leeds against Liverpool in 1995.

August 22

Match of the Day made its first appearance on our screens in 1964, Liverpool's 3-2 win over Arsenal the main event. Vincent Kompany signed for Manchester City from Hamburg in 2008. Germany were the first team to beat England at the newly rebuilt Wembley in 2007.

August 23

Ben Thatcher knocked Pedro Mendes unconscious during Portsmouth's game against Manchester City in 2006 – he was banned for six games. Arjen Robben moved from Chelsea to Real Madrid in 2007. Bayern Munich beat PSG 1-0 in the 2020 Champions League final.

August 24

Jimmy Greaves scored on his senior debut for Chelsea in 1957: he later scored on his Milan, Spurs, West Ham, England U21 and senior debuts. Ole Gunnar Solskjær's proposed move from Manchester United to Tottenham fell through in 1998. Chelsea signed Juan Mata from Valencia in 2011.

August 25

Ruud Gullit's decision to bench Alan Shearer for Newcastle's derby against Sunderland in 1999 backfired: they lost 2-1 and he resigned three days later. Eric Cantona became the first player to score a Premier League hat-trick in 1992, bagging three in a 5-0 win for Leeds over Tottenham.

August 26

Manchester United signed Ángel Di Maria for £59.7 million in 2014 – but on the same day lost 4-0 to MK Dons in the League Cup. Manchester United sold Jaap Stam to Lazio in 2001, one of the few decisions Sir Alex Ferguson says he regrets. Manchester City sacked Peter Reid in 1993.

August 27

Cristiano Ronaldo rejoined Manchester United from Juventus in 2021, a day after it looked likely that he would sign for City. Dennis Bergkamp scored arguably the best Premier League hat-trick ever, for Arsenal against Leicester in 1997. Newcastle sacked Kenny Dalglish in 1998.

August 28

Manchester United dished out a humiliation to Arsenal in 2011, beating them 8-2. United broke the British transfer record in 1989, spending £2.3 million on Gary Pallister. Robbie Fowler scored what was then the Premier League's quickest hat-trick, against Arsenal in 1994.

August 29

In 2009, Arsène Wenger was dismissed from the touchline during Arsenal's 2-1 defeat at Manchester United for the crime of kicking a water bottle. Alexis Sánchez joined Inter on loan from United in 2019. Steve McManaman left Real Madrid to sign for Manchester City in 2003.

August 30

Michael Owen returned to England after a season with Real Madrid, moving to Newcastle in 2005. Newcastle sacked Bobby Robson in 2004. Tottenham paid Leeds £7 million for Robbie Keane in 2002. Christian Eriksen joined Tottenham from Ajax for around £11 million in 2013.

August 31

Manchester United eventually signed Wayne Rooney in 2004 after spending the summer chasing him. Ashley Cole went from Arsenal to Chelsea in 2006, with William Gallas moving the other way. On the same day West Ham surprised the world by signing Carlos Tevez and Javier Mascherano.

September 1

Manchester City were taken over by Sheikh Mansour and signed Robinho in 2008. Real Madrid spent £85 million on Gareth Bale in 2013. Chelsea broke the women's world transfer record by signing Pernille Harder in 2020. Michael Owen scored a hat-trick as England beat Germany 5-1 in 2001.

September 2

Arsenal signed Mesut Özil from Real Madrid for £42.5 million in 2013. In 1997 Rio Ferdinand was about to become England's youngest international since Duncan Edwards, but Glenn Hoddle dropped him after he failed a breathalyser test. Matt Le Tissier made his Southampton debut in 1986.

September 3

Bobby Robson became Newcastle manager in 1999. Alan Curbishley resigned as West Ham manager in 2008, after the club sold Anton Ferdinand and George McCartney. After turning down Thiago Alcântara, David Moyes brought Marouane Fellaini to Manchester United in 2013.

September 4

Kevin Keegan resigned as Newcastle manager for the second time in 2008. Chelsea sealed the £70 million signing of Kai Havertz from Bayer Leverkusen in 2020. Vinnie Jones was sent off for the 12th and final time of his career in 1996 for two yellow cards, both for fouls on Darren Anderton.

September 5

Paul Gascoigne received his first England call-up in 1988, for a game against Denmark. In 1994 Leeds signed Lucas Radebe from South African side Kaizer Chiefs. Costa Rica coach Gustavo Matosas resigned in 2019 saying he 'didn't know being a national team manager was so boring'.

September 6
In 1989 Terry Butcher suffered a cut on his head during England v Sweden, bleeding everywhere and producing some iconic photos. René Higuita performed his scorpion kick in 1995. Wayne Rooney became England's youngest goalscorer against Macedonia in 2003, aged 17 and 317 days.

September 7
Ron Greenwood named an England team to face Switzerland in 1977 featuring six Liverpool players, plus Kevin Keegan who had only just left Liverpool. Northern Ireland shocked England by beating them 1-0 in Belfast during World Cup qualification in 2005, David Healy with the goal.

September 8
The first ever Football League matches were played in 1888. Sky's offer to buy Manchester United for £625 million was accepted in 1998: it was later blocked by the government. Wayne Rooney became England's record goalscorer in 2015 by netting against Switzerland.

September 9
In 1981 Norway beat England 2-1 in a World Cup qualifier, inspiring Bjørge Lillelien's infamous 'Your boys took a hell of a beating' commentary. Four years after winning their first league title since 1974, Howard Wilkinson was sacked by Leeds in 1996 following a bad start to the season.

September 10
ITV broadcast the first ever live Football League game in 1960 as Bolton beat Blackpool 1-0, but clubs refused permission for subsequent games to be broadcast, so it wasn't until 1983 that another live game went out. Theo Walcott scored a hat-trick as England beat Croatia 4-1 in 2008.

September 11

The first ever FA Cup was stolen from a shop window in Birmingham in 1895 – it was never recovered, despite the FA offering a £10 reward for its safe return. Arsenal signed Freddie Ljungberg from Halmstads in 1998. West Ham appointed Gianfranco Zola as manager in 2008.

September 12

Leeds United sacked Brian Clough in 1974 after just 44 days in charge. Liverpool beat Crystal Palace 9-0 in 1989, with eight different players scoring. Emmanuel Adebayor ran the length of the pitch to celebrate scoring for Manchester City in front of fans of his former club Arsenal in 2009.

September 13

Ian Wright broke Cliff Bastin's Arsenal scoring record in 1997, bagging his 178th and 179th goals for the club against Bolton. Robinho scored on his Manchester City debut in 2008, though they lost 3-1 to Chelsea.

September 14

In 1891, Wolves forward John Heath scored the first ever penalty kick in English football, against Accrington. Kidderminster hosted the first FA Cup match under floodlights in 1955. 16-year-old Ansu Fati announced himself by scoring his first ever goal at the Camp Nou for Barcelona in 2019.

September 15

Ruud van Nistelrooy broke Denis Law's European goalscoring record for Manchester United when he bagged two against Lyon in 2004. Claudio Ranieri was appointed as Chelsea manager in 2000. Legendary Swedish striker Gunnar Nordahl, Milan's record goalscorer, died aged 73 in 1995.

September 16

The first ever live televised football game took place, when Arsenal played Arsenal Reserves in a specially arranged fixture in 1937. The first English club to play in the Champions League after it was rebranded in 1992 was Leeds United: they lost 3-0 to Stuttgart.

September 17

Tino Asprilla scored a sensational hat-trick for Newcastle against Barcelona in their first ever Champions League game in 1997, Kenny Dalglish's side winning the game 3-2. In 2007 Derby beat Newcastle 1-0 in the Premier League – it would be their only victory that season.

September 18

Arsenal beat Austria Vienna 6-1 in the European Cup in 1991 and Liverpool beat Finnish side Kuusysi Lahti 6-1 in the UEFA Cup – it was the first time English teams had played in Europe since Heysel in 1985. Fernando Ricksen died in 2019 aged 43 from motor neurone disease.

September 19

The first ever match at San Siro was played in 1926: Inter beat Milan 6-3. Ronny Rosenthal produced one of the great misses in 1992, hitting the bar from an open goal for Liverpool against Aston Villa. Newcastle beat Sheffield Wednesday 8-0 in Bobby Robson's first match in charge in 1999.

September 20

José Mourinho was sacked by Chelsea in 2007 after a poor start to the season/falling out with Roman Abramovich. Reading scored a 'ghost goal' in 2008 when John Eustace put the ball out for a corner but referee Stuart Attwell insisted it had gone in. Brian Clough died in 2004 aged 69.

September 21

Ruud van Nistelrooy missed a penalty and was enthusiastically goaded by Martin Keown in 2003, resulting in a scrap between Manchester United and Arsenal players. Frank Lampard scored against Chelsea while on loan at Manchester City in 2014. Gary Lineker retired in 1994.

September 22

A year after signing but being unable to play due to injuries, Jonathan Woodgate made his Real Madrid debut in 2005: he scored an own goal and got sent off. Liverpool were knocked out of the League Cup by League Two Northampton in 2010 – one of the many low points of Roy Hodgson's tenure.

September 23

Rio Ferdinand missed a drugs test at the Manchester United training ground in 2003 – he would eventually be banned for eight months and missed Euro 2004 because of it. Tony Yeboah scored his second thundering strike in a few weeks for Leeds in 1995, this one against Wimbledon.

September 24

The first ever game at the Camp Nou in 1957 saw Barcelona beat Legia Warsaw 4-2. Arsenal signed Ian Wright from Crystal Palace for £2.5 million in 1991. After Newcastle had won their first six games as a Premier League club in 1994, they were held to a 1-1 draw by Liverpool.

September 25

Massimo Taibi made a disastrous appearance for Manchester United in 1999, letting a Matt Le Tissier shot squirm through his legs. He only played once more for United – a 5-0 defeat to Chelsea. Fabrizio Ravanelli left Middlesbrough for Marseille in 1997 after just a season on Teesside.

September 26

In 1956 Manchester United faced Anderlecht in the first European Cup game in England. Paolo Di Canio pushed referee Paul Alcock after he was sent off for Sheffield Wednesday against Arsenal in 1998. After 24 winless games, Gareth Bale finally played in a winning Spurs side in 2009.

September 27

England manager Sam Allardyce was caught in a *Daily Telegraph* sting that would eventually lead to his sacking in 2016. 'Wimbledon' played their first game in Milton Keynes after moving there in 2003: they drew 2-2 with Burnley and changed their name to MK Dons for the following season.

September 28

Wayne Rooney made one of the all-time great debuts in 2004, scoring a hat-trick for Manchester United against Fenerbahce in the Champions League. The first ever match at Anfield took place in 1884, but not with Liverpool – original tenants Everton beat Earlestown 4-0.

September 29

Bill Shankly died aged 68 in 1981. Portsmouth and Reading set a new record for the highest scoring Premier League game ever when they shared 11 goals in 2007: Pompey ran out 7-4 winners. Manchester United produced one of the great comebacks to beat Spurs 5-3 in 2001.

September 30

Arsenal played their first Champions League game at Wembley in 1998, beating Panathinaikos 2-1. Leeds were knocked out of the Champions League by Stuttgart in 1992 – or so they thought – Stuttgart had fielded one too many foreign players and Leeds won the re-staged game 2-1.

October 1

Arsène Wenger officially arrived at Arsenal in 1996. Eric Cantona returned from his nine-month ban for kicking a Crystal Palace fan in 1995 as Manchester United drew 2-2 with Liverpool. Bayern Munich beat Spurs 7-2 in the Champions League in 2019.

October 2

Red and yellow cards were introduced to the Football League in 1976: George Best and Blackburn's David Wagstaffe were the first to receive reds. Joe Kinnear gave his famous sweary press conference after taking over at Newcastle United in 2008.

October 3

England played their first ever European Championships game in 1962, drawing 1-1 with France in a qualifier at Hillsborough. Dalian Atkinson scored his famous brilliant chipped goal for Aston Villa against Wimbledon in 1992. Aston Villa sacked Steve Bruce after a run of bad results in 2018.

October 4

Arsène Wenger became Arsenal's longest-serving manager in 2009, surpassing George Allison's 13 years in charge. Peter Taylor, Brian Clough's assistant during the glory years of his managerial career, died in 1990 aged 62. Aston Villa thrashed Liverpool 7-2 in the Premier League in 2020.

October 5

Robbie Fowler scored all five goals for Liverpool in a League Cup match against Fulham in 1993. José Mourinho and Arsène Wenger tussled on the touchline during a Chelsea v Arsenal game in 2014. Manchester United signed Edinson Cavani on a COVID-19-delayed deadline day in 2020.

October 6

David Beckham scored a last-minute free-kick to nick a 2-2 draw with Greece and send England to the World Cup in 2001. In 2020 Mesut Özil, frozen out at Arsenal, promised to pay the salary of Jerry Quy, the man who played Gunnersaurus but who had been made redundant by the club.

October 7

After Germany had beaten England 1-0 in the final international at the old Wembley in 2000, Kevin Keegan resigned. Brad Friedel's run of 310 consecutive league games ended in 2012 when Hugo Lloris played for Spurs instead. Juninho signed for Middlesbrough from São Paulo in 1995.

October 8

Jürgen Klopp was appointed Liverpool manager in 2015 after leaving Borussia Dortmund the previous May, replacing Brendan Rodgers. David Beckham became the first England captain to be sent off in 2005, but the 1-0 win over Austria meant qualification for the World Cup.

October 9

Due to a row over floodlights, Estonia refused to play a World Cup qualifier against Scotland in 1996: Scotland kicked off with no opposition present and were awarded the win. David Beckham deliberately got booked for England in 2004, so he'd be suspended for a game he was injured for.

October 10

In 2019 women were allowed to watch a game in Iran for the first time since the 1979 Islamic revolution – Iran thrashed Cambodia 14-0. Aston Villa appointed Dean Smith as manager in 2018. Rob Green became the only goalkeeper to be sent off while playing for England, against Ukraine in 2009.

October 11

Bill Nicholson took charge of his first Spurs game in 1958; they beat Everton 10-4. Duncan Ferguson was jailed in 1995 for head-butting an opponent while at Rangers. In 2006 Paul Robinson's missed clearance saw England lose 2-0 to Croatia, damaging their Euro 2008 prospects.

October 12

Mark Bosnich aimed a Nazi salute at Spurs fans singing Jürgen Klinsmann's name in 1996 – he apologised, saying he thought the crowd was laughing with him, but was fined £1,000. Tony Adams captained England for the first time, as they drew 1-1 with Romania in 1994.

October 13

England were beaten 2-0 by the Netherlands in 1993, effectively ending their hopes of qualifying for the World Cup, immortalised in 'The Impossible Job'. The first Merseyside derby was played in 1894: Everton beat Liverpool 3-0. Thierry Henry was appointed Monaco coach in 2018.

October 14

Petr Čech suffered a fractured skull during Chelsea's 1-0 win over Reading in 2006. Peter Brackley, beloved commentator synonymous with Channel 4's Italian football coverage in the 1990s, died aged 67 in 2018. David Beckham won his 115th and final England cap in 2009.

October 15

Luis Suárez was accused of racially abusing Patrice Evra in 2011 – he was later found guilty by the FA, banned for eight games and fined £40,000. Brian Clough and Peter Taylor resigned from Derby in 1973, a year after winning the title. John Henry took control of Liverpool in 2010.

October 16

Manchester United became the first English club to compete in the Intercontinental Cup in 1968: they drew 1-1 with Estudiantes with Juan Ramón Verón – father of Juan Sebastián – scoring for the visitors, but lost the tie 2-1. Roy Hodgson was appointed Inter manager in 1995, while remaining Switzerland coach.

October 17

Sunderland's Darren Bent scored a goal against Liverpool in 2009 that rebounded in off a beach ball. England drew with Poland in 1973, meaning they would not qualify for the 1974 World Cup: Polish keeper Jan Tomaszewski played brilliantly, despite being dubbed 'a clown' by Brian Clough.

October 18

Ian Rush became Liverpool's record goalscorer in 1992, bagging his 287th for the club against Manchester United, ensuring he overtook Roger Hunt. Thierry Henry also became his club's top marksman: in 2005 he got his 185th and 186th Arsenal goals and moved above Ian Wright.

October 19

Remember the name: Wayne Rooney scored his first league goal, giving Everton a 2-0 win over Arsenal in 2002. The greatest day in Norwich City's history came in 1993, when they became the first English team to beat Bayern Munich in the Olympic Stadium, winning their UEFA Cup first leg 2-1.

October 20

A 21-man brawl between Manchester United and Arsenal in 1990 led to the Gunners being docked two points and United one. Peter Schmeichel became the first keeper to score a Premier League goal, for Aston Villa at Everton in 2001. Newcastle beat Manchester United 5-0 in 1996.

October 21

Rangers won the 'Battle of Britain' in 1992, when they beat Leeds 2-1 in the Champions League. George Reynolds, former Darlington owner who promised Premier League football and built a 25,000 seat stadium but ultimately drove them out of business, was jailed in 2005 for tax evasion.

October 22

Robert Pires and Thierry Henry tried a clever penalty against Manchester City in 2005, but the former made a mess of trying to pass to the latter. Gordon Banks was involved in a car crash in 1972 which resulted in him losing the sight in his right eye, ending his playing career.

October 23

John Terry was accused of racially abusing Anton Ferdinand in 2011: he was found not guilty in court but the FA banned him for four games. On the same day Manchester City beat Manchester United 6-1 at Old Trafford. Kanu scored a 15-minute hat-trick for Arsenal at Chelsea in 1999.

October 24

Manchester United ended Arsenal's 49-game unbeaten run with a 2-0 win at Old Trafford in 2004. Cesc Fàbregas allegedly threw a slice of pizza at Alex Ferguson amid a post-match fracas. Sheffield FC, widely regarded as the world's oldest football club, was established in 1857.

October 25

A big day for Tottenham sacking managers: in 2007 they dismissed Martin Jol, with news leaking during their UEFA Cup game against Getafe. And in 2008 they got rid of Juande Ramos, appointing Harry Redknapp the following day. Leicester beat Southampton 9-0 in 2019.

October 26
In 1863, Ebenezer Cobb Morley chaired a meeting that would establish a standard set of rules that all football clubs in England would follow, thereby forming the FA. Six days after losing 5-0 to Newcastle, Manchester United were thrashed 6-3 by Southampton in 1996.

October 27
Leicester owner Vichai Srivaddhanaprabha, along with two pilots and two members of staff, died in a helicopter crash near the King Power stadium in 2018. On the same day Glenn Hoddle suffered a cardiac arrest in a TV studio, but was saved by a quick-thinking BT Sport employee.

October 28
In 1999 Patrick Vieira was banned for six games and fined £45,000 for spitting at Neil Ruddock and confronting a police officer after Arsenal's game against West Ham. An England Under-17s side featuring Phil Foden and Conor Gallagher won the 2017 World Cup, beating Spain 5-2.

October 29
Julen Lopetegui was sacked as Real Madrid manager in 2018, a 5-1 defeat to Barcelona being the final straw, just four months after he was sacked as Spain coach − for agreeing a move to Real after the World Cup. Chelsea sacked Adrian Mutu in 2004 after he tested positive for cocaine.

October 30
Diego Maradona announced his retirement from professional football in 1997, five days after playing his last game for Boca Juniors. Arsenal came from 4-0 down after 37 minutes to beat Reading 7-5 in a 2012 League Cup game. Nobby Stiles died at the age of 78 in 2020.

October 31

The FA confirmed the appointment of Sven-Göran Eriksson as England manager in 2000: he was due to start in the following July, but ultimately left Lazio early to start in January. After making changes in 99 consecutive games, Rafa Benítez named an unchanged Liverpool side in 2006.

November 1

Spurs sacked Ossie Ardiles in 1994, after a poor start to a season in which they signed Jürgen Klinsmann. Cristiano Ronaldo scored his first Manchester United goal in 2003. In 2018 Jang Hyun-soo was banned from playing for South Korea for life after faking military service documents.

November 2

The origins of the European Super League plans emerged in 2018, as German newspaper *Der Spiegel* published a list featuring 11 of the continent's biggest clubs, led by Real Madrid. Stoke goalkeeper Asmir Begović scored a goal against Southampton in 2013 after just 13 seconds.

November 3

Manchester United were welcomed to hell in 1993, after they faced Galatasaray in a spicy Champions League 0-0 in Istanbul – the Turkish side went through on away goals from the first leg. Blackburn sacked Brian Kidd in 1999 amid fears of a second successive relegation.

November 4

Everton took part in the first ever penalty shootout in the European Cup in 1970: they beat Borussia Mönchengladbach 4-3. Mark Viduka scored four in Leeds United's 4-3 win over Liverpool in 2000. Pep Guardiola tested positive for nandrolone in 2001 but was later cleared.

November 5

Mick McCarthy stepped down from his first spell as Ireland manager in 2002. Jacques Santini was replaced by Martin Jol as Spurs manager in 2004. Bill Shankly was appointed Huddersfield manager in 1956. Gillespie Road tube station next to Highbury was renamed 'Arsenal' in 1932.

November 6

Alex Ferguson was appointed as Manchester United manager in 1986: he would leave 27 years, 13 Premier League and two Champions League titles later. In 1887, The Celtic Football Club was established in Glasgow. Former England striker Tommy Lawton passed away aged 77 in 1996.

November 7

Southend, who were bottom of the Championship, produced one of the great League Cup upsets by beating Manchester United in 2006. Howard Kendall returned for his second spell as Everton boss in 1990, and promptly appointed his sacked predecessor Colin Harvey as his assistant.

November 8

Chelsea made one of the most significant signings in their history when they recruited Gianfranco Zola in 1996. Alex Ferguson took charge of his first Manchester United game in 1986, a 2-0 defeat to Oxford. Steve Coppell left Manchester City after just 33 days in charge in 1996, citing stress.

November 9

Dean Windass received three red cards in the same game while playing for Aberdeen in 1997: one for a second yellow card, a second for dissent and a third for kicking a corner flag. He was banned for six games. Manchester City beat United 3-1 in the final derby at Maine Road in 2002.

November 10

Chelsea's Roy Bentley became the first England player to score a hat-trick at Wembley when he netted all three against Wales in 1954. Joe Royle was appointed as Everton manager in 1994. On the same day, Aston Villa sacked Ron Atkinson. FA chairman Greg Clarke resigned in 2020.

November 11

Chris Coleman came clean in 2007 – after claiming he had been late for a press conference due to a broken washing machine, he admitted it was actually because he had been out until 5am the previous evening. The PFA finally allowed female members for the first time in 2000.

November 12

1881 saw the first game between Newton Heath and St Mark's: they would later become Manchester United and Manchester City. Roy Evans resigned as co-manager of Liverpool in 1998. In 2020 Scotland qualified for their first tournament since 1998 when they beat Serbia to make Euro 2020.

November 13

Newcastle became the first team to lose their first three group games but still qualify for the Champions League knockouts in 2002. In 1999, England beat Scotland 2-0 in the first leg of their Euro 2000 play-off. Arsenal beat Spurs 5-4 in 2004, the game José Mourinho called a 'hockey score'.

November 14

Bobby Moore made his 108th and final appearance for England in 1973: they lost 1-0 to Italy, the goal scored by Fabio Capello. England also faced Italy in 1934, when they named seven Arsenal players in their team. Wayne Rooney was appointed as Derby manager in 2020.

November 15

In 2000, David Beckham captained England for the first time in a 1-0 friendly defeat to Italy in Turin. Kevin Keegan made his senior England debut in 1972, against Wales. Johan Cruyff made his professional debut for Ajax in 1964, aged just 17. Ray Clemence died aged 72, in 2020.

November 16

Arsenal announced that they had identified the site of what would become the Emirates Stadium in 1999. Thierry Henry scored his famous sensational goal against Tottenham in 2002. Willie Hall scored five in England's 7-0 win over Northern Ireland in 1938, including a four-minute hat-trick.

November 17

In 1993 Wales came within a crossbar's width of qualifying for their first World Cup since 1958: Paul Bodin's missed penalty allowed Romania to win and deny the Welsh. England also failed that night, their 7-1 win over San Marino not enough after Davide Gualtieri scored inside nine seconds.

November 18

Roy Keane left Manchester United in 2005, following a disagreement with Sir Alex Ferguson – he would finish his playing career at Celtic. In 2009 Ireland were denied a place at the 2010 World Cup in South Africa after Thierry Henry's handball helped France to win their play-off.

November 19

Tottenham sacked manager Mauricio Pochettino in 2019, six months after he took them to their first ever Champions League final. 22 years earlier in 1997, Christian Gross arrived at Spurs, brandishing his Underground ticket. Pelé scored his 1,000th goal in 1969, for Santos against Vasco da Gama.

November 20

Tottenham replaced Pochettino with José Mourinho in 2019, who had been out of work for nearly a year after leaving Manchester United. Spurs won away at Arsenal for the first time in 17 years, in 2010. West Ham were bought by an Icelandic consortium led by Eggert Magnússon in 2006.

November 21

England lost 3-2 to Croatia in the pouring rain at Wembley in 2007, thus failing to qualify for Euro 2008 – manager Steve McClaren was sacked the next day. Chelsea sacked Roberto Di Matteo in 2012, just six months after winning the Champions League.

November 22

Blackburn lost 3-0 to Spartak Moscow in the Champions League in 1995, but that was the least of their problems: team-mates Graeme Le Saux and David Batty fought on the pitch, with the left-back breaking his hand. Tottenham beat Wigan 9-1 in 2009, with Jermain Defoe scoring five.

November 23

Ali Dia, the man who tricked his way into the Southampton squad after manager Graeme Souness was told he was George Weah's cousin, made his one and only appearance in 1996. He came on as a substitute against Leeds, but was so bad he was taken off before full-time.

November 24

The second leg of the 2018 Copa Libertadores final between Boca Juniors and River Plate was postponed after violence erupted outside the stadium. Graham Taylor resigned as England manager after their failure to qualify for the World Cup in 1993. A John Fashanu elbow broke Gary Mabbutt's cheekbone in 1993.

November 25

Diego Maradona, credited by many as the greatest footballer of all time, died at the age of 60 in 2020, after suffering a heart attack at home in Buenos Aires. Argentina declared three days of mourning and Napoli, with whom he won two Serie A titles, renamed their stadium after him.

November 26

Manchester United signed Eric Cantona from rivals Leeds United in 1992 – a signing that came about after Leeds asked to buy Denis Irwin. A penalty shootout decided an FA Cup game for the first time in 1991, when Rotherham beat Scunthorpe in the first round tie at Millmoor.

November 27

The football world was in shock in 2011 when Wales manager Gary Speed took his own life aged just 42. Future England manager Bobby Robson made his debut as a player for his country in 1957. Dimitar Berbatov scored five for Manchester United as they beat Blackburn 7-1 in 2010.

November 28

In 2016 a plane carrying the Chapecoense side to the Copa Sudamericana final first leg in Colombia crashed on the approach to Medellín airport, killing 71 of the 77 on board. José Luis Chilavert, the Paraguayan goalkeeper, scored a hat-trick of penalties for Vélez Sarsfield in 1999.

November 29

After placing an advert in a Catalan newspaper for fellow football enthusiasts, Swiss accountant Hans Gamper formed FC Barcelona in 1899. Steven Gerrard made his debut for Liverpool in 1998, aged 18. Arsenal sacked manager Unai Emery in 2019, after an unsuccessful 18 months.

November 30

In 1991 the USA won the first Women's World Cup final, beating Norway 2-1 in the final. The first ever official international took place in 1872: England and Scotland drew 0-0. Manchester United became the first English club to win the Intercontinental Cup in 1999 when they beat Palmeiras 1-0.

December 1

Then Second Division side Liverpool appointed Bill Shankly as their new manager in 1959. Quique Sánchez Flores was sacked by Watford for a second time in 2019, having been dismissed by them for the first time in 2016. Fulham sacked manager Martin Jol in 2013.

December 2

The PFA was formed in 1907. In 2010 Russia and Qatar were announced as hosts of the 2018 and 2022 World Cups respectively. In 2018 UEFA announced the formation of a third European competition that would eventually be known as the Europa Conference League.

December 3

Harry Redknapp resigned as Southampton manager in 2005, and four days later he returned to Portsmouth, who he had initially left a year earlier. In 2018 Luka Modrić became the first player not named Cristiano Ronaldo or Lionel Messi to win the Ballon d'Or since 2007.

December 4

Dion Dublin achieved the unusual feat of scoring a hat-trick but ending up on the losing team when his Coventry side lost 4-3 to Sheffield Wednesday in 1995. Liverpool beat Everton 5-2 in 2019, which was the final nail in manager Marco Silva's coffin: he was sacked the next day.

December 5

The infamous ban on women's football being staged at FA member facilities was put in place in 1921 – it lasted until 1971. In 1908 Newcastle lost 9-1 at home to Sunderland – a notable enough scoreline, made more remarkable because Newcastle finished that season as champions.

December 6

Eric Cantona made his Manchester United debut in 1992, coming on as a substitute in their 2-1 derby win over City. In 2014 disgruntled Arsenal fans accosted their players at a train station, one memorably urging Costa Rican forward Joel Campbell to, 'Get out while you can, Joel.'

December 7

Arsenal lost 2-0 to Manchester United in 2002: it was the first time they had failed to score in 55 league matches. Legendary Leeds captain Billy Bremner passed away in 1997 aged 54. Ron Saunders, the man who led Aston Villa to the league title in 1981, died aged 87 in 2019.

December 8

Steven Gerrard scored a last-minute winner against Olympiakos in the Champions League in 2004, keeping Liverpool on track to ultimately win the competition. In 2020 İstanbul Başakşehir's Champions League game at PSG was suspended due to allegations of racism against an official.

December 9

Ledley King scored the fastest Premier League goal when he netted after 9.7 seconds for Spurs at Bradford in 2000 – the record stood for 19 years. The rearranged second leg of the 2018 Copa Libertadores final saw River Plate beat Boca Juniors in Madrid. Newcastle United were formed in 1892.

December 10
In 1998 UEFA added an extra group stage to the Champions League but abolished the Cup Winners' Cup. Jim Smith, the former Derby manager, died aged 79 in 2019.

December 11
Dial Square Football Club played its first game in 1886, a 6-0 win over Eastern Wanderers – they would later be renamed Royal Arsenal, Woolwich Arsenal and finally, simply, Arsenal. Alan Pardew was sacked by West Ham in 2006. Napoli replaced Carlo Ancelotti with Gennaro Gattuso in 2019.

December 12
In 2001 the latest attempt to bring Celtic and Rangers into the English Premier League failed. A game between Burnley and Blackburn in 1891 was abandoned when nine Rovers' players walked off the pitch, either in protest against a sending off, or because it was too cold: reports differ.

December 13
Milan Foot-Ball and Cricket Club, later to be renamed AC Milan, were formed by Englishmen Alfred Edwards and Herbert Kilpin in 1899. A month after buying Blackburn Rovers in 2010 the Venky's group sacked manager Sam Allardyce and replaced him with coach Steve Kean.

December 14
Fabio Capello was confirmed as Steve McClaren's replacement as England manager in 2007. Gary Speed was appointed as Wales boss in 2010. In 1935 Arsenal beat Aston Villa 7-1 with Ted Drake scoring all seven, the record number of goals scored by one player in a top tier match.

December 15
In 1995 the European Court of Justice ruled in favour of Jean-Marc Bosman in his case against RFC Liege, allowing footballers to move freely between clubs at the end of their contracts.

December 16
Paolo Di Canio stopped a game between West Ham and Everton because Toffees' goalkeeper Paul Gerrard was injured, rather than putting the ball into an empty net, in 2000. West Brom sacked Slaven Bilić and appointed Sam Allardyce in 2020. Thierry Henry retired in 2014.

December 17
Seven months after leading them to the Premier League title, José Mourinho was sacked by Chelsea to end his second spell at the club in 2015, following defeat to Leicester. In 2001 Michael Owen became the first English player to win the Ballon d'Or since Kevin Keegan in 1979.

December 18
Manchester United finally ran out of patience with José Mourinho in 2018, sacking him with United 19 points behind league leaders Liverpool. The first ever Ballon d'Or was awarded in 1956: the inaugural award, invented by France Football editor Gabriel Hanot, went to Stanley Matthews.

December 19
Roberto Mancini replaced Mark Hughes as Manchester City manager in 2009. Across Manchester in 2018, United appointed Ole Gunnar Solskjær as interim boss. Joey Barton earned a £60,000 fine in 2004 after stubbing out a lit cigar in team-mate Jamie Tandy's eye during a Christmas party.

December 20

After lengthy negotiations, Mikel Arteta was appointed as Arsenal manager in 2019. In 1996 Middlesbrough called off a game against Blackburn because they had 23 players unavailable with the flu. They were docked three points by the FA – they were eventually relegated by two points.

December 21

Carlo Ancelotti was appointed as Everton manager in 2019. Manchester United won the Club World Cup in 2008, beating LDU Quito of Ecuador. Liverpool won it in 2019. In 1957 10-man Charlton were 5-1 down against Huddersfield with half an hour to go – they went on to win 7-6.

December 22

Jürgen Klinsmann returned to Tottenham in 1997 to help them avoid relegation and himself get ready for the World Cup. Tommy Docherty was appointed Manchester United manager in 1972: he won the FA Cup in 1977 but was sacked for having an affair with physio Laurie Brown's wife.

December 23

In 1995 Newcastle beat Nottingham Forest to go 10 points clear at the top of the Premier League – they would throw away that lead and Manchester United won the title. Tim Sherwood was named permanent Tottenham manager after two games in care-taker charge in 2013.

December 24

Happy Christmas Les Reed: the Charlton manager was sacked in 2006, replaced by Alan Pardew. The same goes for Thomas Tuchel, given his cards by PSG in 2020. Bill Kenwright completed his takeover of Everton in 1999, acquiring a majority stake in the club from Peter Johnson.

December 25

The last Football League match to be played on Christmas Day took place in 1965, as Blackpool beat Blackburn Rovers 4-2, watched by 20,851 Brussels sprout-avoiders. 17-year-old Jimmy Greaves scored four times for Chelsea as they beat Portsmouth 7-4 in 1957.

December 26

A record number of goals for one day in the top flight were scored in 1963: 66 in 10 games. Chelsea fielded the first side entirely of foreigners in an English league game, against Southampton in 1999. Hull's Phil Brown gave his infamous on-pitch team talk against Manchester City in 2008.

December 27

In 2013 Cardiff City owner Vincent Tan sent manager Malky Mackay an email demanding he resigned, or else he would be sacked – he didn't, so he was. Roman Abramovich approached England manager Sven-Göran Eriksson about replacing Claudio Ranieri at Chelsea in 2003.

December 28

In 2013 West Brom's Nicolas Anelka celebrated a goal against West Ham with a 'quenelle', a gesture associated with French comedian Dieudonné that had anti-Semitic associations. He was banned for five games and eventually sacked. Roy Hodgson was appointed Fulham manager in 2007.

December 29

Andy Cole moved from Manchester United to Blackburn in 2001. He made his league debut exactly 11 years earlier, for Arsenal against Sheffield United. West Ham reappointed David Moyes as their manager in 2019, replacing Manuel Pellegrini who had himself replaced Moyes in 2018.

December 30

The first English league game with no English players on either side took place in 2009, as Arsenal faced Portsmouth. Alan Shearer became the first player to score 100 Premier League goals in 1995. Also that day Paul Gascoigne was booked for pretending to book the referee while playing for Rangers.

December 31

After two and a half years and 98 goalless games, John Jensen finally scored his first goal for Arsenal in 1994. Former Scotland, Chelsea and Manchester United manager Tommy Docherty died in 2020, at the age of 92. Michael Owen broke his metatarsal playing for Newcastle in 2005.

THE TOTALLY FOOTBALL BOOK: CREDITS

Editor: Nick Miller

Copy editor: Matt Langham

Production support: Pete South

Editor for Coronet: Erika Koljonen

Contributors: James Richardson, Carl Anka, Daniel Storey, Adam Hurrey, Katie Whyatt, James Horncastle, Tom Williams, Julien Laurens, Elias Burke, Charlotte Harpur, Sasha Goryunov, Flo Lloyd-Hughes, Alvaro Romeo, Maher Mezahi, Dom Fifield, Duncan Alexander, Nancy Frostick, Charlie Eccleshare, Rafa Honigstein and Adrian Clarke.